THE PICTURE LICENSING
GLOSSARY

VERSION 1.0

DEVELOPED AND APPROVED BY THE PLUS COALITION

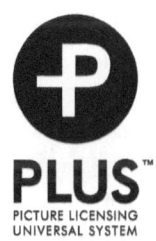

PLUS™
PICTURE LICENSING
UNIVERSAL SYSTEM

PLUS COALITION, INC.
AN INTERNATIONAL NON-PROFIT ORGANIZATION DEDICATED TO
SIMPLIFYING AND FACILITATING PICTURE LICENSING

First Published in the United States of America by
PLUS Coalition, Inc.
940 East 2nd Street, Suite 8
Los Angeles, California 90012
USA

Toll free: 866.669.7587
Telephone: 213.613.1553
www.usePLUS.org

First Edition 2006
Printed in the USA
ISBN 978-1-4303-0115-8

The PLUS Coalition, Inc. is a not-for-profit 501(c) (6) trade association for picture licensors and licensees. Its mission is to establish a universal system of standards designed to simplify and facilitate the licensing of images. The PLUS Picture Licensing Glossary, like all PLUS standards, is developed and maintained cooperatively by picture licensors and licensees, who jointly draft, review, edit and approve all definitions. The PLUS Coalition will not set any pricing policies nor engage in any discussions or activity involving pricing models. It is the policy of the PLUS Coalition to comply with all federal, state and local trade regulations and anti-trust laws.

Glossary Project Manager: Jeff Sedlik
Art Direction & Design: Joseph Gilbert Design
Layout & Production: Sharon Cohen-Powers / Loupe Media
PLUS logo design: Pentagram

Need another copy?
To purchase additional copies of the PLUS Picture Licensing Glossary, visit www.usePLUS.org

CONTENTS

Introduction   4

Acknowledgments   5

How to Become a Part of the PLUS Coalition   6

PLUS Advisory Council   7

How the Glossary was Created   8

Key to Use of the Glossary   9

Glossary Terms   10

Proposed Terms   96

INTRODUCTION

The PLUS Coalition is an international non-profit trade association with a tightly focused mission: "To simplify and facilitate the licensing of images."

In the PLUS Coalition, photographers, illustrators, stock picture agencies, artist representatives, advertising agencies, advertisers, graphic design firms, publishers, and associated industries and initiatives have joined forces to create a universal licensing language.

Through the PLUS Coalition, licensors and licensees are working cooperatively to develop and implement licensing standards and systems that will bring picture licensing into the 21st century.

Picture licensing is an estimated $6-8 billion industry worldwide. Yet, up to this point, artists, distributors and image users have operated without standardized licensing terminology, definitions or image use classifications. Despite the critical importance of image management in our industries, the language of licensing has remained only vaguely defined, with various organizations and companies each offering their own terminology and criteria. Licensing agreements have often included undefined licensing terms, with many companies using different words and definitions to describe the specific reproductive uses of an image in various media. This lack of definition has led to confusion in the marketplace, skepticism among image users, and ultimately to legal disputes and other wasted resources.

The PLUS Picture Licensing Glossary is the core of an integrated system of standards that exists as a comprehensive resource for use by every professional engaged in licensing images, so that we all may speak a common language, avoid misunderstandings, and achieve a precise mutual understanding of the scope of any image license.

Jeff Sedlik
President and CEO
PLUS Coalition, Inc.
www.usePLUS.org

ACKNOWLEDGMENTS

This Picture Licensing Glossary is the result of an unprecedented collaborative effort in the image licensing industries. Hundreds of volunteers from more than a dozen professions in more than ten countries contributed many thousands of hours to reviewing, discussing and revising the terms, phrases, definitions and supplementary information contained in this publication. The PLUS Coalition thanks all those who so generously shared their knowledge and expertise.

The PLUS Glossary Editors dedicated months and years to reviewing proposed terms and definitions, and to making revisions based upon industry consensus.

GLOSSARY EDITORS
Ellie Bair
Niki Barrie
Ellen Boughn
Sharon Cohen-Powers
Jane Kinne (Managing Editor)
Sam Merrell (Managing Editor)
David Riecks (Managing Editor)
Jeff Sedlik (Managing Editor)
Greg Smith

ONLINE GLOSSARY EVALUATION SYSTEMS:
Phil Sedgwick, LW Technologies

Additional logistical assistance provided by Shari Abercrombie, Pam Gligoriu, and Stephanie Howard.

PLUS Development Committee Members during the creation of the Glossary:
Ellen Boughn, Jeffrey Burke, Jane Kinne, Sam Merrell, David Riecks, Jeff Sedlik, Nancy Wolff, Esq

Special thanks to Jane Kinne for her fine work in laying the foundation for the development of this Glossary.

HOW TO BE A PART OF THE PLUS COALITION

In the PLUS Coalition, photographers, illustrators, stock agencies, publishers, art buyers, designers, researchers, educators, artist representatives, application developers, attorneys and their trade associations work together cooperatively towards creating and maintaining industry standards for image licensing. PLUS welcomes all organizations and individuals as members. PLUS members have the opportunity for in-depth participation in the development of the PLUS standards, and receive voting privileges in the organization. In addition to General Membership, Sustaining Membership opportunities exist for those individuals and organizations that are in a position to partner with the Coalition by providing substantial financial and/or logistical support in the development of this important initiative.

Join PLUS
Find out more at www.usePLUS.org

866.669.7587
213.613.1553
info@useplus.org

The PLUS Coalition thanks our Leadership Circle members for their generous financial and logistical contributions.

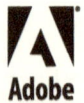

jupiterimages.

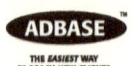

Pentagram

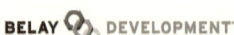

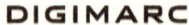

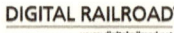

IPNSTOCK.COM

PhotoServe.com

BOARD OF DIRECTORS: Chair: Jeffrey Burke • Vice Chair: Jane Kinne • Secretaries: Roger & Judy Feldman, American Society of Picture Professionals (ASPP) • Directors: Bonnie Beacher, American Association of Publishers (AAP) • Patrick Donehue, Picture Agency Council of America (PACA) • Richard Grefé, American Institute of Graphic Arts (AIGA) • Gene Mopsik, American Society of Media Photographers (ASMP) • President & CEO: Jeff Sedlik

ADVISORY COUNCIL

ADVISORY COUNCIL TRADE ASSOCIATIONS: Advertising Photographers of America (APA)* • American Institute of Graphic Arts (AIGA)* • American Society of Media Photographers (ASMP)* • American Society of Picture Professionals (ASPP)* • Association of American Publishers (AAP)* • Association of Illustrators (AOI) * Association of Photographers (AOP)* • Australian Commercial and Media Photographers Association (ACMP)* • Australian Institute of Professional Photography (AIPP) • British Association of Picture Libraries & Agencies (BAPLA)* • Canadian Artists Representation Copyright Collective (CARCC) • Canadian Association of Photographers & Illustrators In Communications (CAPIC) • Coordination of European Picture Agencies Press Stock Heritage (CEPIC) • Editorial Photographers (EP) • Editorial Photographers United Kingdom & Ireland (EPUK)* • Graphic Artists Guild (GAG)* • Illustrators' Partnership of America (IPA) * • International League of Conservation Photographers (ILCP) • International Press Telecommunications Council (IPTC)** • Japan Photographers Union (JPU) * • National Association of Professional Photographers of Italy (TAU Visual) • National Press Photographers Association (NPPA)* • National Union of Journalists (NUJ)* • Newspaper Association of America (NAA) • North American Nature Photography Association (NANPA)* • Picture Archive Council of America (PACA)** • Picture Research Association (PRA) * • Professional Photographers of America (PPA)* • Professional Photographers of Canada (PPOC) • Pyramide • Society of Photographers & Artists Representatives (SPAR) • Stock Artists Alliance (SAA)* • Union des Photographes Createurs (UPC)* • United States Digital Imaging Group (USDIG)* • Visual Artists & Galleries Association (VAGA) • Wedding and Portrait Photographers International (WPPI) * • Women in Photography International (WIPI)

OTHER VALUED COUNCIL PARTICIPANTS: James Alexander, Director, Adobe Stock Photos, Adobe Systems** • Stephanie Anderson, Artist Representative, Anderson/Hopkins • Michael Ash, Director, Print Division, Radical Media • Chris Bain, Photography Director, Barnes & Noble Publishing • Julie Barnwell, Art Buying Manager, Digitas • Niki Barrie, Principal, Loupe Media • Morton Beebe, Morton Beebe & Associates* • Howard Bernstein, CEO, Bernstein Andriulli • Ellen Boughn, Vice President, SuperStock • Jigisha Bouverat, Director, Art Buying, TBWA/Chiat/Day • Elaine Brown, Art Producer, Eisner Communications • Barbara Brundage, President, Pacific Stock Photography* • Geoff Cannon, Executive Vice-President, Masterfile Corporation** • Jean-Francois Cardella, The Data Archive* • Richard Cardinali, Senior Art Buyer, J. Walter Thompson • Kate Chase, Kate Chase Presents • Beate Chelette, President, Beateworks* • Lily Cheung, IP Relations Manager, NewsCom** • John Clarke, McGraw-Hill* • Sharon Cohen-Powers, Principal, Loupe Media • James Cook, HindSight • Tad Crawford, Attorney, Publisher, Allworth Press • Robin Daily, Freelance Art Buyer • Kat Dalager, Creative Wrangler, Best Buy • Lisa Dapolito, Art Buying Manager, Foote Cone & Belding • Doug Dawirs, Consultant • Meghan DeBruler, Art Buying Manager, Ogilvy & Mather • Chris DeLellis, CIO, Superstock • Steven Diamond, Executive Director of Photography, Scholastic, Inc. • Laurent Di Costanzo, Managing Director, Agence Images • Nicole Elovitz, Product Marketing Manager, Digimarc Corporation • Gary Elsner, VP/Sales & Marketing, StockPhotoFinder** • Lynn Eskenazi, Director of Photography, JupiterImages** • Jean Ferro, Photo Artist, President, WIPI • Bahar Gidwani, CEO, Index Stock Imagery • Daniel Gluckman, Director, Imagen y Publicaciones S.L. • Michael Grecco, President, Michael Grecco Photography, Inc.* • Matthew Goodrich, Marketing Director, Stockland Martel • John Greim, Chairman, Creative Eye • Tim Grey, Director, Professional Photography Community, Microsoft Corporation • Robert Gubas, VP/Product Marketing, Getty Images** • Eyal Gura, CEO and Co-Founder, PicScout** • Prof. Christopher R. Harris, Electronic Media Communication, MTSU* • Joel Hecker, Attorney, Russo & Burke • Grant Heilmann, Grant Heilmann Photography* • Michal Heron, Photographer, Author • Kit Hinrichs, Partner, Pentagram** • Maggie Hunt, President, StockShop LLC* • Eric Hyman, President, Bibble Labs • Mark Ippolito, Consultant • Bruce Isaacs, Attorney, Wyman & Isaacs LLP • Beth Johnson, Artist Representative, Friend & Johnson • Dennis Keeley, Chair, Photography Department, Art Center College of Design • Karen Kirsch, Art Buyer, Cramer Krasselt • Julieanne Kost, Photo Illustrator, Educator • James Kozyra, Senior Art Buyer, Young & Rubicam • Mary Kuch-Nagel, Digimarc** • Karin Larin, Artist Representative, Kane Larin Reps* • Josette Lata, Head of Art Buying, J. Walter Thompson • Jain Lemos, Founder, Reality Books • Kevin Lipskin, Copyright Attorney • Steve Liska, Founder, Lisa + Associates, Inc. • Chrissy Borgatta Liuzzi, Senior Art Buyer, Doner • Tony Luna, Creative Consultant, Representative • Kathy Lyons, VP/ Art Buying Manager, BBDO • David MacTavish, Attorney, Author • Carl May, Photo Agent, Biological Photo Service* • Sam Merrell, Principal, Synthetic Imaging • Barbara Mikula, Project Manager, Acclaim Images* • Sybille Millard, Director, Visual Resources, Reader's Digest Association • Peter Miller, President, Actionpix* • Clement Mok, CEO, CMCD • Brian Moorhead, Director, Focus New Zealand Photo Library Limited* • Chad Newell, CEO, Media Bakery • Evan Nisselson, Founder, CEO, Digital Railroad** • Dr. Norman Paskin, Founding Director, International DOI Foundation • Shel Perkins, Founder, Shel Perkins & Associates • Wanda Pion, Macmillan/McGraw-Hill • Jim Pickerell, Author & Consultant, Selling Stock • Maria Piscopo, Creative Services Consultant • Bill Radcliffe, Director, Technology Development, Corbis Corporation** • Don Resnick, President, 20/20 Software • Seth Resnick, Photographer, Co-Founder, D-65 • David Riecks, Principal, Controlled Vocabulary • Bob Roberts, President, H. Armstrong Roberts Company* • Jeffrey Roberts, Publisher, American Photo • Tony Rodriguez, Chief Technologist, Digimarc** • Cindy Rowe, Manager of Art Buying, Saatchi & Saatchi • Greg Samata, Principal, SamataMason, Inc. • Grover Sanschagrin, PhotoShelter* • Joanna Santander, Business Development Manager, Alamy • David Schimmel, Presidente & Creative Director, And Partners, Inc. • Alexis Scott, President, Workbookstock** • Phil Sedgwick, Founder, CTO, LW Technology • Joshua Shaw, President, Belay Development** • Jeff Shear, CTO, ImageSpan** • Dean Siracusa, President, Transtock, Inc.* • Greg Smith, Owner, mediaSmith • Blake Springer, CTO, Veer • Bill Stockland, President, Stockland Martel • Steve Stone, Consultant, InFlows • Monica Suder, Creative and Business Coach • Mary Virginia Swanson, Consultant • Lubomir Synek, ArchArt • Randy Taylor, President, Stock Photofinder** • Paula Voorhies, Art Producer, Fitzgerald+CO • George Watson, Artist Representative, Watson & Spierman • Debra Weiss, Creative Consultant • Lauren Wendle, Publisher, Photo District News (PDN)** • Kristine Wilson, Art Buyer, Ogilvy & Mather • Nancy Wolff, Attorney, Cowan, DeBaets, Abrahams & Sheppard, LLP • Tracy Wong, Chairman, Creative Director, WongDoody** • Carolyn E. Wright, Esq., Photoattorney.com

*Member **Sustaining Member

HOW THE GLOSSARY WAS CREATED

The Picture Licensing Glossary was initially created by merging a number of glossaries and term lists contributed by participating organizations in the photography, illustration, advertising, design and publishing sectors. After an initial edit, the first draft of the Glossary was submitted for review by hundreds of volunteer "Glossary Reviewers" from a broad spectrum of professions involved in making, distributing and using images. Drafts were presented in a custom-built, online "Glossary Review and Comment System" allowing reviewers to enter comments on terms and respond to comments made by others. Reviewers also proposed hundreds of additional terms for inclusion in the Glossary. After the initial industry review, comments were processed and terms and definitions were edited by a supervised team of editors, based upon the consensus expressed in the comments received. Following this process, a second and third draft were submitted for industry review. The Glossary was further refined at each stage. A fourth draft was submitted for final review by the PLUS Glossary Working Group. After revisions requested by consensus of the Working Group were completed by the editors, the final version was submitted to the PLUS Board of Directors for review and approval. The PLUS Board, comprised of one seat for each industry sector, unanimously approved the draft, and the world's first image licensing standard was born.

It should be noted that as this is a Picture Licensing Glossary, the definitions of terms in this Glossary are intended to apply only in the context of picture licensing transactions. Finally, it should be noted that the definitions in this Glossary may or may not match dictionary definitions. The PLUS Glossary definitions are achieved by consensus. With the exception of terms defined by law, what any term "means" is up to those who use it. The users have cooperatively drafted each definition in this Glossary.

PLUS is an international image licensing standard, and this Glossary was created with worldwide participation. But by necessity, Glossary version 1.0 was first created in a single language. With this version in place as a starting point, regional "Working Groups" are forming in several countries to Draft 2.0 of this Glossary, complete with regionally specific terms and definitions.

This Glossary will never be completed. The standard will be periodically submitted for industry review and will be updated to accommodate new terms and evolving definitions. At the back of this volume, you will find a list of terms that are currently queued for inclusion or revision in Draft 2.

To participate as a PLUS Glossary Reviewer, visit the PLUS website at www.useplus.org and submit a Reviewer Application.

KEY TO THE USE OF THE GLOSSARY

To use the Glossary, look up any term in alphabetical order. The elements of each listing are described in detail below. Where a term's definition varies based upon the context in which the term is used, there will be multiple listings for that term, each indicating a different "facet" (context) of the term. Where a term is used in several formats (hyphenated, abbreviated, etc), each such "variation" will be separately listed in alphabetical order within the Glossary, and each term record will provide a listing of all variations on the term. PLUS identifies each term with a PLUS Glossary ID ("PGID"). These ID codes may be used in place of the actual terms, to allow precise communication. The PGID codes will also facilitate worldwide, multilingual use after the Glossary is translated. The first four digits of the PGID indicate the term number. The 5th and 6th digit indicate the facet number, and the 7th and 8th digit indicate the variation number. The final four digits indicate the Glossary version number, an essential reference, as definitions may be revised in future editions by industry consensus. PLUS also applies a "Usability Rank" to many terms. In ranking terms, PLUS does not recommend or discourage any business practice. Rather, PLUS applies a rank of "Cautioned" or "Discouraged" to terms that are ambiguous, outdated or otherwise often result in misunderstandings. In such instances, PLUS provides a "Preferred Term" designed to facilitate the clearest possible communication.

SAMPLE TERM

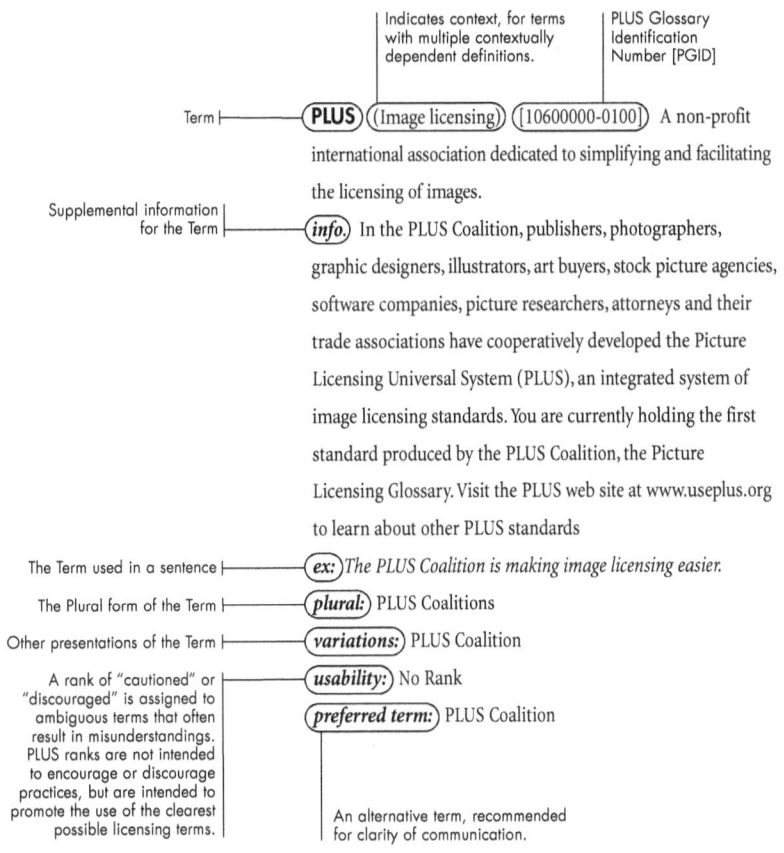

16mm [1333-00-00-0100] Motion picture film, 16 millimeters wide, 40 frames per foot. *info:* Used traditionally by educational, industrial, government, scientific, and student filmmakers. Improvements in grain structure have made 16mm practical for stock footage and commercial productions as well as some television shows and independent motion pictures. *ex: 16mm film transfers well to video tape.*

3-D [4410-01-00-0100] Abbreviation for Three-Dimensional *ex: The image was enhanced to appear as 3-D.*

35mm [1336-00-00-0100] Film stock that is thirty-five millimeters wide, used for still photography, motion picture, and television production. *info:* The most common still frame format is 24mm by 36mm, with up to 36 frames fitting in a 135 roll film cassette. Motion picture projection film is standardized at 16 frames per foot, but the frame size varies between several formats. Term sometimes used when referring to digital cameras with designs based on 35mm film camera bodies. *ex: 35mm still camera film is available in 135 cassettes and in 100-foot rolls.*

3:2 Pulldown [1335-00-00-0100] The technique used to convert 24-frames-per-second film to 30-frames-per-second video. *info:* Every second film frame is held for three video fields, resulting in a sequence of three fields, two fields, three fields, etc. *ex: The action sequence looked great after 3:2 pulldown. **plural:** 3:2 Pulldowns*

70mm [1337-00-00-0100] Motion picture film seventy millimeters wide. Generally used for release prints of large-budget feature films. *info:* 70mm prints are made from 65mm negatives or enlarged from 35mm negatives. For many years, 70mm transparency film was used by stock photo agencies to duplicate original transparencies for distribution to clients and to sub-agents. *ex: The 70mm prints are back from the processing lab.*

8mm [1338-00-00-0100] Motion picture film, eight millimeters wide, 80 frames per foot. *info:* Primarily used by amateur and home movie makers. There are also several formats of video tape with the 8mm designation, but they are largely obsolete. *ex: The old 8mm movies are upstairs in the attic.*

A-V [1084-04-00-0100] Abbreviation for Audiovisual *ex: The A-V presentation included slides and music. **plural:** A-Vs*

A3 [3090-00-00-0100] An international standard page size, measuring 297 by 420 millimeters (11.7 by 16.5 inches). *ex: The poster will be an A3 size and inserted in magazines.*

A4 [3100-00-00-0100] An international standard paper size of 210 by 297 millimeters (8.3 by 11.7 inches). *info:* A common finished (single page) size for magazines. *ex: The license is for a full page in an A4 book.*

A5 [3110-00-00-0100] An international standard paper size of 148 by 210 millimeters (5.8 by 8.3 inches). *info:* Also known as a half page, which it is for magazines printed to finish in the A4 size. If you fold an A4 sheet in half, then the folded size is equivalent in size to an A5. *ex: The table cards will fold to A5 and feature an image on the front.*

A6 [3120-00-00-0100] An international standard paper size of 105 by 148 millimeters (4.1 by 5.8 inches). *info:* Also known as a quarter page, which it is for magazines printed to finish in the A4 size. Four A6 sheets set together will be 1 millimeter smaller (210 x 296) than the 210 by 297 millimeters size of an A4. *ex: The note card will fold to A6 and feature your image on the front.*

ABC [1002-01-00-0100] Abbreviation for Audit Bureau of Circulations ex: *ABC was founded in 1948 to confirm circulation figures.*

Above the Line

(1) Above the Line (Advertising) [1079-00-01-0100] Budget term denoting the traditional five advertising uses for which commission is paid to advertising agents. They include: press, TV, radio, cinema and outdoor. *ex: The above the line advertising budget will include press, TV and radio.*

(2) Above the Line (Production) [1079-00-02-0100] Budget term denoting the licensing and creative fees for a production. *info:* The categories of fees that comprise this figure often vary from project to project. Many prefer to itemize each category, rather than lump all as above the line. Does not include production costs. *ex: The above the line budget for this shoot includes fees for the photographer, producer and two models. **preferred term:** Creative Fee **usability:** Caution*

Abridged [3130-00-00-0100] A work that has been reduced in size or scope while retaining essential elements. *info:* An abridged edition of a book may or may not include all images that were in the original edition. *ex: The publisher wants to license five of the images for an abridged edition.*

Academic Book [2747-00-00-0100] A printed or electronic volume containing information on one or more subjects used in a real or virtual classroom by students and teachers. *info:* Usually includes images.

Ancillaries, which require specific licenses, might include other edition(s), such as instructor handbooks, a student edition, an edition in another language or an electronic edition. *ex: This academic book is for sixth graders.* *plural:* Academic Books *preferred term:* Textbook *usability:* Discouraged

Acknowledgment [1753-00-00-0100] The mention within a work of a contributor, colleague, supportive person or organization. *info:* This may be required by contract to appear in a specific location within the work. *ex: The acknowledgment thanked two additional contributors and the author's spouse.* *plural:* Acknowledgments

Active Picture Area

(1) Active Picture Area (Television) [1339-00-01-0100] The part of a television image that contains actual image as opposed to sync or other data (487 vertical lines for NTSC and 576 lines for PAL). *info:* The inactive area of the image is called blanking. *ex: If the TV set is properly tuned, viewers see only the active picture area.* *plural:* Active Picture Areas

(2) Active Picture Area (Photo) [1339-00-02-0100] The area of a photograph that contains the actual image, as opposed to the border area or frame around the image. *info:* In some cases, such as Polaroid frames showing in-camera borders or prints made from filed-out negative carriers, a border may be considered part of the active image area. *ex: A full-frame crop does not remove or hide any of the active picture area.* *plural:* Active Picture Areas

Ad [1819-01-00-0100] See Advertisement [1819-00-00-0100] *ex: The image was licensed for that ad which will appear in four national magazines.* *plural:* Ads

Ad Slick [1078-00-00-0100] A prepared, camera-ready advertisement sent to franchises, distributors, dealers, resellers and area product representatives for placement in media at their discretion. *info:* Traditionally on paper but increasingly in digital form, ready to print or insert in electronic layout. Contains white space for the local dealer or franchise to insert its address, telephone number, etc. No distribution or additional placement information is furnished to the licensor. *ex: The ad slick was sent to all distributors yesterday.* *plural:* Ad Slicks

Additive Color [1340-00-00-0100] A system for reproducing hues based on the three primary colors of light: red, green and blue. *info:* When fully saturated and pure RGB colors combine, they yield white. *ex: Computer monitors use an additive color system.* *plural:* Additive Colors *preferred term:* RGB *usability:* Caution

Address Book

(1) Address Book (Print) [1200-00-01-0100] A printed and bound volume in which to record a list of contacts, including addresses and other information. *info:* Many organizations distribute an address book containing members' contact information. Many address books include blank pages or page areas for adding personal entries. *ex: The address book will include all members' key information, along with photographs of them.* *plural:* Address Books

(2) Address Book (Software) [1200-00-02-0100] A computer or other electronic file in which one can record a list of contacts, including addresses and other information. *info:* Numerous computer programs offer competing and often incompatible digital address book formats. Many also include a digital calendar. *ex: My address book has over 100 names, with street and email addresses, and I can find anything almost instantly.* *plural:* Address Books

Advance [1572-00-00-0100] A payment made by a buyer to a seller prior to production, usage or actual sales. *info:* Generally not refundable. The amount paid is then deducted from payments for remaining balances due on any fees, expenses and/or royalties. Advance amounts and calculation methods vary; both are negotiable. Examples: on a complex production project, between 50% and 100% of expenses; for less elaborate or expensive projects, between 33% and 50% of creative fees and expenses. *ex: We received their check which covers the advance.* *plural:* Advances

Advance Copy [1535-00-00-0100] A finished copy of a work that is distributed for review or other purposes before the work is made widely available. *ex: The advance copy arrived one week before the book went into general circulation.* *plural:* Advance Copies

Advanced Reader's Copy [2703-00-00-0100] A mid-production, unbound version of a work that is distributed for marketing, review or public relations purposes. *ex: Here is the advanced reader's copy of the new book.* *plural:* Advanced Reader's Copies *variation:* ARC

Advanced Reader's Edition [2702-00-00-0100] A mid-production, unbound version of a work that is distributed for marketing, review or public relations purposes. *ex: Here is the advanced reader's edition of the new book.* *plural:* Advanced Reader's Editions *preferred term:* Advanced Reader's Copy *usability:* Caution *variation:* ARE

Advert [1819-02-00-0100] See Advertisement *ex: The image was licensed for that advert, which will appear in four national magazines.* **plural:** Adverts

Advertisement [1819-00-00-0100] An instance of advertising expressed in a particular design. May include text, photography, illustration or other graphic elements. *info:* Where individual elements are licensed for use, such licenses may define or limit the use of the particular design. *ex: The image was licensed for the advertisement, which will appear in four national magazines.* **plural:** Advertisements *variation:* Advert, Ad

Advertiser Copy [1001-00-00-0100] A printed example of a magazine, or other periodical publication, containing a commercial announcement, sent to whomever contracted and/or paid for the placement. *info:* Used to verify an advertisement was presented properly, as promised. Not to be confused with advertising copy, which refers to text within an ad. *ex: Ship them an advertiser copy, so they can see the ad was printed correctly.* **plural:** Advertiser Copies

Advertising [1628-00-00-0100] The activity of attracting public attention to a product, idea or business using announcements in print, broadcast or electronic media. *info:* In most cases, advertising is clearly different from editorial content and is paid for by an advertiser, who controls its appearance and content. This distinguishes it from public relations content, which can be edited by a media outlet and is inserted without payment. *ex: Advertising is one element in an overall marketing strategy.*

Advertorial [1081-00-00-0100] Paid advertising or public relations created and designed (often by the staff of a magazine or other media in which it appears) to resemble editorial material. *info:* The publication reproducing the advertorial typically receives an insertion fee or enters a barter arrangement and receives in-kind goods or services. The publication may also offer advertorial insertions as incentives to advertisers who purchase a certain amount of advertising. By law in some countries, an advertorial page must be marked advertisement. *ex: The advertorial was on page five of the September issue.* **plural:** Advertorials **preferred term:** Advertisement **usability:** Caution

Aerial Photography [1341-00-00-0100] Images created with the visual impression of no physical connection to the Earth's surface, usually from an aircraft, building rooftop or cherry picker. *ex: Aerial photography shows a bird's-eye view of the ground.*

Afterword [1514-00-00-0100] A section at the end of a written work by the author or a third party that comments on the work or the process of its creation. *ex: In the book's afterword, the author mentions how difficult it is to write good examples.* **plural:** Afterwords

Agency [4200-00-00-0100] A company authorized to act for another company or individual within the scope of an assignment or project. *ex: The agency commissioned the photographs on behalf of its client.* **plural:** Agencies

Agent [1570-00-00-0100] A party authorized to act for or in place of another. *info:* The scope of an agent's authorization is typically limited by contract. *ex: My agent is a brilliant negotiator, watching out for my bottom line interests.* **plural:** Agents **preferred term:** Representative **usability:** Caution

Agreement [1573-00-00-0100] The act of two or more people or entities uniting to express a common and mutual purpose, and/or the writing that is evidence of their common and mutual purpose. *info:* An agreement must have the elements of: offer, acceptance, consideration. It involves terms and conditions that two or more parties agree to, rather than something that might be only arranged or understood. *ex: Our agreement states the delivery date and each of our responsibilities.* **plural:** Agreements **preferred term:** Contract **usability:** Caution

Airport Display [1082-00-00-0100] A work that is installed for viewing at an airport. *info:* If promotional, the usage is airport terminal advertising. *ex: Our images will be used for airport display in kiosks at five different terminals.* **plural:** Airport Displays

Airport Terminal Advertising [1848-00-00-0100] A marketing or promotional piece, usually poster sized or larger, placed on the structure of a public airport stop or terminal. *info:* May be printed, or displayed on monitors or other digital devices. *ex: The campaign includes posters for airport terminal advertising.*

Album

(1) Album (Music) [2751-00-01-0100] A paperboard sleeve used to package a vinyl record or other recording. *info:* Usually contains information about the performers or contents, often with images. *ex: His image was licensed for the cover of the band's album.* **plural:** Albums

(2) Album (Photo) [2751-00-02-0100] A book used for collecting photographs, letters, stamps and other printed materials, or a selection of digital images on a computer or other electronic device. *info:* New album products allow design of finished pages—both printed and electronic—on a computer. May be bound or use one of a variety of expandable formats. In the case of a digital album, may not be printed but shared online, on CD or on a specialized display device—including mobile phones and other personal electronic devices. *ex: We are making an album of our vacation photographs.* **plural:** Albums

All Media [1229-00-00-0100] Licensing language granting use in all types of communication. *info:* May be limited by time, geography, size or restrictions, but meaning can be unclear. *ex: The license includes usage in all media.* **preferred term:** Unlimited Use **usability:** Caution

All Media Known or Unknown [1554-00-00-0100] Every type of communication method, whether or not that method has been discovered or developed at the time a license is granted. *ex: The license includes usage in all media known or unknown.* **preferred term:** Unlimited Use **usability:** Caution

All Reproduction Rights [4530-00-00-0100] Denotes right to create unlimited copies, without restriction on media, size, placement or distribution unless otherwise specified. Not a copyright transfer. Non-exclusive unless otherwise specified. *info:* Not recommended for use in a license. An ambiguous term that frequently results in misunderstandings. Often confused with buyout and copyright transfer. *ex: The client requires a license for all reproduction rights to avoid any delays in releasing the pictures for future publication.* **preferred term:** Unlimited Use **usability:** Caution

All Rights [1230-00-00-0100] The unrestricted right to reproduce, distribute, display, and perform a work for any purpose, unless restrictions or limitations are specified. Not a copyright transfer. Not exclusive unless otherwise specified. *info:* Not recommended for use in a license. An ambiguous term that frequently results in misunderstandings. Often confused with buyout and copyright transfer. *ex: The client asked to license all rights.* **preferred term:** Unlimited Use **usability:** Discouraged

All Rights in Perpetuity [1555-00-00-0100] The unrestricted right to reproduce, distribute, display, and perform a work for any purpose, for an unlimited time period, unless restrictions or limitations are specified. Not a copyright transfer. Not exclusive unless otherwise specified. *info:* Not recommended for use in a license. An ambiguous term that frequently results in misunderstandings. *ex: The client asked to purchase all rights in perpetuity.* **preferred term:** Unlimited Use **usability:** Discouraged

Amendment [3140-00-00-0100] Formal revision or addition to an agreement or contract. *info:* As with other legal matters, any amendment is best made in writing and signed by representatives of all parties. *ex: We agreed to make an amendment to the contract, allowing more time to complete the project.* **plural:** Amendments

Analog [1342-00-00-0100] A form of information conveyed by a continuous and variable signal that can represent an infinite range of values. *info:* When duplicated from one generation or medium to another, the quality of analog information frequently degrades. In photography, film cameras are analog systems. *ex: Most silver-based photographic imaging is an analog system.*

Ancillary Product [2698-00-00-0100] New products or presentations, based on those existing, to extend brand awareness for publishers, manufacturers and service providers, or additional items included with a product to enhance its sales. *info:* Some examples include special magazine issues, custom books, trade show displays, merchandise (such as T-shirts and mugs) and electronic presentations such as a CD or website. Some books and periodicals include ancillary CD-ROMs, workbooks or field guides. *ex: We want to reuse the magazine cover image on at least one ancillary product, a rack card, and we're considering reuse on others, including T-shirts and tote bags.* **plural:** Ancillary Products

Ancillary Rights [1231-00-00-0100] An extension of a right to material in a main or primary work for appearance in subordinate, helping, auxiliary, consequent or resultant materials that accompany or relate to the primary work. *info:* Examples include a student edition, teacher's edition, educational software, table of contents and collateral. *ex: The publisher licensed ancillary rights to include the image in the book's table of contents and sales brochures.*

Animatic [1083-00-00-0100] A test TV commercial based on story boards, with frames of images filmed in stop-motion, accompanied by the audio portion of the script. *info:* Used also to describe a still image series edited into a sequence for a finished TV commercial. *ex: The animatic uses 10 photographs, two illustrations and the client logo.* **plural:** Animatics

Animation [1343-00-00-0100] The technique of synthesizing the optical illusion of mobility using a series of still images that depict movement of inanimate objects through cinematography, video or specialized computer software. *info:* Animation has evolved from hand-drawn and photographs of objects to computer images. The computer is programmed with scene, lighting, model and movement information. It then renders individual frames in a sequence of images. *ex: The animation used a panoramic still photo as the background.* **plural:** Animations

Annual [3720-00-00-0100] A publication with a unique title that is issued once a year. *ex: This annual shows the best illustration used in print for the entire year.* **plural:** Annuals

Annual Report [1184-00-00-0100] A document issued once each year by a corporation, outlining details of the company's income, expenditures, long-range plans, etc. *info:* For distribution to shareholders, the press and others. Required for public and certain non-profit companies; annual reports from a private company might be classified as advertising or public relations. *ex: The annual report has more photographs than last year.* **plural:** Annual Reports

Anthology [1134-00-00-0100] A collection of selected works or parts of works that are produced or published as a single unit. *info:* Copyright may be claimed for the unit, even if copyrights to the individual pieces are held by others. An anthology requires separate permission from the copyright holder of each work it includes. *ex: The student course pack is effectively an anthology.* **plural:** Anthologies

Appendix [1515-00-00-0100] Additional, relevant information added to a written work, usually at the end. *ex: Appendix B includes pictures of each species, organized by dominant color.* **plural:** Appendices

Arbitration [1232-00-00-0100] A dispute resolution process during which both parties are heard by a neutral third party (arbitrator) who renders a decision. *info:* When arbitration is voluntary, the disputing parties select one or more arbitrators, who have the power to render a decision that may be binding or not, depending upon prior agreement. *ex: The contract included a clause requiring arbitration of any dispute.* **plural:** Arbitrations

ARC [2703-01-00-0100] Abbreviation for Advanced Reader's Copy *ex: Here is the ARC of the new book.* **plural:** ARCs

Archive [1135-00-00-0100] To organize a repository of images, other materials and/or electronic data so it is indexed for easy retrieval and reuse of the materials and/or data; or a repository of such images, materials or data. *info:* Retrieval and use subsequent to an initial usage influences licensing. Many editorial clients archive past issues, online or otherwise, for public viewing, which requires a license. Hence, the ability to add a work to an archive may be restricted under a license. Offline (or physical) archives may not necessarily be organized for easy retrieval. *ex: The image is in our archive and available for reuse.* **plural:** Archives

ARE [2702-01-00-0100] Abbreviation for Advanced Reader's Edition [2702-00-00-0100] *ex: Here is the ARE of the new book.* **plural:** AREs **preferred term:** Advanced Reader's Copy

Arrears [1625-00-00-0100] An unpaid, overdue debt, or the state of being behind in fulfilling contracted obligations or payments. *ex: Some of the bill has been paid but the balance is in arrears*

Art Buyer [4720-00-00-0100] An advertising agency or creative department employee, or a contractor, with duties including but not limited to identifying artists and stock images in relation to the production of advertisements, negotiating agreements with vendors involved in the production of artwork, and in some cases supervising production of artwork. *info:* The role and responsibilities of the art buyer position vary from company to company. *ex: The art buyer negotiated a license agreement with the artist representative to commission a photograph from the photographer.* **plural:** Art Buyers

Art Framing Print [4280-00-00-0100] An image rendered on paper or other material (such as canvas) that is prepared for display within a constructed border (of materials such as metals, woods and plastics) or on a heavy substrate, as a work of art or wall decor in a private or gallery setting. *info:* Does not include prints intended for display within a frame for the express purpose of selling that frame (packaging). An art framing print is generally sold for private display without any license to reproduce. *ex: The art framing print will arrive in a protective sleeve with mat board to protect it.* **plural:** Art Framing Prints **preferred term:** Art Print usability: Caution

Art Print [1136-00-00-0100] An image on paper or other substrate (such as canvas) intended for collection or display in a public or private setting, such as wall decor, or in a museum or gallery. *info:* Does not include display within a frame for the express purpose of selling that frame (packaging). Note that the markets for home decor and art collecting have very different pricing levels. *ex: This art print is designed to hang above a living room couch.* **plural:** Art Prints

Art Producer [4740-00-00-0100] A person or company who works with an illustrator or photographer to ensure the client's concept is reflected in the finished artwork. *info:* The art producer usually negotiates the agreement between the creator (or stock house) and the client or agency contracting the work, as well as overseeing arrangements for props, rentals, talent and other services required to complete the project. *ex: The art producer made sure everyone was on the set and ready in time for the shoot.* **plural:** Art Producers

Art Reference [1058-01-00-0100] See Artists' Reference [1058-00-00-0100] *ex: To draw the beak correctly, the illustrator looked at an art reference photograph of a parrot.* **plural:** Art References

Art Rendering [1138-00-00-0100] A work in the same or a different medium that is a copy or reproduction in its entirety of another original work. *info:* Under Copyright Law, an art rendering is a derivative work copied from the original and requires written permission from the copyright holder. *ex: Although it is a pencil drawing, this art rendering looks exactly like the original photograph.* **plural:** Art Renderings

Artifact [1344-00-00-0100] An undesirable visual effect (a specific blemish or general degradation) caused by an error or limitation in a capture, processing, storage, transport or transmission system. *ex: There is some sort of artifact in the upper left corner of the image.* **plural:** Artifacts

Artist [3890-00-00-0100] A person who creates an original work. *info:* Term has connotations that reflect on the quality of creativity, and it has no basis in law. Best avoided. *ex: The client needed to hire an artist to come up with a more creative game plan for the campaign.* **plural:** Artists **preferred term:** Creator **usability:** Discouraged

Artist's Reference [1058-00-00-0100] A licensed image, typically a photograph, from which an artist may extract visual information for use in creating an illustration. *info:* A license to use a work as an artist's reference does not grant the right to reproduce, display, distribute or make any other use of a work, unless such rights are separately granted. *ex: To draw the beak correctly, the illustrator worked from an artist's reference photograph of a parrot.* **plural:** Artist's References **variation:** Art Reference

Artwork [3950-00-00-0100] A general term for completed creative efforts, including electronic and/or digital media, especially photographs and illustrations being reproduced. *info:* Sometimes used to refer to a layout or comp. *ex: Has the agency sent us the artwork we licensed?* **plural:** Artworks

As Is [1727-00-00-0100] A basis on which images and/or services are provided, usually without any warranties or undertakings of any kind. *ex: The goods will be received on an as is basis.*

Aspect Ratio [1345-00-00-0100] The ratio of width to height in an image. *info:* Theater screens generally have aspect ratios of 1.85:1, wide-screen TV (16x9) of 1.77:1 and traditional (NTSC, PAL) TV (4x3) of 1.33:1. Still photography offers many aspect ratios, from square format (such as 6x6 cm) to various panoramic formats. *ex: The image must fit a 3:2 aspect ratio.* **plural:** Aspect Ratios

Assign [2684-00-00-0100] To transfer to another all or part of one's property, interest, responsibilities or rights. *ex: The clients want us to assign the rights to them.*

Assignment

(1) Assignment (Production) [1803-00-01-0100] An agreement to produce creative works according to client specifications, to be used only in the manner described by a grant of usage rights. *info:* Typically, the usage rights granted with an assignment are part of the assignment agreement. *ex: The assignment is to shoot an interior location.* **plural:** Assignments

(2) Assignment (Rights) [1803-00-02-0100] The act of transferring intellectual property rights or ownership from the owner to one or more other parties. *info:* Any assignment must be in writing and specify exactly which rights are transferred. *ex: We made the assignment official after the client paid the appropriate fee.* **plural:** Assignments

Assignment Confirmation [3970-00-00-0100] A written document that specifies agreed terms, conditions and expected results for a contracted creative project, stating approval by the contracting party to proceed. *info:* Should be signed by all parties, but may be enforceable without signatures. Typically follows acceptance of an estimate by a client and precedes an invoice and delivery memo for the project. *ex: We've received your signed assignment confirmation, and we'll begin work on the project tomorrow.* **plural:** Assignment Confirmations

Assignment of a Copyright Interest [2683-00-00-0100] A transfer of one or more, but not all, rights in a work (such as a photograph or illustration) from the copyright holder to another party. *info:* An interest may include one or more exclusive rights but not necessarily ownership. Must be in writing and signed by the copyright holder. *ex: My agent asked for the assignment of a copyright interest in my images.* **plural:** Assignments of Copyright Interest

Assignment of Copyright Ownership [2815-00-00-0100] A complete transfer of copyright in a work (such as a photograph or illustration) from the copyright holder to another party. *info:* Must be in writing and signed by the copyright holder. *ex: The client asked about the price for an assignment of copyright ownership.* *plural:* Assignments of Copyright Ownership

Assigns [2755-00-00-0100] The persons or entity to whom property of another party is given or transferred on a voluntary basis, generally as a result of a term in an agreement. *ex: This agreement shall inure to the benefit of myself and my assigns.*

Attached Invoice [2731-00-00-0100] A renewal promotion attached to a magazine or mailed with it in a polybag, or in place of or in addition to a direct mail effort. *info:* Attached renewal is a clearer term. *ex: The attached invoice was distributed with last month's issue.* *plural:* Attached Invoices *preferred term:* Attached Renewal *usability:* Discouraged

Attached Renewal [1802-00-00-0100] A promotion encouraging readers to continue their subscription, attached to a magazine or mailed with it in a polybag. *info:* Often used in place of or in addition to a direct mail or telemarketing effort. *ex: Our cover image is also being used on their attached renewal.* *plural:* Attached Renewals

Audience [1044-00-00-0100] The number of people or homes who might see an image, publication, advertisement or display. *ex: That magazine has a large audience.* *plural:* Audiences

Audio Visual [1084-01-00-0100] See Audiovisual [1084-00-00-0100] *ex: The audio visual presentation included slides and music.* *plural:* Audio Visuals

Audio-Visual [1084-03-00-0100] See Audiovisual *ex: The audio-visual presentation included slides and music.* *plural:* Audio-Visuals

Audiovisual [1084-00-00-0100] A work combining sound and images, produced for presentation at events, at meetings or in retail outlets. *info:* Can be an advertising, editorial, educational or corporate use, and include slides, video, film and/or digital media. *ex: The audiovisual presentation included slides and music.* *plural:* Audiovisuals *variation:* AV, Audio Visual, Audio-Visual, A-V

Audit Bureau of Circulations [1002-00-00-0100] One of two independent organizations (the other is BPA worldwide) that verify magazine publishers' circulation numbers for advertisers. *ex: The Audit Bureau of Circulations was founded in 1948.* *variation:* ABC

Author [1719-00-00-0100] As used in licensing, a legal term referring to the initial copyright owner of a copyrightable work. *info:* With a work made for hire, the employer of the creator is the author. *ex: She is the author of the photograph.* *plural:* Authors

AV [1084-02-00-0100] Abbreviation for Audiovisual [1084-00-00-0100] *ex: The AV presentation included slides and music.* *plural:* AVs

Back Cover [1346-00-00-0100] The rear-facing, outer-page wrapping of a book, magazine, catalog, etc. *info:* More prominent than an interior page usage. *ex: The photograph will appear on the back cover of the book.* *plural:* Back Covers

Back Matter [1516-00-00-0100] All material added to the end of a book, beyond its main story or information. *info:* Includes but is not limited to an appendix, afterword or colophon, index and bibliography. *ex: The back matter in the book is 20 pages long.* *plural:* Back Matters

Background [1660-00-00-0100] The portion of a pictorial representation that appears behind the main subject and is arranged to provide relief for the principle objects or text. *info:* When two or more images are merged together in a composite, the portion of the image that appears behind a foreground image or graphic is called the background. *ex: The background behind the people is a cloudy blue sky.* *plural:* Backgrounds

Backlist [1587-00-00-0100] Books from previous seasons that are still in print. *ex: My book is on the publisher's active backlist.* *plural:* Backlists

Backlit Print [2804-00-00-0100] A large positive transparency designed to be lighted from behind; used for advertising or promotion purposes. *info:* Also known as Duratrans(TM), a trademarked brand name owned by Eastman Kodak Company. *ex: This image will be used for a backlit print displayed on a lightbox at the airport.* *plural:* Backlit Prints

Bandwidth [1347-00-00-0100] Digital communications capacity. *info:* A high bandwidth network connection can transmit or receive more data in a given amount of time than a low bandwidth connection. *ex: Cable Internet service usually delivers high bandwidth.* *plural:* Bandwidths

Bang Tail [1003-00-00-0100] A direct mail piece that includes an attached reply envelope. *info:* No separate envelope means lower cost compared to a business reply envelope. *ex: The bang tail includes an area for filling in address information.* *plural:* Bang Tails

Banner

(1) Banner (Print Placement) [1348-00-01-0100] Across the entire page or spread in a magazine or newspaper, often above a headline or any story content. *ex: The ad ran as a banner at the very top of the page.* *plural:* Banners

(2) Banner (Web Placement) [1348-00-02-0100] Across the width of a major portion of an entire web page, usually above other content. *ex: The banner ad includes animation that marches across the web page.* *plural:* Banners

(3) Banner (Display) [1348-00-03-0100] A flag or large canvas displaying a printed design and/or image, often placed above, either indoors or outdoors. *info:* May include promotion or advertising. *ex: This banner will hang above the trade show floor.* *plural:* Banners

Belly Band [1004-00-00-0100] A printed promotional advertisement that is physically wrapped around a magazine, catalog or product before shipment to a subscriber or retail outlet. *info:* Other promotional use might include a press kit or sales kit. *ex: To attract attention, the belly band will be bright, fluorescent green.* *plural:* Belly Bands

Below the Line

(1) Below the Line (Advertising) [1085-00-01-0100] Budget term denoting non-commissionable advertising use outside the five traditional areas: press, TV, radio, cinema and outdoor. *ex: The below the line budget includes brochures and post cards.*

(2) Below the Line (Production) [1085-00-02-0100] Budget term denoting expenses for a production's costs, such as equipment rental, film or tape stock and technical crew salaries. *info:* Usually does not include creative costs, such as photographer, producer and talent. *ex: The below the line budget includes a stylist, grip and grip truck.*

Bi-Monthly [4120-01-00-0100] See Bimonthly [4120-00-00-0100] *ex: The engineering journal is a bi-monthly, coming out every two months.* *plural:* Bi-Monthlies

Bi-Weekly [4130-01-00-0100] See Biweekly [4130-00-00-0100] *ex: The newsletter came out bi-weekly, giving the editor two weeks to prepare each issue.* *plural:* Bi-Weeklies *preferred term:* Biweekly *usability:* Caution

Bibliography [1517-00-00-0100] A listing of work consulted during the preparation of and/or cited within the body copy of a written work. *info:* Frequently part of a work's back matter. *ex: The bibliography is 10 pages long, listing 60 books and 15 periodicals.* *plural:* Bibliographies

Bid [1059-00-00-0100] A pre-production document formulated by a licensor based on a project description provided by the licensee, including the scope of the license, and any applicable terms and conditions. Also, the act of formulating and presenting such a document. *info:* Unlike an estimate, if actual costs are higher than those cited in the bid, the licensor may not add to the bill, unless additional charges are approved by the licensee. If actual costs are lower than those bid, the licensee remains obligated to pay the entire approved bid amount. A bid may be legally binding if not signed by a licensee, provided the licensee indicates acceptance of its terms and conditions, and authorizes the licensor to proceed. *ex: The customer has asked us to provide a bid.* *plural:* Bids *preferred term:* Estimate *usability:* Caution

Billboard [1086-00-00-0100] A large, permanent outdoor display structure with advertising signage installed, usually for a one- or three-month period. *info:* Can also be inside large arenas or stadiums. May be printed, painted, projected, illuminated or three-dimensional. *ex: The billboard is 40 feet long and 30 feet high.* *plural:* Billboards

Bimonthly [4120-00-00-0100] A publication with a unique title that is distributed every other month. *info:* Some refer to a semi-monthly (twice a month) publication as a bimonthly. It's best to be clear which period is intended. *ex: The engineering journal is a bimonthly, coming out every two months.* *plural:* Bimonthlies *variation:* Bi-monthly

Bind in Card [1811-00-00-0100] One or several subscription or promotional postcards physically bound into a magazine (or inserted across the magazine spine) so they will not fall out. *ex: To increase return rates, the next bind in card will be postage paid.* *plural:* Bind In Cards *variation:* Bind-In Card

Bind-In Card [1811-01-00-0100] See Bind In Card *ex: To increase return rates, the next bind-in card will be postage paid.* *plural:* Bind-in Cards

Binding

(1) Binding (Legal) [1518-00-01-0100] Describes a legal obligation that continues while an agreement is in force. *ex: The contract was binding on both parties.*

(2) Binding (Print) [1518-00-02-0100] The materials that hold a book or other publication together, typically including a front cover, the spine and a back cover. *ex: The book title is often printed two or more places on the binding. plural:* Bindings

Bit [1349-00-00-0100] A single unit of digital information. *info:* Digital information is recorded using binary notation, so a single bit has a value of either zero or one. *ex: Some scanners produce 48 bit scans, offering a wealth of color data. plural:* Bits

Bit Depth [4330-00-00-0100] Refers to the amount of tonal or color information associated with a digital image. *info:* An image with a higher bit depth can display more gradations or nuanced colors. The most common color bit depth for exchanged files (especially JPEGs) is 8 bits per color, or 24-bit color (for an RGB image). Professional digital cameras typically capture 10 bits or more per color, which can be imported and/or converted with professional software to 16 bits or more per color for editing. *ex: We need an image with a high bit depth to be sure we can match color exactly. plural:* Bit Depths

Bit Rate [1350-00-00-0100] The rate at which data are encoded or transported in a given amount of time, specified as bits per second (BPS), kilobits per second (KBPS) or megabits per second (MBPS). *info:* Usually expressed as a theoretical maximum; actual data throughput is often lower. *ex: If you transmit the image at a higher bit rate, it will reach its destination sooner. plural:* Bit Rates

Bitmap [1351-00-00-0100] An image represented by rows and columns of dots called pixels. *info:* Enlarging or reducing a bitmap in size (as measured by the number of pixels across and down) results in image degradation and the more bits associated with each pixel, the more possible colors can be displayed. Many use this term to refer specifically to images in which the dots are bi-level (pure black or white with no shades of gray) and the image can be represented with one bit per dot (e.g.: a fax image). *ex: The resolution of a bitmap image is determined by how many pixels it contains. plural:* Bitmaps

Biweekly [4130-00-00-0100] A publication with a unique title that is issued every two weeks. *info:* Some use this term for a publication (a semi-weekly) that comes out twice a week. It's best to specify which period is intended. *ex: Since the newsletter came out biweekly, the editor had two weeks to prepare each issue. plural:* Biweeklies *variation:* Bi-weekly

Black and White Image

(1) Black and White Image (Digital) [1817-00-01-0100] An image whose pixel data comprises only levels of luminance, without color data. *info:* Typically, a black and white, or grayscale, image has eight bits of luminance data per pixel to produce 256 shades of gray. More bits per pixel are possible and frequently yield smoother results, particularly when editing an image's tone and contrast. *ex: Downloading your black and white image will take one-third as long as downloading a comparable RGB image. plural:* Black and White Images

(2) Black and White Image (Print) [1817-00-02-0100] An image printed using only black ink, or an image printed with multiple ink colors that appear as shades of gray. *info:* May be enhanced by adding one, two or three shades of ink (from gray or black to warm or cold colors) to become, respectively: duotone, tri-tone or quadtone images. Process color inks can also simulate the appearance of black and white printing. *ex: Look at the black and white image on the second page of the brochure. plural:* Black and White Images

(3) Black and White Image (Photo) [1817-00-03-0100] A photographic image that contains only white, black and shades of gray. *info:* May be recorded on black-and-white materials or electronic systems, or on color materials or systems that are converted to shades of gray during processing. May be printed on black-and-white or color materials, depending upon processing methods. *ex: We will ship the black and white image to you. plural:* Black and White Images

Black and White Print [1352-00-00-0100] An image reproduced on black and white or color photographic materials using black, shades of gray and white—or neutral amounts of color. *ex: The photographer delivered the image as a black and white print. plural:* Black and White Prints

Black Compression [1353-00-00-0100] The loss of detail in dark areas when an original image is reproduced. *ex: Black compression during reproduction eliminated shadow detail that is clearly visible in the original image.*

Blast [2777-00-00-0100] Bulk distribution of promotional, marketing or advertising messages, usually by fax or email. *ex: The blast was sent to 7,000 fax machines last night. plural:* Blasts

Blast Date [2738-00-00-0100] The calendar day when a marketing, sales, mail, fax or email campaign is actually distributed to the target audience. *ex: The blast date is next Thursday.* *plural:* Blast Dates

Bleed [1354-00-00-0100] Image placement on a page so that the edge of the page cuts off the edge of the picture. *info:* A bleed may run off one or more sides of a page. *ex: The layout called for a right-edge bleed, so we allowed for a 1/4-inch crop on the right of the picture.* *plural:* Bleeds

Blog [5150-00-00-0100] A personal or professional diary or running commentary on an Internet page that may contain words, images, or other content. *info:* A blog is usually published and updated on a frequent basis. *ex: I saw the story on our company blog.* *plural:* Blogs

Blow In [1107-02-00-0100] See Blow In Card *ex: The blow in was printed on plain, white paper for insertion in next month's issue.* *plural:* Blow Ins

Blow In Card [1107-00-00-0100] An advertising or subscription card inserted, but not bound, into a magazine or periodical. *ex: The Blow In card was printed on plain, white paper for insertion in next month's issue.* *plural:* Blow In Cards *variation:* Blow In, Blow-In Card, Blow-In

Blow-In [1107-04-00-0100] See Blow In Card *ex: The blow-in was printed on plain, white paper for insertion in next month's issue.* *plural:* Blow-Ins

Blow-In Card [1107-03-00-0100] See Blow In Card *ex: The blow-in card was printed on plain, white paper for insertion in next month's issue.* *plural:* Blow-In Cards

Blue [1527-01-00-0100] See Blueline *ex: Check the blue before the end of the day, so we can get this project on the press.* *plural:* Blues

Blueline [1527-00-00-0100] A final, preproduction copy of a work, used to verify there are no last-minute errors. *info:* Typically created by a printer on blueprint paper. *ex: Check the blueline before the end of the day, so we can get this project on the press.* *plural:* Bluelines *variation:* Blue

Board Book [1519-00-00-0100] Book printed on robust, stiff card stock and intended for very young children. *ex: Our illustrations will be used throughout the board book.* *plural:* Board Books

Body Copy [1580-00-00-0100] The majority of the text in a book, magazine or periodical that appears between the front matter and back matter. *info:* Does not include headline, title or other type that stands out from the textual matter. Often used also to refer to the text on a web page, advertisement or other media that is neither headline, navigation nor boilerplate information. *ex: The body copy begins on page one.*

Body of Work [3270-00-00-0100] A collection of creative efforts fixed in tangible form, such as an entire photography session, assignment or archive. *info:* It's important both licensor and licensee understand everything included in a body of work as well as the license to use it. *ex: The client wants to license the entire body of work from our latest stock production.* *plural:* Bodies of Work

Boilerplate [1510-00-00-0100] Colloquial for the standard terms and conditions that appear in almost every contract, or the standard form of agreement sent to a party before negotiation. *ex: The boilerplate on the back is set in very tiny type.*

Book

(1) **Book (Publishing)** [1139-00-01-0100] Any work that is printed and bound, distinguished from a magazine, tract, etc. *info:* Images may be used on the front cover, back cover, jacket or inside. Usually has a unique ISBN reference number. *ex: Her memoirs were published in a book.* *plural:* Books

(2) **Book (Production)** [1139-00-02-0100] The act of reserving a service, a professional's time or a location. *ex: Be sure to book the talent, grip truck and town park well in advance.* *plural:* Books

(3) **Book (Marketing)** [1139-00-03-0100] A common term for a portfolio or other collection of sample work by a photographer, illustrator, designer or other creator. *ex: Drop off your book for review at the advertising agency, and you may just see some work from them.* *plural:* Books

Book Signing [1512-00-00-0100] A marketing event at which an author signs copies of his or her book for the general public. *ex: The author left the book signing late in the afternoon.* *plural:* Book Signings

Bottlenecker [1087-00-00-0100] An advertising tag specifically designed to encircle or hang from the neck of a glass or plastic vessel. *ex: Each bottlenecker has a one-inch hole through which a bottle passes.* *plural:* Bottleneckers

Bound-in Insert [4750-00-00-0100] A piece that is printed separately, then glued and/or stitched together with other pages in a periodical. *info:* Often used for advertising projects. *ex:* *The bound-in insert is printed on different paper than the magazine it's stitched into.* *plural:* Bound-In Inserts

BPA [1622-01-00-0100] Abbreviation for BPA Worldwide *ex:* *BPA is authorized to verify that a publication qualifies for postal service periodicals mailing class privileges.*

BPA Worldwide [1622-00-00-0100] One of two media auditing companies that verify newspaper, magazine and website circulation numbers on behalf of advertisers. *info:* The other company that verifies audience numbers is the Audit Bureau of Circulations. *ex:* *BPA worldwide is authorized to verify that a publication qualifies for postal service periodicals mailing class privileges.* *variation:* BPA.

Brand Extension [1007-00-00-0100] To increase revenues and awareness, brand owners (publishers or manufacturers) create special magazine issues, books, trade shows, merchandise or electronic products (CD or website) that carry the brand name and deal with topics that are related to the brand. *ex:* *The adventure travel guide is a brand extension of the country's oldest sport's periodical.* *plural:* Brand Extensions

BRC [1008-01-00-0100] Abbreviation for Business Reply *ex:* *The BRC, printed on plain, white paper, is set for insertion next month.* *plural:* BRCs

BRE [1009-01-00-0100] Abbreviation for Business Reply Envelope *ex:* *The BRE, printed on plain, white paper, is set for insertion next month.* *plural:* BREs

Breach [1233-00-00-0100] By action or failure to act, the breaking or violation of a law, right, engagement, obligation or duty. *info:* Exists if one party to a contract fails to carry out a term, promise or condition of the contract. *ex:* *Breach of contract can have serious legal ramifications.* *plural:* Breaches

Broadcast Email [1838-00-00-0100] Email distribution of a large quantity of messages containing promotion, marketing or advertising. *info:* May link to a web page. The use of broadcast email may be restricted by legislation, such as that requiring an existing business relationship with the recipient. *ex:* *The broadcast email was sent out last night to 70,000 addresses.* *plural:* Broadcast Emails

Broadcast Fax [1607-00-00-0100] Bulk fax distribution of promotion, marketing or advertising messages. *info:* The use of broadcast fax may be restricted by legislation, such as that requiring an

existing business relationship with the recipient. *ex:* *The broadcast fax was sent last night.* *plural:* Broadcast Faxes

Broadsheet

(1) Broadsheet (Journalism) [2741-00-01-0100] A traditional, folded newspaper format that unfolds in two directions for reading the inside pages. *info:* Usually distributed in sections that are inserted inside each other. Several standard web widths exist, with corresponding standard advertising sizes. *ex:* *The Wall Street Journal is a broadsheet financial newspaper.* *plural:* Broadsheets

(2) Broadsheet (Advertising) [2741-00-02-0100] A large sheet of paper, usually printed on one side, containing advertising or a public notice. *ex:* *The broadsheet for the benefit concert includes pictures of the performers.* *plural:* Broadsheets

Broadside [1759-00-00-0100] A large sheet of paper, usually printed on one side, containing advertising or a public notice. *ex:* *The concert broadside includes an image of the performers.* *plural:* Broadsides

Brochure [1088-00-00-0100] A pamphlet, usually promotional or advertising in nature, with a front cover, back cover and content inside. *info:* Usually folded or bound. *ex:* *One side of the brochure is printed in color.* *plural:* Brochures

Buckslip [2739-00-00-0100] A small, printed booklet advertising a product or service. *info:* Usually distributed by hand or placed in kiosks and other high-traffic areas. *ex:* *We ordered 5,000 copies of the buckslip.* *plural:* Buckslips

Budget [1608-00-00-0100] The itemized sums of money and/or other resources (such as time) estimated and set aside for a particular purpose, project or timeframe. *ex:* *We will not exceed the budget for this project.* *plural:* Budgets

Building Wrap [4760-00-00-0100] Rolls of vinyl or other flexible, durable and printable material that can be draped on or around a building to create large signs. *info:* Usage is similar to a billboard on a building. *ex:* *The building wrap showing our ad could be seen for 20 blocks.* *plural:* Building Wraps

Bulk Circulation [1045-00-00-0100] A quantity of magazine, newspaper or other printed matter delivered to one location for redistribution to multiple parties. *ex:* *The magazine is shipped to a bulk circulation distributor.* *plural:* Bulk Circulations

Bus Advertising [1852-00-00-0100] A marketing or promotional piece, usually poster size or larger, displayed on the interior or exterior of a public transportation, or on the exterior of other large vehicles. *info:* May be printed, or displayed on monitors or other digital devices. *ex: The campaign includes bus advertising on vehicles throughout the metro area.*

Bus Stop Advertising [1855-01-00-0100] See Bus Terminal Advertising *ex: The campaign includes bus stop advertising on the walls of each shelter.*

Bus Terminal Advertising [1855-00-00-0100] A marketing or promotional piece, usually poster size or larger, placed on the structure of a bus terminal, station, platform or stop. *info:* May be printed, or displayed on monitors or other digital devices. *ex: The campaign includes bus terminal advertising on each shelter, as well as in regional lobbies.* *variation:* Bus Stop Advertising

Business Card [1185-00-00-0100] A small, printed card used as a means of communicating contact information about a specific person and/or company. *ex: She gave her business card to the client, so he would know how to contact her.* *plural:* Business Cards

Business Reply Card [1008-00-00-0100] Postcards included in a magazine, brochure or other printed matter for use by recipients to request information or to order products, subscriptions or services. *info:* Usually includes a prepaid business reply postage permit number. *ex: The business reply card, printed on plain, white paper, is set for insertion next month.* *plural:* Business Reply Cards *variation:* BRC

Business Reply Envelope [1009-00-00-0100] Flat, folded paper containers included in magazines, brochures and other printed matter for use by recipients to request information, or to order products, subscriptions or services. *info:* Usually includes a prepaid business reply postage permit number. *ex: The business reply envelope, printed on plain, white paper, is set for insertion next month.* *plural:* Business Reply Envelopes *variation:* BRE

Butt Against [1358-00-00-0100] To place immediately against adjoining matter with no white space between. *ex: On the layout, the two photos butt against each other.* *variation:* Butt To

Butt To [1358-01-00-0100] See Butt Against [1358-00-00-0100] *ex: On the layout, the two photos butt to each other.*

Button

(1) Button (Online) [1694-00-01-0100] An icon on a web page that, when selected, submits data entered on a form to a server, or via an HTML link, and allows users to view a particular associated web page or image. *info:* Sometimes includes an image. *ex: The button that links to the website has a drop shadow.* *plural:* Buttons

(2) Button (Promotion) [1694-00-02-0100] A small, printed piece, attached to a pin, that carries text, graphics and/or images as part of a promotion or marketing campaign. *info:* Sometimes includes an image. *ex: A political campaign button usually includes the candidate's name in bold type.* *plural:* Buttons

Buy Out [1060-00-00-0100] An imprecise term used to describe acquisition of broad usage rights to a work, sometimes in a particular market or medium. *info:* Buy Out is a slang term, often misinterpreted as a transfer of copyright ownership of a work from the copyright holder to the client or client's agent. In the absence of a specific copyright transfer agreement executed by the copyright holder there is no copyright transfer. If this term is used, an additional, precise list of rights granted or transferred should accompany any license. *ex: The clients asked for a buy out but agreed to a time-based license for a single campaign.* *plural:* Buy Outs *preferred term:* Unlimited Use *usability:* Discouraged *variation:* Buyout, Buy-Out

Buy-Out [1060-02-00-0100] See Buy Out [1060-00-00-0100] *ex: The clients asked for a buy-out but agreed to a time-based license for a single campaign.* *plural:* Buy-Outs *preferred term:* Unlimited Use *usability:* Discouraged

Buyout [1060-01-00-0100] See Buy Out [1060-00-00-0100] *ex: The clients asked for a buyout but agreed to a time-based license for a single campaign.* *plural:* Buyouts *preferred term:* Unlimited Use *usability:* Discouraged

Byte [4340-00-00-0100] A unit of digital information comprising an arbitrary number of bits (usually eight). *info:* A byte can theoretically be almost any size, although bytes with few bits can't define as many different data variations—such as typographical characters—as larger bytes. File sizes and storage capacities are commonly described in thousands of eight-bit bytes (kilobytes), millions (megabytes), billions (gigabytes) or trillions (terabytes). *ex: The file was just a byte or so too big to fit on that disk.* *plural:* Bytes

Calendar [1091-00-00-0100] Any formal listing of the months and days in each year. *info:* Retail calendars are sold to the general public and to businesses; promotional calendars carry advertising, promotion or marketing messages from one or more sponsors. Size varies. Single-hanger calendars usually feature a single image and list each month on a separate page. Multiple-hanger calendars typically feature a different image for each month. Desk calendars may have different images each week or even every day. *ex: The company sends out a promotional calendar each year.* *plural:* Calendars

Camera Format [1629-00-00-0100] The size, shape and aspect ratio, and/or perceived quality of an image produced on film or recorded by digital capture. *info:* Typically stated as large format, medium format or 35mm, but determined by the dimensions of the focal plane or image sensor. Digital capture technologies are blurring the traditional distinctions, since an image sensor may be small but pack many pixels. *ex: The images were made in 35mm camera format.* *plural:* Camera Formats

Camera Ready [3280-00-00-0100] Describes an advertisement, book, periodical or other layout fully prepared for reproduction. *info:* Traditionally on paper, but may sometimes refer to digital formats, such as PDF. Additional prepress work on a project promised as camera-ready can be expensive. *ex: Please send us camera ready artwork, unless you wish to pay us for typesetting and design.*

Cancellation Fee [1574-00-00-0100] A sum agreed to be paid when a procuring party cancels the services of the providing party. *info:* Typically applicable when there is a short period before the production or due date, in order to offset costs and inconvenience to the seller. Cancellation fees typically are not refundable. *ex: The amount of the cancellation fee is reasonable, considering how much work was done in advance.* *plural:* Cancellation Fees

Cap [1201-00-00-0100] A retail shelf location at the end of an aisle of shelves. *ex: The food store cap shows our logo and a picture of our soup cans.* *plural:* Caps *variation:* End Cap

Caption [4170-00-00-0100] Information describing the content, context and/or details of a picture. *info:* May be printed below a picture, elsewhere on a page, in an appendix or in a POP up online. Can be included in appropriate metadata with digital images. *ex: Make sure every picture has a complete caption.* *plural:* Captions

Card [1760-00-00-0100] A flat, usually rectangular piece of stiff paper, cardboard or plastic. *ex: We will enclose this card with our annual report.* *plural:* Cards

Cardbound Book [1140-00-00-0100] A book with a stiff, hard cover. *ex: That cardbound book should hold up well in the waiting room.* *plural:* Cardbound Books

Cassette [1359-00-00-0100] Plastic case system that holds, protects and manages spools of magnetic tape for easy insertion into data, music or video tape players or recorders. *ex: Insert the cassette into the player and wind it forward to the program.* *plural:* Cassettes

Casting [4770-00-00-0100] The act of interviewing or otherwise reviewing potential talent for a project. *info:* May be the responsibility of a photographer, art producer, client or agency, depending upon an agreement associated with the project. *ex: The producer will handle all casting of talent at least two weeks before the shoot date.*

Catalog

(1) Catalog (Print) [1804-00-01-0100] A printed listing of one or more companies' products or services, or the act of producing such a listing. *info:* Descriptive text and images usually accompany entries in a catalog. *ex: The catalog includes more than 100 products.* *plural:* Catalogs

(2) Catalog (Electronic) [1804-00-02-0100] An electronic or online listing of products or services, a similar listing of digital assets (such as image files), or the act of creating or adding to such listings. *info:* Descriptive text and images usually accompany entries in a catalog. *ex: The catalog includes more than 100 products.* *plural:* Catalogs

CD [1092-02-00-0100] Abbreviation for CD ROM *info:* CD also is short for manufactured compact discs that store music and have replaced vinyl record albums. *ex: The CD containing the image data was stored in a paper sleeve. plural:* CDs

CD ROM [1092-00-00-0100] Compact disc—read only memory/media: an electro-optical data storage medium with the same physical format as an audio disc and a capacity of approximately 650–700MB of data. *info:* Often used in advertising, PR, marketing, sales or other promotion activities, and for delivery of large quantities of content (including digital photographs). There are several types of compact discs, some of which include the ability to erase and record data many times. *ex: The CD ROM containing the image data was stored in a paper sleeve.* *plural:* CD ROMs *variation:* Compact Disc, Compact Disk, CD-ROM, CD

CD-ROM [1092-01-00-0100] Acronym for CD ROM *ex: The CD-ROM containing the image data was stored in a paper sleeve.* **plural:** CD-ROMs

CDB [1559-03-00-0100] Abbreviation for Cost of Doing Business *ex: Understanding your CDB is only one step in setting prices.*

Cellular Phone [4780-00-00-0100] A communications device that allows users to talk and send data with a low-power radio signal that links to a network of antennas and computers. **info:** Operates much as a wired telephone from the user's perspective. Cellular phones are a subset of mobile communications devices, using one of several cellular communications methods. Many such devices—including most recent models—can display images and access the Internet, and some can capture and transmit a digital image or video. *ex: The photographs will be available to cellular phone users of our service.* **plural:** Cellular Phones

Centerfold [1360-00-00-0100] A spread of two or more pages bound into a saddle-stitched magazine at the point where its stitches show inside. *ex: This image will appear as the March centerfold.* **plural:** Centerfolds

Chain [1544-00-00-0100] Any retail company having multiple locations, either owned or franchised. **info:** Typically, the same advertising and logo are used for each location. *ex: Most large shopping malls have at least one large chain store.* **plural:** Chains

Change Order [1730-00-00-0100] A specification of modifications to a contract after the terms and conditions are set and agreed upon. **info:** If the original agreement includes a term that states no changes except in writing, a change order must be in writing and executed by all parties. *ex: The change order includes more work to be performed.* **plural:** Change Orders

Chapter Book [1550-00-00-0100] A book tailored for young children, ages 6 to 13, that is divided into chapters, with one or two drawings or images at the beginning or in the middle of each chapter. **info:** Some are released one chapter at a time, using various media (print, email or online). *ex: My second-grader brought home a chapter book from school.* **plural:** Chapter Books

Chapter Opener [1361-00-00-0100] Special, prominent use of an image to designate the beginning page of a portion of a work. **info:** Often treated as a special design element. *ex: The image will be used as a chapter opener.* **plural:** Chapter Openers

Check [1202-00-00-0100] A draft for monetary funds from a bank or other financial institution. **info:** Often includes an illustration, image or design on the front face. *ex: The check for the payment owed is in the mail.* **plural:** Checks

Checking Copy [2695-00-00-0100] A printed example of a magazine or other periodical publication containing a commercial announcement, sent to whomever contracted and/or paid for the placement or needs to verify placement. **info:** Used to verify an advertisement was presented properly, as promised. *ex: A checking copy was shipped to all companies that had an ad in the last issue.* **plural:** Checking Copies **preferred term:** Advertiser Copy [1001-00-00-0100] **usability:** Caution

Children's Book [3990-00-00-0100] A trade book published for children, often for a specific age group. *ex: The children's book will be heavily illustrated, since it's aimed at early readers.* **plural:** Children's Books

Choice of Law [1234-00-00-0100] A contractual clause that specifies which law (usually the law of a specific state, county and/or nation) will govern disputes arising under a contract. *ex: Both parties were located in Los Angeles, so they specified California law in the choice of law clause in their contract.*

Chrome [2803-00-00-0100] A positive transparency designed to be viewed when lighted from behind. **info:** Term used frequently to describe positive camera film, which is sold as slide film. Large chromes are used for advertising or promotional purposes, and are sometimes known by the trademarked brand name Duratrans(TM), which is owned by Eastman Kodak Company. *ex: This image will be used for a chrome to be displayed for three months in a lightbox in the boarding terminal.* **plural:** Chromes

Circulation [1288-00-00-0100] The number or amount of reproductions displayed or distributed. **info:** Related but not synonymous with frequency. While frequency might be used to refer to the number of insertions in a magazine (or whether the insertions are monthly, bimonthly, etc.), circulation for the magazine focuses on quantity of each issue distributed. *ex: The magazine has a circulation of one million.* **plural:** Circulations

Clear [4810-00-00-0100] To ensure that no existing usage license conflicts with a potential license. *ex: We need to clear and reserve this exclusive license before we can offer it to the client.*

Clearance [4790-00-00-0100] Confirmation that prior or current use of an image will not conflict with a pending exclusive usage license. *ex: The client has received clearance to use the picture for six months in shoe advertising.* **plural:** Clearances

Clearing Party [4800-00-00-0100] The person or entity responsible for granting clearance for a usage license. *ex: The clearing party assures us the image is available for our exclusive use.* **plural:** Clearing Parties

Client [4820-00-00-0100] The person or entity seeking to license or assign creation of a work. *info:* A photographer or illustrator might work directly with a client, or through an agent or representatives. *ex: The client wants to be present during production to ensure we produce the pictures she wants.* **plural:** Clients

Clip Art [3300-00-00-0100] A descriptor for royalty free works purchased in bulk. *info:* The term clip art originated with large books of mostly generic artwork, arranged on pages that purchasers cut apart to obtain specific images for mechanical layout and reproduction. Used often in local advertising. Also applied to collections of digital illustrations, photographs and even video clips sold on CD or DVD, or downloaded, with unlimited reproduction rights licensed to the buyer. *ex: We can't afford to commission an image for this ad; we'll have to go with clip art.* **plural:** Clip Art

Clipping Path [1363-00-00-0100] A graphics software function that allows a shape to mask part of an image. *info:* Used to isolate an object from its original background so that it can be dropped into a composite or page design. *ex: Some image files include a clipping path that makes it easy to knock out the background.* **plural:** Clipping Paths

CMS [1364-01-00-0100] Abbreviation for Color Management System *ex: Make sure your CMS is set up properly for your monitor and output systems.*

CMYK [1365-00-00-0100] A method of representing color using the four standard printing ink colors. *info:* CMYK color is based on the primary colors of pigment—cyan, magenta and yellow—which combine in their purest forms to make black. In practice, black ink is added, since impurities mean most CMY inks combine to make a muddy brown. The range of possible colors in CMYK is much less than in RGB color, making problematic anything more than minor color adjustment of digital images in CMYK color. *ex: We had a CMYK color separation made for offset printing.* **variation:** Cyan Magenta Yellow and Black

Co-Op [1012-00-00-0100] Advertising or promotion in which several advertisers, one or more media outlets, manufacturers, or distributors share the costs and/or message. *info:* Participants can also include wholesalers and local retail outlets, different brands, related products or services. Typically, all participants share the costs. *ex: The manufacturer offers a 50-50 co-op advertising program.* **plural:** Co-Ops **variation:** Cooperative

Co-op Money [1818-00-00-0100] Funds available from a company or distributor for retail outlets to help promote a product. *info:* May include funds advanced or reimbursed in part or in whole by a manufacturer, distributor, wholesaler or franchiser to a local retail outlet. Typically, all participants share the costs. Some manufacturers reduce advertising costs using cooperative promotion across different brands, related products or services. *ex: We should spend the co-op money this quarter on advertising that includes our store and the brand name.* **plural:** Co-Op Monies

CODB [1559-02-00-0100] Abbreviation for Cost of Doing Business *ex: Understanding your CODB is only one step in setting prices.* **plural:** CODBs

Coffee Table Book [1141-00-00-0100] Term used to describe a large-format volume, usually heavily illustrated. *ex: A coffee table book can help build a photographer's reputation.* **plural:** Coffee Table Books

Collage [1142-00-00-0100] A composition of materials, objects or images (or parts thereof) arranged together, often with unifying lines or colors, and reproduced as a single unit. *info:* If any elements are protected by copyright, then including those elements usually requires permission from the copyright holder(s). *ex: The artist produced a collage of magazine pictures and type, graphically arranged against a plain, black background.* **plural:** Collages

Collateral [1061-00-00-0100] Printed marketing and advertising pieces for use in direct request and personal contact, not in publications. *info:* Often reflects a larger broadcast, print or direct mail campaign. May include leaflets, brochures, pamphlets and business cards, among many other possible uses. However, collateral is often misunderstood to comprise an even longer list of uses. Listing individual uses may be more practical for most licensing situations. *ex: Collateral is delivered directly to the consumer or dealers rather than via mass media.* **usability:** Caution

Collective Licensing [4000-00-00-0100] A system for cooperative administration of copyrights. *info:* License fees may be set by the cooperative or by individual participants, who often share the burden of marketing and sales administration. *ex: Some collective licensing solutions aim to help control individual work and pricing, while reaching a larger market as a group.*

Collective Work [1715-00-00-0100] A legal term referring to a publication, such as an issue of a newspaper, magazine or anthology, in which separate and independent works are assembled as contributions to a larger whole. *info:* A type of compilation. Publisher typically owns copyright in the publication, but copyright ownership in each element remains with its contributor unless otherwise negotiated. *ex: Our new magazine will be a collective work, including articles and pictures from many sources. plural:* Collective Works

Colophon [1520-00-00-0100] A summary of information related to a book's production, usually placed at the end of the book. *info:* Example content might include typefaces used or illustrations that appear in the book. *ex: The colophon begins on page 233 and lists 75 photographs. plural:* Colophons

Color Correction [1366-00-00-0100] The changing of hues and tones in an image to achieve optimum printed results. *info:* Can include adjustments to brightness, contrast, midlevel grays, hue and saturation. *ex: A small color correction can sometimes vastly improve image reproduction. plural:* Color Corrections

Color Fidelity [4840-00-00-0100] The desired result of color management software; an assurance that images will look the same regardless of the reproduction medium. *info:* A relative term. Different media reproduce color using different processes, and perfect matches are rare. *ex: The color fidelity of the images is outstanding in the latest edition of the book.*

Color Image

(1) Color Image (Digital) [1827-00-01-0100] A digital image comprising levels of hues and tones. *info:* The most common color modes are RGB or CMYK, typically with eight bits of luminance data per pixel for each of the colors. More bits per pixel are possible and frequently yield better results, particularly when adjusting tone and color. *ex: That color image looks great on the monitor. plural:* Color Images

(2) Color Image (Photo Technical) [1827-00-02-0100] A photographic image produced using color film or other color imaging systems, or a full-tone color image printed on color photographic paper or duplicating film. *ex: This color image was made on negative film, which we can ship to you for scanning. plural:* Color Images

(3) Color Image (Print) [1827-00-03-0100] An image that is printed using process color. *info:* May be enhanced by adding one or several additional special colors. *ex: Look at the richness of the color image on page two of the brochure. plural:* Color Images

Color Management System [1364-00-00-0100] A system for communicating color reproduction information about digital images between input, display and output devices. *info:* Improves fidelity of image reproduction when properly configured and used by all involved in a production workflow. *ex: Make sure your color management system is set up properly for your monitor and output systems. plural:* Color Management Systems *variation:* CMS

Color Profile [1744-00-00-0100] A standardized digital file containing color space information. *info:* Can improve color fidelity when embedded into a digital image file and referenced during reproduction. *ex: Be sure your system properly translates the color profile embedded in that image. plural:* Color Profiles

Color Proof [1367-00-00-0100] A representation of a final printed piece, used for checking color accuracy and other elements. *info:* May not be as accurate as a contract proof. *ex: The text on the color proof was correct and the pictures looked good. plural:* Color Proofs

Color Separation [1368-00-00-0100] The process of transforming full-color artwork into screened, CMYK components, the digital file that results from that process, or the set of films that results and are used to burn plates for printing a process color image. *ex: The printer shipped us the color separation. plural:* Color Separations

Color Space [1369-00-00-0100] A three-dimensional representation of a color profile, useful in imaging to understand color performance across a variety of input, display and output devices. *ex: A CMYK color space reflects the ink and paper being used. plural:* Color Spaces

Column Inch [1370-00-00-0100] The unit used to measure the running length of a piece as it appears (or will appear), set in type, in column(s) in a newspaper or other publication. *ex: The piece is one column inch too long for the layout. plural:* Column Inches

Commercial

(1) Commercial (Broadcast) [1093-00-01-0100] An advertisement on television or radio. *ex: The image will appear in a television commercial. plural:* Commercials

(2) Commercial (General) [1093-00-02-0100] A descriptor for image uses that are part of sales or marketing efforts. *ex: Commercial use requires releases for all recognizable models and property.*

Commercial Misappropriation [1237-00-00-0100] Using another's property for commercial purposes without consent. *info:* The basis for protection of trademark, intellectual property, the right of publicity and the right of privacy. *ex: My lawyer said it was a clear-cut case of commercial misappropriation of my work. plural:* Commercial Misappropriations

Commission [1609-00-00-0100] A payment to a sales agent or agency, usually a percentage of the gross or net sales amount. *info:* Can also be a fixed-dollar amount per item sold. *ex: My agent receives a 20 percent commission on all sales. plural:* Commissions

Commissioned Work [1718-00-00-0100] A work created by an independent contractor to satisfy an order placed by a customer or client. *ex: That assignment was a commissioned work for this year's annual report. plural:* Commissioned Works

Comp

(1) Comp (Publishing) [1143-00-01-0100] A complimentary copy of a magazine or a book. *ex: I received this copy of the magazine as a comp. plural:* Comps

(2) Comp (Production) [1143-00-02-0100] Visual rendering of a proposed advertisement or other printed piece. *info:* Usually indicates the planned placement of each photograph, each illustration and/or all copy, along with examples of each. May have two stages: a rough outline (called a mock up or visual), followed by the proposed or finished artwork (called a comp). *ex: The art director showed the comp to the client. plural:* Comps

Comp Use [1144-00-00-0100] Image reproduction in one or a very few copies of a layout or dummy that shows headlines, images, type and text. *info:* Purpose of comp is to secure approval from all concerned parties prior to final production. An image delivered for comp use is typically, but not always, delivered at low resolution and a fee is sometimes charged. *ex: The image was licensed for comp use in a proposed layout for an advertisement. plural:* Comp Uses *variation:* Comprehensive Use

Compact Disc [1092-03-00-0100] See CD ROM *ex: The compact disc containing the image data was stored in a paper sleeve. plural:* Compact Discs

Compact Disk [1092-04-00-0100] See CD ROM *ex: The compact disk containing the image data was stored in a paper sleeve. Plural:* Compact Disks

Compendium [1238-00-00-0100] A summary or abridgment of a book or other publication, sometimes including images. *ex: We need compendium rights to the license, so we can reuse the pictures in our condensed edition. plural:* Compendiums

Compilation [1716-00-00-0100] A work formed by the collection and assembly of pre-existing materials or data that are selected, coordinated or arranged, so the resulting work as a whole constitutes an original work of authorship. *info:* Includes a collective work and usually requires a license for any copyright material included. *ex: In their next compilation, my photo will be used with the original article that accompanied it. plural:* Compilations

Composite [1657-00-00-0100] An image made up of separate, distinct visual elements merged into one visually continuous, seamless image. *ex: A colleague has licensed one of my images for use in a composite with his pictures. plural:* Composites *variation:* Photo Composite

Compositing [1371-00-00-0100] The act or process of combining images. *info:* Now usually accomplished with digital tools, but can also use photo-mechanical methods. *ex: She makes a good living as an independent contractor compositing images into new scenes.*

Comprehensive Use [1144-01-00-0100] See Comp Use *ex: The image was licensed for comprehensive use in a rough layout for an advertisement. plural:* Comprehensive Uses

Compression [1372-00-00-0100] The act of making something smaller. A digital file is compressed by removing redundant information. *info:* Some image file compression methods discard visually redundant information and may degrade image quality. *ex: JPEG compression makes image files smaller but discards some data, possibly leaving artifacts. plural:* Compressions

Compression Ratio [1373-00-00-0100] The amount of data in an original video or digital file divided by the amount of data in a version after compression. *info:* Higher ratios indicate more compression and may degrade image quality. But note that some measures of compression ratios, such as those commonly applied to JPEG image files, rate lower compression ratios as high quality or a higher number. *ex: A compression ratio of less than 4:1 is usually safe. plural:* Compression Ratios

Computer Game [1820-00-00-0100] Interactive computer software (together with instructions and packaging) designed specifically for entertainment, educational, or sometimes, marketing. *info:* Distributed on CD ROM or DVD (frequently inside a jewel case), or via download from the World Wide Web. Some games are played on the web. *ex: These images will appear as backdrops in a new computer game.* *plural:* Computer Games

Computer Presentation [1094-00-00-0100] Audiovisual presentation composed (and perhaps also delivered) using a computer and/or projection system. *ex: The computer presentation will begin in 15 minutes.* *plural:* Computer Presentations

Computer Software [2818-00-00-0100] Coded procedures (together with any instructions and packaging) that control computer hardware and provide access to interactive digital entertainment, education and information processing tools. *info:* Distributed on CD ROM or DVD (usually packaged in a jewel case), or via download from the World Wide Web. *ex: The new computer software will display our photographs during start up.*

Concept [1732-00-00-0100] The underlying, abstract idea for a promotion, advertisement, editorial package or the components that comprise it, or a category of communication that focuses on such ideas, rather than on specific motivation of the audience. *info:* A concept is the idea a client wishes to illustrate. But the term also may describe a campaign that focuses, for example, on the idea that fuel economy helps the environment, rather than on the particularly fuel efficient vehicles the sponsor manufactures. *ex: The image will be used in a concept advertising campaign.* *plural:* Concepts *variation:* Conceptual

Concept Book [1551-00-00-0100] Book designed for toddlers and very young children, with minimal, easy-to-read text and numerous images. *info:* Subject matter is usually limited to one specific idea or concept (e.g.: simple counting, ABCs, colors, familiar animals or objects). *ex: The image will be used in our concept book about cleanliness.* *plural:* Concept Books

Conceptual [1732-01-00-0100] See Concept *ex: The image will be used in a conceptual advertising campaign.*

Confidential [3320-01-00-0100] See Confidentiality [3320-00-00-0100] *ex: Before you can work in our plant, you must agree not to photograph certain areas and keep what you see in those areas confidential.*

Confidentiality [3320-00-00-0100] Describes an agreement that limits how information or images may be shared with others. *info:* Confidentiality may be a condition set in a license, contract, model release, property release, or in exchange for access to a particularly valuable property or technology. *ex: Before you can photograph next year's fashions for us, you must sign a confidentiality agreement.* *variation:* Confidential

Conflict [1235-00-00-0100] When a requested license overlaps or is incompatible with an existing exclusive license. *info:* There are four possible types of conflict: spot, use, territory and industry. *ex: Using that image in a real estate ad would create a conflict.* *plural:* Conflicts

Consideration [1239-00-00-0100] Something of value given by one party to another as part of a contract. The inducement to a contract. *info:* The cause, motive, price or impelling influence that induces a contracting party to enter into a contract. *ex: They agreed $10,000 was reasonable consideration.* *plural:* Considerations

Consumer Advertisement [1062-00-00-0100] Commercial communication that is directed to members of the general public. *ex: The consumer advertisement will appear in several popular magazines.* *plural:* Consumer Advertisements

Consumer Goods [1204-00-00-0100] Packaged products intended for mass markets, and for consumption by an individual or household for personal, family or household purposes. *ex: This image is being used in the packaging comp for a new line of consumer goods.*

Consumer Magazine [2808-00-00-0100] A periodical targeted toward, marketed and distributed to the public at large. *ex: This advertisement is geared to a consumer magazine.* *plural:* Consumer Magazines

Consumer Print Advertising [1095-00-00-0100] Advertising in newspapers, magazines and/or other consumer publications targeted to the general public. *ex: The image will be used for the company's consumer print advertising.*

Consumer Publication [1145-00-00-0100] A periodical targeted toward, marketed and distributed to the public at large. *ex: This advertisement is geared to a consumer publication.* *plural:* Consumer Publications

Contents Page [2797-00-00-0100] A listing, usually at the beginning of a work, of the titles and/or short descriptions of chapters, sections and/or articles within. *info:* Often includes a repeat use of images from within the work. *ex: The illustration will appear on the contents page.* **plural:** Contents Pages

Continuity [1010-00-00-0100] Buyers agree to receive products for review over a set period and to buy an agreed quantity. **info:** Examples include book and music clubs. *ex: The goal in continuity marketing is for customers to keep and pay for the goods shipped to them.*

Continuous Tone Image [1375-00-00-0100] An image containing smooth gradient tones from black to white. *ex: That continuous tone image reproduces well.* **plural:** Continuous-Tone Images

Contract [1556-00-00-0100] A legally binding agreement, involving two or more competent people or entities, with terms and conditions that state what the parties will or will not do, and which specifies consideration (some form of benefit to each party) for their performance. **info:** A contract requires: an offer, acceptance of that offer, agreement and consideration. Acceptance can include a signature (printed or electronic), taking an action (such as clicking an I agree online button), or in some cases, oral affirmation. *ex: The contract is 10 pages long and includes penalties for any delays.* **plural:** Contracts

Contract Proof [1648-00-00-0100] A high-quality print, made with careful color management, of an image or layout, sometimes with text and graphics, intended to convey accurate predictions of how a press will reproduce color, registration, text and other visual elements. **info:** Depending on contract terms and conditions, commercial printers may or may not guarantee final printed results will match the contract proof closely. *ex: We approved the contract proof yesterday and have assurance our work will print beautifully.* **plural:** Contract Proofs

Contrast [1376-00-00-0100] The extent of tonal gradation between the highlight and shadow regions in an image. *ex: That contrast will be corrected when the image is reproduced.*

Contributor [1240-00-00-0100] An author whose work is published as a part of a collective work, such as a book, magazine or advertisement. *ex: As a contributor, he supplied two pictures and wrote a chapter of the book.* **plural:** Contributors

Controlled Circulation [1011-00-00-0100] Describes a periodical targeted at a particular consumer or trade product category, vertical industry, or profession. **info:** Distributed at no charge to subscribers who have verified they fit a social, professional or economic target audience and are qualified to receive the periodical. *ex:*

The magazine has a controlled circulation of 450,000 homeowners. **plural:** Controlled Circulations

Cooperative [1012-01-00-0100] See Co-Op [1012-00-00-0100] *ex: The manufacturer offers a 50-50 cooperative advertising program.* **plural:** Cooperatives

Copy

(1) Copy (Text) [1684-00-01-0100] In advertising, the text portion of an advertisement including headline. In editorial and book, the entire text or narrative portion of the work. *ex: We're expecting to read the copy this morning.* **plural:** Copies

(2) Copy (Reproduction) [1684-00-02-0100] A material object in which a work is fixed by any method, and from which the work can be perceived, reproduced and/or otherwise communicated with the aid of a machine or device. **info:** Includes the material object in which the work is first fixed. Prevailing interpretation of Copyright Law indicates that an image stored temporarily or permanently in digital form on a hard drive, in computer memory or on any other storage media constitutes a copy, provided the storage is more than transitory. *ex: Here is a copy of the piece, with a license to reproduce it.* **plural:** Copies

Copy Transparency [1377-00-00-0100] A copy of a transparency, usually in a different camera format than the original. *ex: Ship a copy transparency to the printer.* **plural:** Copy Transparencies

Copyright [1241-00-00-0100] A legal property right in an original work of authorship fixed in any tangible medium of expression, such as photographs, illustrations, architectural works, literary works, musical scores and recordings, and motion pictures. **info:** Copyright is more than the right to copy, it is a divisible bundle of exclusive rights. The owner of copyright in a work holds the exclusive right to reproduce, publicly display, adapt, distribute and/or publicly perform the work, and to authorize others to do the same. *ex: She owns the copyright to those images.* **plural:** Copyrights

Copyright Infringement [1557-00-00-0100] The act of violating any of the exclusive rights of a copyright owner. **info:** Reproduction, public display, adaptation, distribution or public performance of a work without advance permission from the copyright owner is a copyright infringement, unless such use constitutes fair use or a compulsory license under Copyright Law. *ex: Use of the photograph without the copyright holder's consent is a copyright infringement.* **plural:** Copyright Infringements

Copyright Notice [1666-00-00-0100] Printed text adjacent to the reproduction of a work that indicates the work is copyright protected. *info:* Consists of the copyright symbol (or the word copyright or abbreviation copr.), the year of first publication and the name of the copyright owner. This is not required to protect copyright, but it may provide legal benefit to the copyright owner. Can appear on or adjacent to the reproduction of a work, or on a separate page. *ex: The copyright notice appears in a small typeface below the image. plural:* Copyright Notices

Copyright Page [1521-00-00-0100] A page in a book, magazine or website containing publisher contact information, copyright statements, publication history, library information, and perhaps copyright information about texts or images appearing in the work and an ISBN number. *ex: The copyright page is usually in front matter, often on the back of the title page. plural:* Copyright Pages

Copyright Registration [1558-00-00-0100] In the United States, the process of registering and filing tangible copies of creative works with the Library of Congress Copyright Office. *info:* Registration is a practical prerequisite to bringing a claim against another party for copyright infringement in the U.S. Without timely registration, only actual damages may be awarded in a successful copyright suit filed in a U.S. District Court. Registration allows a successful plaintiff to seek the recovery of attorney fees and court costs, and to elect to recover statutory damages instead of actual damages, including enhanced damages for willful infringement. *ex: The U.S. Copyright Office is the office of public record for copyright registration and deposit of copyright material. plural:* Copyright Registrations

Copyright Transfer [1242-00-00-0100] An assignment of copyright ownership or an assignment of a copyright interest in a work (such as a photograph or illustration) from the copyright holder to another party. *info:* Often misunderstood because the term does not specify exactly which rights are being transferred. Use of more specific language may prevent misunderstandings. *ex: The clients asked about the cost of a copyright transfer for the image. plural:* Copyright Transfers *preferred term:* Assignment of Copyright Owners [2815-00-00-0100] *usability:* Discouraged

Copyrighted [1724-00-00-0100] Describes a work protected by copyright, whether or not a copyright registration has been submitted to record ownership of the work. *info:* Copyright in a work exists from the moment that the work is fixed in tangible form. *ex: As soon as a photograph is made, it is copyrighted.*

Copyrighted Work [2712-00-00-0100] A work protected by copyright, whether or not a copyright registration has been submitted to record ownership of the work. *info:* Copyright in a work exists from the moment that the work is fixed in tangible form. *ex: As soon as a photograph is taken, it is a copyrighted work. plural:* Copyrighted Works

Corollary Rights [2706-00-00-0100] An extension of a right to material in a main or primary work for appearance in subordinate, helping, auxiliary, consequent or resultant materials that accompany or relate to the main work. *info:* Examples include student guides, instructor's manuals, educational software and duplicate transparencies. *ex: The corollary rights include in-class audiovisual presentations.*

Corporate Card [1186-00-00-0100] A small card, usually sent through the mail as an invitation to corporate events, as thank you notes, etc. *ex: The corporate card will be back from the printer tomorrow. plural:* Corporate Cards

Corporate Invitation [2762-00-00-0100] A small card, usually sent through the mail, to encourage attendance at a sponsored event. *ex: The corporate invitation will be back from the printer tomorrow and sent out two weeks before the party. plural:* Corporate Invitations *variation:* Corporate Invite

Corporate Invite [2762-01-00-0100] See Corporate Invitation [2762-00-00-0100] *ex: The corporate invite will be back from the printer tomorrow and mailed two weeks before the party. plural:* Corporate Invites

Cost of Doing Business [1559-00-00-0100] The sum of money required to open a business, and over time, keep it running and solvent. *info:* Includes rent, utilities, labor, taxes and other costs that are not part of the cost of goods sold. Generally expressed as dollars per day. *ex: Understanding your cost of doing business is only one step in setting prices. plural:* Costs of Doing Business *variation:* CDB, CODB

Cost Per Thousand [1014-01-00-0100] See CPM *ex: The cost per thousand is $1.53 for that magazine. plural:* Costs Per Thousand

Counter Card [1096-00-00-0100] A small, printed promotional piece placed where a product is sold. *ex: The counter card is printed on bright orange paper to help attract attention. plural:* Counter Cards

Coupon [1205-00-00-0100] Printed ticket that promises a discount or special promotion to a consumer when redeemed at a retail outlet. *ex: This coupon will appear in the Sunday newspaper. plural:* Coupons

Course Pack [1146-00-00-0100] A compilation or anthology of photocopied selections from various sources that are bound, or left unbound, and distributed to students. *info:* A separate license is needed for any image used in a course pack. *ex: Pick up your course pack of important articles and chapters at the bookstore.* **plural:** Course Packs *variation:* Coursepack

Coursepack [1146-01-00-0100] See Course Pack *ex: Pick up your coursepack of important articles and chapters at the bookstore.* **plural:** Coursepacks

Covenant [1243-00-00-0100] In its broadest usage, any formal agreement or contract. *ex: We will enter into a covenant between all parties once we all agree on the terms.* **plural:** Covenants

Cover [1378-00-00-0100] The outer page or wrapped pages of a book, magazine, catalog or other printed piece, usually made of heavier materials than the inside pages, and which readers see before opening the piece. *info:* More prominent than an interior page usage. Cover is a general term that includes both the front and back of a printed piece. *ex: This image was licensed for the cover.* **plural:** Covers

Cover Wrap [1013-00-00-0100] A special promotional sheet attached to the outside of a magazine. *info:* Often used on sample copies or for subscription renewal. *ex: To attract attention, the cover wrap is bright orange.* **plural:** Cover Wraps

CPM [1014-00-00-0100] Refers to the price an advertiser pays for reaching 1,000 target audience members through a given advertising medium. *info:* The cost per thousand impressions, or CPM (M is the roman numeral for thousand), is calculated as ad cost divided by circulation. Used as a basis to compare advertising cost and to price subscriber list rentals. *ex: The CPM is $1.53 for that magazine.* *variation:* Cost Per Thousand

Creative Commons [1736-00-00-0100] An organization that proposes a license method allowing use without permission under certain circumstances. *info:* Enables copyright holders to grant some of their rights to the public while retaining others, through a variety of different license and contract arrangements. See http://creativecommons.org. *ex: Creative commons licenses are used widely for web pages.*

Creative Fee [1560-00-00-0100] A charge by a creator for his or her efforts to complete a project, which is not based on time alone. *info:* Factors may include compensation for trade experience and special capabilities, or for any creative effort, contribution or process required to complete a project. Typically does not include a licensee or usage fee. *ex: The estimate included the photographer's creative fee based on production of ten images for the campaign.* **plural:** Creative Fees

Creator [1720-00-00-0100] A person or entity causing an original work to be fixed in tangible form. *info:* Under the Copyright Law, the creator of a work is the author and copyright owner of that work upon its creation. Exception: if a work is a work made for hire made by an employee in the course of his or her employment, the employer of the creator is the author of the work and owns the copyright upon creation. *ex: A creator produces original works.* **plural:** Creators

Creator Restriction [4290-00-00-0100] A restriction required by artists or third-party image providers that can limit the availability of specific images for particular industries, territories, uses and/or time frames. *ex: Because of the creator restriction on this image, it cannot be licensed for use in anything related to the tobacco industry.*

Credit [2767-01-00-0100] See Credit Line *ex: The image has a proper credit, including the photographer's name, copyright and affiliation.* **plural:** Credits

Credit Card [1206-00-00-0100] A rectangular piece of stiff plastic, sometimes decorated with an image, used to draw funds against the credit line of an individual or company as payment for goods and services. *info:* Sometimes combined with a debit card. *ex: He used a credit card with a picture of the ocean on it to buy gasoline.* **plural:** Credit Cards

Credit Line [2767-00-00-0100] A line of text identifying the copyright holder (and, optionally, the date of the copyright). *info:* Usually placed near an image, at the bottom of a page or screen on which the image appears, or in a separate area of the publication. Some licenses require specific wording, placement, size of type and/or other details for a credit line. Many credit lines include a creator that differs from the copyright holder, such as one whose creation was a work made for hire or who has assigned the copyright. Some credit lines include an image provider, such as an agency or archive, that is not the copyright holder. *ex: The image has a proper credit line, including the photographer's name, copyright and affiliation.* **plural:** Credit Lines *variation:* Credit

Credit Page [5160-00-00-0100] A page, usually inthe back matter of a book or magazine with many contributors, listing contributions and their sources. *info:* A listing on such a page may be required by contract. This page is often in addition to a copyright page that appears in the front matter. *ex: The credit* page lists 40 photographers and 97 pictures that are in the book. *plural:* Credit Pages

Crop [1379-00-00-0100] To trim an image to a specific size to fit a layout or to focus the viewer on a specific portion of the content, or the version of an image that has been trimmed. *ex: The art director wants a tight crop around the model's head.* *plural:* Crops

Custom Publishing [1147-00-00-0100] Providing individualized content (such as a personal, city or state edition) by assembling various pieces of information from a database. *info:* In some models, consumers select from a variety of content to suit personal taste or need. Consumer selections might then be printed and bound. Such assemblies usually require a license from the copyright owner(s). *ex: These sales packages were produced using our new custom publishing system.*

Cut Out [3340-00-00-0100] A shape or object removed from its background in order to insert it into another image or background. *info:* A digital image may contain clipping paths to make producing a cut out easier. *ex: The catalog project requires a cut out as the finished image for each product.* *plural:* Cut Outs

Cutline [3330-00-00-0100] Traditional term for a caption, particularly one directly beneath a halftone in a publication. *info:* Derived from old printing term for halftone engravings, which had to be cut into a printing plate. A line or two of descriptive type beneath a cut became a cutline. *ex: Make sure the cutline for that picture is complete and accurate.* *plural:* Cutlines

Cutout [1097-00-00-0100] A specially designed print advertisement that includes an area intended for physical separation. *ex: The cutout has a perforated edge to make it easier to separate.* *plural:* Cutouts

Cyan Magenta Yellow and Black [1365-01-00-0100] See CMYK *ex: We had a cyan magenta yellow and black color separation made for offset printing.*

Daily [3350-00-00 0100] A publication with a unique title that has a new edition every day or each weekday. *ex: The press kit photo will be in every daily tomorrow.* *plural:* Dailies

DAM [4850-01-00-0100] Acronym for Digital Asset Management System *ex: Our DAM allows us to quickly locate and repurpose previous projects, in whole or in part.*

Damages [1245-00-00-0100] Harm, injury and/or loss suffered by someone or an entity, and the money paid to compensate for a harm, injury or loss. *info:* There are many kinds of damages. *ex: We won our*

case in court and were awarded damages, including legal fees.

Dangler [1098-00-00-0100] An advertising tag designed to hang from a retail display of products for sale, most often clothing. *ex: The dangler hangs from a shelf display for men's shirts.* *plural:* Danglers

Day

(1) Day (Duration) [1504-00-01-0100] A single, 24 hour period, generally from 00:00:01 a.m. Until midnight. *ex: Shipping typically occurs within one day.* *plural:* Days

(2) Day (Production) [1504-00-02-0100] An eight hour work period. *ex: That job will require one full day.* *plural:* Days

Day Rate [1561-00-00-0100] A pre-agreed, flat-rate fee paid for up to one day of production work. *info:* Generally based on an 8-hour production day, but may require specific negotiation. *ex: The day rate for the project covers production efforts, but the usage fee is additional.* *plural:* Day Rates *preferred term:* Creative Fee *usability:* Caution

Debit Card [1677-00-00-0100] A rectangular piece of stiff plastic, often decorated with an image. Draws against the bank deposits of an individual or company when used at a point of sale as payment for goods or services. *info:* Sometimes combined with a credit card. *ex: Pay for the groceries with the debit card that has a picture of a skier on it.* *plural:* Debit Cards

Dedication [1581-00-00-0100] A creator's statement of acknowledgment or appreciation for one or more people to whom a project or product is addressed. *ex: The dedication is at the front of the book.* *plural:* Dedications

Defamation [1246-00-00-0100] A false statement that could damage the reputation of a person or other legal entity within the community. *ex: Libel and slander both involve defamation.* *plural:* Defamations

Defamatory Use [1247-00-00-0100] Use of a work in a derogatory context, such as part of a false statement concerning a person that could damage that person in the eyes of the community. *ex: Printing that photograph with this headline might be a defamatory use.* *plural:* Defamatory Uses

Delete [2780-00-00-0100] To remove or cancel. *ex: The client is required to delete these images files from his hard drive after publication.*

Delivery Contract [1562-00-00-0100] A document that describes a work or materials delivered by an owner or the owner's representative to another party. *info:* Contains terms and conditions relating to the delivery of the property and limitations on its use. *ex: The delivery contract was signed by the client.* *plural:* Delivery Contracts

Delivery Memo [2717-00-00-0100] A document that describes a work or materials delivered by an owner or the owner's representative to another party. *info:* Contains terms and conditions relating to the delivery of the property and limitations on its use. However, the title memo has caused problems enforcing such terms and conditions, especially when a signed copy is not returned. Use delivery contract instead. *ex: The client received a delivery memo with the prints but failed to sign and fax the document back.* *plural:* Delivery Memos *preferred term:* Delivery Contract *usability:* Discouraged

Derivative [1630-01-00-0100] See Derivative Work *info:* Used for image files that are derived by subsampling or oversampling an original or archive master digital image. Previews, thumbnails and fingernails are all examples of derivative files. *ex: This thumbnail is a derivative of the original, high-resolution file.*

Derivative Work [1630-00-00-0100] A work derived from or based upon one or more pre-existing works. An alternative version of a copyrighted work. *info:* The right to prepare a derivative work is reserved exclusively for copyright owners. Permission from all copyright owners of pre-existing works involved is required before preparing a derivative work, unless the derivative work constitutes a fair use under the Copyright Act. The owner of the copyright in a derivative work does not acquire ownership of the copyright in the preexisting works. *ex: This image is a derivative work.* *plural:* Derivative Works *variation:* Derivative

Desktop [1661-00-00-0100] The default view on a computer monitor when no application windows are visible. *info:* More loosely, refers to a personal computer that requires more than battery power. *ex: There are file icons on the desktop.* *plural:* Desktops

Desktop Publishing [1389-00-00-0100] A workflow that uses personal computers to arrange text and graphics for printing in a magazine, newsletter, brochure, web page, poster, etc. *ex: We have converted from paste-up production to desktop publishing.* *variation:* DTP

Detail [1381-00-00-0100] Describes the smallest visual elements in an image that can be clearly recognized or defined and reproduced. More generally, a minor portion of a larger work. *ex: It's easy to make out the detail in a high-resolution image.* *plural:* Details

Digital [1382-00-00-0100] The representation of information using binary numbers (zeros and ones) that correspond to a voltage being either on or off in computers and associated processing, storage and transmission technologies. *info:* Digital information may be copied many times with no loss of quality or degradation, and it can be altered in ways that are difficult to detect. *ex: Publishing and imaging have widely adopted digital technologies and depend on computers.*

Digital Asset Management System [4850-00-00-0100] A database or similar program designed for tracking and organizing digital files, including documents, images, video, animations and more. *ex: Our digital asset management system allows us to quickly locate and repurpose previous projects, in whole or in part.* *plural:* Digital Asset Management Systems *variation:* DAM

Digital Capture [1631-00-00-0100] The process of acquiring visual information with a digital camera, or an image that results from such photography. *ex: We will use digital capture because it gets images into our computers faster.* *plural:* Digital Captures

Digital Fee [1646-00-00-0100] A charge made by a photographer for digital capture and subsequent processing or rendering of the digital image. *info:* A digital fee might be a lump-sum charge or a tally of itemized charges, such as downloading files from camera to computer, RAW file post-processing and editing, digital darkroom processing to enhance the digital capture, data storage, proof prints, delivery and other services. *ex: The invoice includes a digital fee for postproduction of the captured images.* *plural:* Digital Fees

Digital File [1805-00-00-0100] An ordered set of binary numbers representing information in active computer memory, or stored on magnetic, optical or other media. *info:* Can be electronically transferred, or translated into a facsimile of an original analog form (on paper or a computer display). Digital files can be altered in ways that can be difficult to detect. *ex: We are downloading the digital file now.* *plural:* Digital Files

Digital Image [1651-00-00-0100] A visual recording of objects, scenes and/or people that is encoded into a digital file. *info:* Can result from a digital scan, digital capture, original input of artwork on a computer or combinations of several sources. *ex: We will email you a digital image.* *plural:* Digital Images

Digital Image Management System [4860-00-00-0100] A database or similar software program for tracking and organizing digital image files. *info:* Many digital asset management systems can handle image files. A digital image management system is more specialized. *ex: Thanks to keywording, we can locate any one of the 50,000 pictures in our digital image management system.* *plural:* Digital Image Management Systems *variation:* DIM

Digital Imaging [1652-00-00-0100] A catch-all term that includes all electronic production processes associated with pictures captured or created with binary systems. *info:* Can include a scan, digital capture, as well as retouching, enhancement, compositing, resizing and other modifications. *ex: We have a large digital imaging operation.*

Digital Mechanical [1437-01-00-0100] See Mechanical [1437-00-00-0100] *ex: Because the digital mechanical was missing the specialized fonts used for the job, the piece was on hold until the fonts could be procured.*

Digital Negative [1741-00-00-0100] A digital image file format akin to a digital original. Similar to a RAW file but an open format that does not include manufacturer-specific proprietary technologies. *info:* A digital negative requires post-processing before it can be used. Capable of delivering more color, dynamic range and resolution than a TIFF or JPEG digital image file. Adobe Corp.'s DNG is one such format. *ex: Few photographers deliver a digital negative file to a client.* *plural:* Digital Negatives

Digital Rights Management [1763-00-00-0100] The use of encryption or other technological means to regulate access to a licensable digital work, such as images, songs, movies, other software or sensitive documents. *info:* Typically, special computer software enforces time limits and permits viewing, yet denies copying, or it ties usage to a particular device. *ex: The DVD uses digital rights management that prevents copying on a computer.* *variation:* DRM

Digital Scan [1842-00-00-0100] Visual information acquired with a device that passes light through or reflects light off an analog original, capturing its tone and color information with a light-sensitive digital sensor or sensor array. *info:* The resulting digital information is typically sent to an attached computer, where it is stored as a digital image. *ex: We will make a digital scan of that print for reproduction.* *plural:* Digital Scans

Digital Versatile Disc [1392-01-00-0100] See DVD *ex: The digital versatile disc includes both the still images and a video that incorporates them.* *plural:* Digital Versatile Discs

Digital Versatile Disk [1392-02-00-0100] See DVD *ex: The digital versatile disk includes both the still images and a video that incorporates them.* *plural:* Digital Versatile Disks

Digital Video Disc [1392-03-00-0100] See DVD *ex: The digital video disc includes both the still images and a video that incorporates them.* *plural:* Digital Video Discs

Digital Video Disk [1392-04-00-0100] See DVD *ex: The digital video disk includes both still images and a video that incorporates them.* *plural:* Digital Video Disks

Digitally Alter [1383-00-00-0100] To use computer software to change a digital version of an original work. *info:* The process may create a derivative work that requires permission from the copyright holder for any element appearing in the finished piece. Digital alteration can be difficult to detect. *ex: We have secured licenses to digitally alter the image for our needs.* *preferred term:* Digitally Modify *usability:* Discouraged

Digitally Change [2771-00-00-0100] To use computer software to change a digital version of an original work. The process may create a derivative work that requires permission from the creator of any element appearing in the finished piece. *info:* Digital changes can be difficult to detect. *ex: We have secured licenses to digitally change the image for our needs.* *preferred term:* Digitally Modify *usability:* Caution

Digitally Enhance [2772-00-00-0100] To use computer software to remove blemishes or artifacts in a digital image and to make other minor changes before distribution, delivery or use. *info:* Requires specialized computer software and operator expertise. Refers to edits and adjustments that do not materially affect the content of the image. *ex: We will digitally enhance the image to improve the contrast.*

Digitally Modify [2770-00-00-0100] To use computer software to change a digital version of an original work. The process may create a derivative work that requires permission from the copyright holder of any element appearing in the finished piece. *info:* Digital modifications can be difficult to detect. This term is often confused with digitally enhance, making digitally alter preferred. *ex: We have secured permission to digitally modify the image to include the missing board member.* *preferred term:* Digitally Alter *usability:* Caution

Digitally Retouch [1840-00-00-0100] To use computer software to remove digital image blemishes or artifacts and make other desirable changes before distribution, delivery or use. *info:* Requires specialized computer software and operator expertise. Term does not describe material changes to the primary content of the image, although it may describe changes to a distracting background or foreground. *ex: We will digitally retouch the image to remove the scar from the CEO's nose. variation:* Retouch

Digitize [1384-00-00-0100] To convert analog content into digital form. *info:* Typically involves a digital scan or digital photography. *ex: We will digitize this illustration for insertion in the layout.*

DIM [4860-01-00-0100] Acronym for Digital Image Management System *ex: Thanks to keywording, we can locate within a few minutes any one of the 50,000 pictures in our DIM. plural:* DIMs

Dimensions [1385-00-00-0100] With a given digital image file, denotes the number of pixels across width and depth. *info:* Together with an output DPI, allows the calculation of the reproduction size of the given digital image. Much confusion comes from defining digital image size by resolution (such as 300 PPI), which does not describe an image's size without the addition of its physical dimensions at that resolution. An image that is 4x6 inches at 300 PPI is actually the same size as an image that is 8x12 inches at 150 PPI, or 1,200 pixels by 1,800 pixels. *ex: The dimensions of that file are 1,200 pixels by 1,800 pixels.*

Direct Debit [1612-00-00-0100] A payment method. Customers instruct their bank to authorize an individual or organization to collect regular or occasional payments from their bank account. *info:* Bank customers must be notified in advance regarding the collection amount and date of collection. *ex: We will use direct debit to pay our account each month. plural:* Direct Debits

Direct Mail [1830-00-00-0100] Advertising or marketing materials mailed directly to a specific market, target audience, group or list of names, usually in large volume. *info:* Examples include (but are not limited to) a brochure, catalog, flyer, postcard and CD ROM. ex: *That postcard is part of our direct mail campaign. plural: Direct Mailings*

Direct Request [1015-00-00-0100] Describes a list of customers who verify in writing or electronically that they desire and are qualified to receive a magazine or product. *info:* Of great appeal to advertisers and marketers. *ex: The magazine has a high percentage of direct request subscribers.*

Direct Response Television [1017-00-00-0100] An extended-length television advertisement used by magazine, product and service marketers to increase brand awareness, sell subscriptions or promote a brand extension. *info:* The ads ask viewers to place a phone call or respond online to order the magazine, product or service. *ex: Many direct response television ads run late at night and include a toll-free number for orders. variation:* DRTV

Directory [1187-00-00-0100] A listing of services or information, usually arranged alphabetically or as a classified list. May be printed, on a CD ROM or online. *info:* Typically contains telephone numbers, addresses and names of persons and businesses. *ex: Our company directory will be reprinted next week, but the online version is current. plural:* Directories

Directory Advertising [1100-00-00-0100] Commercial communication that appears in a directory. *ex: The ad campaign includes directory advertising.*

Display

(1) Display (Media) [2816-00-01-0100] Information or a work exhibited for groups of people to view, generally, but not always, in public. *info:* May include advertising or other marketing messages. *ex: This image will be used as part of a display in a shopping mall. plural:* Displays

(2) Display (Production) [2816-00-02-0100] A device for visually representing information. May be electronic (such as a video or computer monitor), electric (such as a light box), or as simple as a frame surrounding an image on a stand. *ex: The image looks perfect on our computer display. plural:* Displays

Display Chrome [1101-00-00-0100] A large, positive transparency designed to be lighted from behind, and used for advertising, promotion, editorial or fine art purposes. *info:* Sometimes referred to as a Duratrans(TM), which is a trademarked brand name owned by Eastman Kodak Company. *ex: This image will be used for a display chrome. plural:* Display Chromes

Display Print [2812-00-00-0100] A printed copy of an image, intended for viewing by an audience, usually in a public place, rather than reproduction. *info:* Does not include display within a frame for the express purpose of selling that frame (packaging) or for fine art. *ex: The display print will be mounted in a train station kiosk. plural:* Display Prints

Display Print Advertising [1102-00-00-0100] Promotional materials presented in a form that is relatively large and viewable in person, usually from a distance and in public. *info:* Generally refers to reflected art, as opposed to a display chrome. *ex: The marketing campaign includes lots of display print advertising.*

Distribution [2690-00-00-0100] The process or act of moving a work, goods or services, usually from manufacturer or publisher to wholesale or retail outlets (but also to end users), or a description of how widely the goods or services will be delivered. *info:* In image licensing, often refers to the geographical area in which reproductions (such as a publication) will be sold and/or circulated, and is a key factor in pricing a license. *ex: That movie goes into North American distribution next week. plural:* Distributions

Distribution Right [1249-00-00-0100] Refers to a specific geographic region in which copies of an image or other work may be distributed by a license holder. *info:* Often associated with language rights, but distinct. The name of the area(s) should be specified, as well as the language(s) for which the image is licensed. Does not grant the right to distribute for reuse by a third party or parties. *ex: The client purchased a North American distribution right. plural:* Distribution Rights

Distributor [5120-00-00-0100] A company that stores, catalogs, markets, sells and/or licenses on behalf of a number of creators or producers, consolidating costs for those services. *info:* May work through sub-distributors, who require additional fees for their services. *ex: We sell our products through a distributor. plural:* Distributors

Division [1536-00-00-0100] A section or business group within an organization that specializes in a certain product, a kind or type of activity, or perhaps a specific geographic region. *ex: The image was licensed to only the western division of the company.* plural: Divisions

DMM [1613-01-00-0100] Abbreviation for Domestic Mail Manual [1613-00-00-0100] *ex: See the DMM for the cost of shipping your express package. plural:* DMMs

Documentary [3360-00-00-0100] A sequence of images, audio and/or video that tells a factual story of a place, person, event, etc. *info:* Also used to describe a style of photography that records what the photographer finds in a situation, rather than what he or she might arrange, control or contrive. *ex: The producer wants to license two pictures for a documentary on eagles. plural:* Documentaries

Domain [1689-00-00-0100] A group of networked computers and the data they make available that share a common communications address. *info:* Users apply to one of several sanctioned domain registrars for name assignments. If available, the name is granted to the applicant. Special Internet servers translate the words and punctuation of a domain name into a set of numbers more readily used by computers. *ex: Our domain name is usePLUS.org. plural:* Domains

Domestic Mail Manual [1613-00-00-0100] The U.S. Postal service guide to the rules and regulations of the postal system. *ex: See the domestic mail manual for the cost of shipping your express package. plural:* Domestic Mail Manuals *variation:* DMM

Dot Gain [1653-00-00-0100] A printing effect that sometimes causes a printed image to grow denser or darker. *info:* When ink is applied to paper on a printing press, it tends to spread slightly across the paper, and the dots comprising a printed image sometimes increase in diameter. A prepress operator or photographer preparing images for specific press conditions can compensate for this effect by reducing color saturation or density during halftone or color separation setup. More porous papers tend to have higher dot gain figures. *ex: Please make sure you use proper dot gain settings or the pictures will appear too dark or too light. plural:* Dot Gains

Dots Per Inch [1388-01-00-0100] See DPI *ex: Many computer monitors display at 72 dots per inch.*

Double Page Spread [1387-00-00-0100] A piece that covers two facing pages in a magazine, newspaper, book or other printed publication. *ex: The advertisement will be a double page spread on pages 10 and 11 of the magazine. plural:* Double Page Spreads

Double Postcard [1016-00-00-0100] A two-part, printed promotional or advertising piece on heavy paper stock, with an attached reply postcard designed to be separated and mailed back to the sponsor. *ex: The double postcard was printed on plain, white paper. plural:* Double Postcards

Double Truck [1386-00-00-0100] A piece that covers two facing pages in a magazine, newspaper, book or other printed publication. *ex: The story and pictures will run as a double truck on pages 10 and 11. plural:* Double Trucks

Download [1704-00-00-0100] To use a computer or other digital device to retrieve digital data from a server or another computer. *ex: Please download the image from our website.* **plural:** Downloads

DPI [1388-00-00-0100] A measurement unit describing the resolution of a hardware device, such as a computer monitor or digital printer, that renders digital imagery as output using binary values for each colorant. *info:* Often used incorrectly as the resolution unit for a digital image, in which case the correct units would be PPI (pixels per inch). *ex: Many computer monitors display at 72 DPI.* **variation:** Dots Per Inch

DRM [1763-01-00-0100] Abbreviation for Digital Rights Management *ex: The DVD uses DRM that prevents copying on a computer.*

Drop Out [4150-00-00-0100] A picture of a shape, person or object removed from its background in a work and integrated into a page design. *info:* A Drop Out may be placed on a white background or on any other color or pattern, even another image. Sometimes a Drop Out is wrapped with text or headline type. Many pictures are made against white, green or other solid backgrounds, so that creating a Drop Out will be easy. Sometimes images include clipping paths that make a Drop Out easier to accomplish. *ex: The designer wants to use the picture of the girl as a drop out.* **plural:** Drop Outs

DRTV [1017-01-00-0100] Abbreviation for Direct Response Television *ex: Many DRTV ads run late at night and include a toll-free number for orders.*

Drum Scan [1764-00-00-0100] A high-end digital scan produced by mounting the original to a transparent cylindrical drum, which rotates at high speed and moves in small steps across the path between a light source and digital sensor. *ex: We are sending the transparency out for a drum scan.* **plural:** Drum Scans

DTP [1389-01-00-0100] Abbreviation for Desktop *ex: We have converted from paste-up production to DTP.*

Dummy [1390-00-00-0100] A prototype of a proposed book, magazine or other graphical page, with or without a cover. *info:* Sometimes includes sample images and text to indicate the bulk and format of the intended finished piece. *ex: Here is the dummy for the new book, showing the proposed placement of all images.* **plural:** Dummies

Duotone [1148-00-00-0100] A two-color halftone reproduction of an image. *info:* Used to add a tint, such as a sepia tone look, or richer tones to a black and white original image. *ex: Let's print that image as a duotone, using black and silver inks.* **plural:** Duotones

Dupe [1391-01-00-0100] See Duplicate *ex: A high-quality dupe should be suitable for reproduction.* **plural:** Dupes

Duplicate [1391-00-00-0100] An exact copy of a transparency or negative, usually in the same format. *info:* More generally, a very close and accurate copy of something else. *ex: A high-quality duplicate should be suitable for reproduction.* **plural:** Duplicates **variation:** Dupe

Duration [2692-00-00-0100] Stated in days, weeks, months or years, the period during which a license is active. The end date of a license is defined by the duration and start date. *info:* May be limited by the number of allowable insertions during that time period. *ex: The duration of the license is two months.* **plural:** Durations

Duration Exclusive [5190-01-00-0100] See Duration Exclusivity *ex: The client wants to purchase a duration exclusive for five months.* **plural:** Duration Exclusives

Duration Exclusivity [5190-00-00-0100] A right that, when granted, limits the rights of the licensor (and other parties offering licenses of the work) to further license or otherwise permit any third party to use the work during a specified time period. *ex: The client wants to purchase duration exclusivity for five months.* **variation:** Duration Exclusive

Dust Jacket [2793-00-00-0100] Paper cover of a book that slips over its bound cover. *ex: The image will run on the dust jacket, but not on the cover it wraps around.* **plural:** Dust Jackets

DVD [1392-00-00-0100] A type of high-capacity, electro-optical data storage media. *info:* Initially capable of storing approximately 4.7GB, enough for a full length movie on a 5-inch disc using MPEG (or other) compression. Recent iterations of the technology can store more. Some types can be erased and recorded again many times. *ex: The DVD includes both the still images and a video that incorporates them.* **plural:** DVDs **variation:** Digital Versatile Disk, Digital Video Disc, Digital Video Disk, Digital Versatile Disc

DVD Packaging [2765-00-00-0100] The container and/or wrapping for a consumer digital versatile disc. *ex: Our image is used on the front cover of the DVD Packaging.*

E-Book [3380-00-00-0100] A long document delivered and designed for viewing by electronic means *info:* May be saved in a common document or multimedia format, or in a proprietary format. Delivered by CD

ROM, DVD or other electronic storage method, or by download. May require special software or hardware for viewing, and may be copy protected. *ex: The e-book includes text, pictures and video clips.* *plural:* E-Books *variation:* eBook, Electronic Book

E-Commerce [1189-01-00-0100] Acronym for Electronic Commerce *ex: Our web site allows you to license a photograph and pay for the license using e-commerce.*

E-mail [1188-01-00-0100] See Email *ex: The image will serve as a signature on all e-mail sent by the client's staff.* *plural:* E-Mails

E-mail Advertising [1103-01-00-0100] See Email Advertising *ex: E-mail advertising is governed by U.S. Law concerning digital communications and privacy.*

E-zine [1154-01-00-0100] See Ezine *ex: My image is being used in her e-zine, which receives thousands of online visits each month.* *plural:* E-Zines

Ebook [3380-01-00-0100] Acronym for E-Book *ex: The ebook includes text, pictures and video clips.*

Ecommerce [1189-02-00-0100] Acronym for Electronic Commerce *ex: Our web site allows you to license a photograph and pay for the license using ecommerce.*

Edition

(1) Edition (Magazine) [1018-00-01-0100] Adaptations of a magazine that are tailored to a different region or demographic. *info:* Some magazines create a different edition for retail vs. subscription sales. *ex: Our advertisement will appear in the northeastern edition.* *plural:* Editions

(2) Edition (Book) [1018-00-02-0100] A version of a book or given title that remains substantially the same over a period. *info:* Succeeding editions of books, especially textbooks, are usually numbered. Image rights for books are usually specified for one or a larger number of editions. A license often defines a percentage or other measure that must be changed before a reprint is termed a new edition. *ex: The paperback edition will be published after the hardbound edition.* *plural:* Editions

(3) Edition (Broadcast) [1018-00-03-0100] The date and/or time of day in which a regularly scheduled or episodic program, such as a newscast, is broadcast or transmitted to its audience. *ex: The morning edition of the news program begins at 8 a.m.* *plural:* Editions

Editorial [1833-00-00-0100] Describes work in a periodical, online, on electronic media, presentation and/or broadcast that is educational or journalistic in nature, and which does not promote a product, person, service or company based on sponsorship. *ex: The client wants to license the image for an editorial use in a magazine.*

Editorial Use [1149-00-00-0100] A use whose purpose is to educate and/or convey news, information or fair comment opinion, and which does not seek or accept sponsorship to promote a product, person, service or company. *ex: The license specifies editorial use only in a newspaper.* *plural:* Editorial Uses

Education Magazine [1151-00-00-0100] A periodical printed with the express intention of conveying educational material. *info:* Content is usually tailored to specific age ranges or audiences. *ex: The image will appear in an education magazine for fourth graders.* *plural:* Education Magazines *variation:* Educational Magazine

Educational Book [1152-00-00-0100] A volume in printed or electronic form containing information on one or more subjects used in a real or virtual classroom by students and teachers. *info:* Usually includes images. Ancillaries, which require specific licenses, might include other edition(s), such as instructor handbooks, a student edition, an edition in another language or an electronic edition. Major categories include K-8, high school, college and professional. *ex: This educational book is for sixth grade language arts.* *plural:* Educational Book *preferred term:* Textbook *usability:* Discouraged

Educational CD [1150-02-00-0100] See Educational CD ROM *ex: The image will be used as a welcome screen on an Educational CD.* *plural:* Educational CDs

Educational CD ROM

(1) Educational CD ROM (Academic) [1150-00-01-0100] A CD ROM or DVD containing information or programming specifically intended for classroom or other use within an academic setting. *ex: The image will be used to illustrate a testing screen on an educational CD ROM that accompanies a textbook.* *plural:* Educational CD ROMs variation: Educational CD-ROM, Educational CD

(2) Educational CD ROM (Retail) [1150-00-02-0100] A CD ROM or DVD containing information or programming that is intended to teach skills or impart knowledge, and is intended for retail sale to consumers. *ex: The image will be used as a welcome screen in an Educational CD ROM sold in department* stores. *plural:* Educational CD ROMs variation: Educational CD-ROM, Educational CD

Educational CD-ROM [1150-01-00-0100] See Educational CD ROM *ex: The image will be used as a welcome screen on an Educational CD-ROM. plural:* Educational CD-ROMs

Educational Magazine [1151-01-00-0100] See Education Magazine *ex: The image will appear in an educational magazine for fourth graders. plural:* Educational Magazines

Effective Date [4900-00-00-0100] The date when the terms of a contract or agreement begin to be in force. *info:* In some contracts, the effective date differs from the date of signing. It might come in the future, or the contract may be retroactive to some date in the past. *ex: Although we signed our contract in March, the effective date was not until mid-April. plural:* Effective Dates

Effort [1019-00-00-0100] A single promotion or advertising message sent to a subscriber list or other prospects. *info:* Several messages about the same theme are known as several efforts or a campaign. *ex: That effort reached our target audience last week. plural:* Efforts

Electronic Book [3380-02-00-0100] See E-Book *ex: The electronic book includes text, pictures and video clips. Plural:* Electronic Books

Electronic Commerce [1189-00-00-0100] The conducting of commercial business transactions and the resulting transfer of funds and/or digital assets across digital communications networks using online computers and software. *ex: Our website allows you to license a photograph and pay for the license using electronic commerce. variation:* Ecommerce, E-Commerce

Electronic Comp [2750-00-00-0100] An image file that is less than one megabyte (1,024KB) in size when opened in digital image viewing or editing software and intended as a proof. *info:* Useful for presentation purposes but generally insufficient for high quality printed reproduction, except at very small size. *ex: The clients requested an electronic comp file so they could be sure the picture fit their needs. plural:* Electronic Comps

Electronic Duplicate [4910-00-00-0100] A digital reproduction of a work. *info:* May be a copy of an existing digital image, a digital scan or a digital photograph made of artwork. *ex: We will make an electronic duplicate of the illustration and promptly return the original. plural:* Electronic Duplicates

Electronic Rights [1251-00-00-0100] Permission that applies to an end use that includes digital media, such as online, CD ROM, DVD and email. *info:* This term is sometimes understood to include broadcast. Clarification with the client is recommended regarding what is included in electronic rights or use of another term. *ex: The client wants the license to include electronic rights for his website. preferred term:* Online *usability:* Discouraged

Element [1393-00-00-0100] An individual image part that can be combined with other parts in a composite, collage or montage image, or on a page. *info:* Use of an element from one image to create a new image for reproduction requires permission of the copyright holder, unless its reproduction is considered fair use. *ex: We will use the car in your illustration as an element in the final image. plural:* Elements

Elevator Advertising [4930-00-00-0100] A commercial marketing or promotional communication, displayed inside an elevator. *info:* Elevator advertising may be printed or in electronic form, such as on a video display. *ex: The images will be used as posters for elevator advertising.*

Email [1188-00-00-0100] A communication sent via a specific Internet protocol to specific recipient addresses with the help of computers and appropriate software. *info:* Used by individuals and organizations to exchange or disseminate messages, memos, information, editorial, promotional or advertising content. *ex: The image will serve as a signature on all email sent by the client's staff. plural:* Emails *variation:* E-Mail

Email Advertising [1103-00-00-0100] A commercial communication sent via a specific Internet protocol to specific recipient addresses with the help of computers and appropriate software. *info:* Usually distributed to large lists of Internet addresses. Unsolicited or unauthorized commercial email messages, often referred to as spam or unsolicited commercial email, can be illegal. May include marketing and promotional messages. *ex: Email advertising is governed by U.S. Law concerning digital communications and privacy. variation:* E-Mail Advertising

Email Blast [2798-00-00-0100] Distribution of a promotional, marketing, sales or advertising message to a large quantity of specific recipients via a specific Internet protocol. *info:* May link to a web page. Unsolicited or unauthorized commercial email messages, often referred to as spam, can be illegal. *ex: The email blast was sent out last night to 70,000 addresses. plural:* Email Blasts

Embargo Period [1563-00-00-0100] A period of time during which a work or a product may not be licensed, published and/or distributed. *info:* Usually specified in a contract or invoice. Can be complete or partial—such as restricting use in a particular publication or medium. *ex: The embargo period for this image ends next week, so we can't license it to you until then.* *plural:* Embargo Periods

Employee [1564-00-00-0100] Someone who works under supervision of another in return for a salary, wage or other regular compensation. *info:* Work produced by a professional creative who is an employee is usually work made for hire. Labor officials have specific criteria for determining whether someone is an employee or not. *ex: An employee produced those images, so we have license to use them as we wish.* *plural:* Employees

Encapsulated Postscript [1395-01-00-0100] See EPS [1395-00-00-0100] *ex: We will send you an encapsulated postscript file to import into your page layout.*

Encryption [1394-00-00-0100] A method of encoding information so that it can be read only by those who have appropriate translators—such as special software. *info:* Used to protect data as it travels over intranets and the Internet. Provides privacy for email, electronic commerce transactions, online banking and other online commercial communications. Prevents unauthorized users from accessing proprietary information, such as high-resolution image files. *ex: To secure transactions, our website includes encryption software.* *plural:* Encryptions

Encyclopedia [1153-00-00-0100] A book, set of books, website, CD ROM (single or set) or DVD (single or set) that delivers information on many branches of knowledge. *info:* Subject matter is usually arranged in alphabetical order. *ex: They licensed several illustrations for their upcoming encyclopedia.* *plural:* Encyclopedias

End Cap [1201-01-00-0100] See Cap *ex: The food store end cap shows our logo and a picture of our soup cans.* *plural:* End Caps

End Date [1252-00-00-0100] The day when a contract or rightful usage duration of a creative work expires. *ex: The end date for this agreement will be December 31.* *plural:* End Dates

End User [4030-00-00-0100] A member of the target audience for a work or product or the client of an agency licensing or contracting work. *info:* An agency's end user—a client—may have end users for their product or communication. *ex: All of the background computations on the website will be hidden from the end user.* *plural:* End Users

Epilogue [2806-00-00-0100] A section by the author or a third party at the end of a written work that comments on the work, the future of its characters or the process of its creation. *ex: In the book's epilogue, the author tells of how his lead character went on to become a successful agent.* *plural:* Epilogues

EPS [1395-00-00-0100] A graphics file format that can include type, other vector graphics and images. *ex: We will send you an EPS file to import into your page layout.* *plural:* EPSes *variation:* Encapsulated Postscript

Estimate [1063-00-00-0100] A pre-production document formulated by a licensor based on a project description provided by the licensee. Typically describes work to be produced and licensed, the scope of the license to be granted, any terms and conditions applicable to the transaction, and the fees and costs for the project and license. *info:* Unlike a bid, an estimate is a best effort approximation of fees and costs—expected to be reasonably accurate but not necessarily precise. Estimates are typically subject to variance, which may or may not be negotiated in advance. An estimate may be legally binding whether or not it is signed by a licensee, provided the licensee is presented with the estimate, indicates acceptance of the terms and authorizes the licensor to proceed. It is best to ensure that estimates or job confirmations are signed by the commissioning party or licensee. *ex: We told the customer we could provide an estimate for producing 10 photographs on location.* *plural:* Estimates

Event Program [1104-00-00-0100] A printed piece, often small, that contains the order of performance and/or other information about a performance, public event or social function. *info:* Often includes advertising. *ex: Our image is on the cover of their event program for the new musical.* *plural:* Event Programs

Exam [2760-01-00-0100] See Examination [2760-00-00-0100] *ex: The image will be used on their exam materials, which are included with the textbook.* *plural:* Exams

Examination [2760-00-00-0100] A series of questions or problems designed to determine knowledge, intelligence or ability. *info:* May be an ancillary product to other educational products. *ex: The image will be used on their examination materials, which will be included with the textbook.* *plural:* Examinations *variation:* Exam

Exclusive [2720-01-00-0100] See Exclusivity *ex: The agency wants to purchase an exclusive for using the image in printed matter.* **plural:** Exclusives

Exclusive License [4960-00-00-0100] A privilege that, when granted, limits how a copyright holder (and other parties permitted) can offer a work to a third party for reproduction. *info:* An exclusive license may be broad or specific. The rights grant may provide the licensee with exclusive rights to use a work singly or in any combination of: a specified media, industry, territory, language, time period, product and any other specific right negotiated by the licensor and licensee. *ex: The client needs an exclusive license for the image, restricting all other licenses for real estate advertising.* **plural:** Exclusive Licenses

Exclusive Rights [2718-00-00-0100] A privilege that, when granted by a licensor to a licensee, limits the right of the licensor (and other parties offering licenses of the work) to license rights in a work to a third party. *info:* An exclusive right may be broad or specific. The rights grant may provide the licensee with exclusive rights to use a work singly or in any combination of: a specified media, industry, territory, language, time period, product and any other specific right negotiated by the licensor and licensee. *ex: The agency wants to purchase exclusive rights for using the picture in resort advertising for two years.*

Exclusivity [2720-00-00-0100] Describes a right that, when granted by a licensor to a licensee, limits how the licensor (and other parties offering licenses of the work) may license rights in a work to a third party. *info:* Exclusivity may be broad or specific. The rights grant may provide the licensee with exclusive rights to use a work singly or in any combination of: a specified media, industry, territory, language, time period, product and any other specific right negotiated by the licensor and licensee. *ex: The advertising agency wants to license exclusivity for using the image in printed matter.* **plural:** Exclusivities **variation:** Exclusive

Exposure

(1) Exposure (Legal) [4240-00-01-0100] A single photographic work. *info:* Different exposures may appear similar, but each is treated separately, unless agreed to otherwise. *ex: We want to license only that one exposure from the set up.*

(2) Exposure (Photo Technical) [4240-00-02-0100] Refers to camera settings used to capture light reflected off a subject and render it as an image on a photo-sensitive material (such as film) or device (digital imaging chip), or the quantity of light available for such capture. *info:* Correct exposure depends on the sensitivity of the imaging device or material to light, the amount of light reflected off the photographic subject, the amount of reflected light transmitted (usually through a lens) to the photo-sensitive device or material, and the amount of time the device or material is open to the reflected light. *ex: A very short exposure will freeze action, while a longer one blurs it.*

(3) Exposure (Advertising and PR) [4240-00-03-0100] A viewing, hearing or other perception of an advertising, marketing or public relations piece. *ex: Sometimes the second or third exposure to our message counts more than the first.*

Extranet [1190-00-00-0100] A private digital network that uses the same kind of software and communications technologies as the Internet, but shares data only with a company's clients, vendors or suppliers. *ex: Post that information on our extranet for all our buyers to see.* **plural:** Extranets

Ezine [1154-00-00-0100] A magazine or other periodical published only on the World Wide Web or in other digital media. *info:* Usually a number of web page articles with links or Adobe Acrobat(TM) PDF files. May be delivered on CD ROM or other digital media. *ex: My image is being used on her ezine, which receives thousands of online visits each month.* **plural:** Ezines **variation:** E-Zine, Webzine

Fair Use [1565-00-00-0100] A doctrine under U.S. Copyright Law that permits the use of copyrighted materials without permission from the copyright owner under certain circumstances and for certain purposes such as scholarship, news reporting, reviews, parody, teaching activities. *info:* Not all such uses will qualify as fair use. See section 107 of the Copyright Act, listing the factors that determine a fair use. For more information, see publication no. Fl-102, available at www.copyright.gov. *ex: Your reproduction of my photograph in a review of my exhibition is fair use.* **plural:** Fair Uses **usability:** Caution

Fee [1623-00-00-0100] A sum of money charged for a professional service or license. *ex: The photographer's fee is on the fourth line of the invoice.* **plural:** Fees

Ferry Advertising [1851-00-00-0100] A marketing or promotional piece, usually poster-size or larger, displayed on the interior or exterior of a public transportation vehicle. *info:* May be printed, or displayed on monitors or other digital devices. *ex: The campaign includes ferry advertising throughout the region.*

Ferry Terminal Advertising [1847-00-00-0100] A marketing or promotional piece, usually poster size or larger, placed on the structure of a public ferry stop or terminal. *info:* May be printed, or displayed on monitors or other digital devices. *ex: The campaign includes ferry terminal advertising.*

File Format [1398-00-00-0100] A form or type of digital file used to store images and other information on computers. *info:* Some examples of image file formats are TIFF, JPEG, PSD and DNG. *ex: Save the image in the JPEG file format, which the client can easily open. plural:* File Formats

File Transfer Protocol [1703-01-00-0100] See FTP *ex: Please upload those files using file transfer protocol.*

Film

(1) Film (Media) [1859-00-01-0100] An audiovisual medium that enacts a story with sequences of images, usually accompanied by audio. *info:* When a film includes a still image, that usage is identified as a film still. *ex: We will watch the film with the lights off. plural:* Films

(2) Film (Production) [1859-00-02-0100] Photographic material with a flexible, transparent celluloid backing, coated with a light-sensitive emulsion. *ex: Please get me another roll of film so we can keep making pictures. plural:* Films

Film Still

(1) Film Still (Usage) [1655-00-01-0100] Image use as content in a motion picture or video production. *ex: The image is being licensed for use as a film still in a PBS documentary. plural:* Film Stills

(2) Film Still (Advertising and PR) [1655-00-02-0100] A photograph taken during film production that is subsequently used to publicize or advertise the film. *ex: The image is being licensed for use as a film still to promote the movie. plural:* Film Stills

Fine Art [1155-00-00-0100] Work in any medium created more for aesthetic appreciation than for commercial use, or a description of a market and items in it that are intended for private or gallery display, rather than reproduction. *info:* Generally (but not necessarily), fine art is generated and often funded based on the whims of the artist, as opposed to a client. *ex: Her photographs were produced as fine art, but they might have commercial value. plural:* Fine Arts

Fine Art Print [4050-00-00-0100] A reproduction of an original two-dimensional work, made with a high-quality process and materials. *info:* Usually refers to prints licensed only for private use and/or

gallery display. *ex: I made the picture as photojournalism, but it has sold quite well as a fine art print. plural:* Fine Art Prints

Fingernail [1507-00-00-0100] A miniature version of an image, smaller than a thumbnail. *info:* Generally smaller than 1 inch by 1 inch (24mm by 24mm). *ex: This image will be used as a fingernail on our home page. plural:* Fingernails

Finished Work [4950-00-00-0100] A completed image, illustration or layout submitted for reproduction. *ex: The finished work reflects our best efforts to realize the image concept. plural:* Finished Works

First Rights [1254-00-00-0100] The right to publish, before others do, an image, article, product or project. *info:* First rights need to be defined specifically, noting whether they are regional, global, in one medium or many. *ex: The first rights to this image in North America have already been sold.*

First Serial Rights [1255-00-00-0100] Prepublication of selected parts of a book or other creative work (including an image) in a magazine, other periodical or online. *ex: The client wants to license first serial rights.*

Flap [1400-00-00-0100] Part of a book jacket, usually containing a precis or summary of the contents, and a biography and image of the author. *ex: The flap is printed with type reversed out of the cover picture background. plural:* Flaps

Flash

(1) Flash (Television) [1105-00-01-0100] Use of an image in a television advertisement or program in which the image appears for no more than five seconds. *ex: The image will be used in a three second television flash.*

(2) Flash (Online) [1105-00-02-0100] A digital file format used on the World Wide Web and in other digital presentation applications. It can contain animated text, graphics, sound, still images or video. *info:* Flash™ is a trademark of Macromedia, now a subsidiary of Adobe corp. It can be produced and edited with Macromedia software, as well as with some third-party products. The file format is also known as SWF (for Shockwave Flash) and it's turning up in a variety of devices and media, including mobile communications. *ex: This image will be used as background in a flash animation.*

(3) Flash (Photo Technical) [1105-00-03-0100] A brief, high-intensity form of illumination used by photographers. *ex: The scene was lighted with flash.*

Flat Bed Scan [1766-01-00-0100] See Flatbed Scan *ex: We will make a flat bed scan of that print.* **plural:** Flat Bed Scans

Flat Rate Fee [4010-00-00-0100] A fee, including all creative and licensing charges, involved in creating and/or delivering a work or works. *info:* A flat rate fee typically precludes separate line items on an invoice for creative and licensing fees, and may include some or all production expenses. Such a fee is usually negotiated in advance of an assignment, and it typically does not include extra payments for extra time required due to changes in the job requirements. Terms, conditions and licenses accompanying invoices for a flat rate fee should specify all that is included, especially the terms of the license. *ex: We agreed on a flat rate fee that will cover the photographer, his staff and the usage we need.* **plural:** Flat Rate Fees

Flat Rate Image [1256-00-00-0100] A stock picture, licensed on a non-exclusive basis, allowing multiple uses by a licensee, typically with few restrictions and no requirement that the licensee contact the licensor for permission prior to each use. *info:* License may or may not specify a license period. *ex: The clients asked for a flat rate image license for a dozen images they planned to use broadly.* **plural:** Flat Rate Images

Flatbed Scan [1766-00-00-0100] A digital scan produced by laying the original on a flat glass panel, the length of which is a digital sensor array and light source, then move in small steps, recording image data. *info:* Generally not a preferred method for scanning transparent materials, although many flatbed scanners have film adapters. *ex: We will make a flatbed scan of that print.* **plural:** Flatbed Scans *variation:* Flat Bed Scan

Flexible License Pack [1257-00-00-0100] A license model permitting the use of one or more images in multiple media without requiring individual license fees for each image or use. *info:* A number of different flexible license pack variations have been developed, presenting a wide variety of media combinations, such as unlimited usage in selected territories, industries or timeframes. *ex: We purchased a flexible license pack for these images.* **plural:** Flexible License Packs

Flip [4970-00-00-0100] To turn an image over from side to side, mirroring the original image, or an image that has been reproduced in this manner. *info:* Type that reads correctly in an original reads backwards in a flip. *ex: We had to flip the image to make its action lead to the right rather than left.* **plural:** Flips

Floor Graphic [1106-00-00-0100] An advertising piece designed for physical placement onto the floor of a retail outlet. *info:* Often a freestanding, die-cut board that promotes a specific product or service. *ex: The automotive floor graphic is a half-size reproduction of the car.* **plural:** Floor Graphics

Flop [4980-00-00-0100] To turn an image over from top to bottom or an image that has been reproduced in this manner. *info:* Subjects that were right side up in an original are upside down in a flop. *ex: The image includes a scene reflected on a pond, so be careful not to flop it.* **plural:** Flops

Flyaway Card [2697-00-00-0100] A subscription, advertising or promotional postcard inserted, but not bound, into a magazine or periodical. *ex: The flyaway card was printed on plain white paper and inserted in 10,000 targeted copies of the magazine.* **plural:** Flyaway Cards

Flyer [1117-00-00-0100] A single-page advertisement meant to stand alone or to be inserted into a publication. *ex: We ordered 5,000 copies of the flyer for insertion in the local weekly and another 200 for posting around town.* **plural:** Flyers

Focus

(1) Focus (Photo) [1401-00-01-0100] Refers to the acuity of lines and detail in the subject matter of an image. *info:* If the lines and detail are sharp and clearly resolved, the image is said to be properly focused or in focus. *ex: When you take the picture, make sure that the subject matter is in focus.*

(2) Focus (Production) [1401-00-02-0100] The degree of acuity with which an output device (such as a computer monitor, paper print, projection screen or film emulsion), displays an image. *info:* If lines and detail are sharp and clearly resolved when displaying an image that is known to be sharp, a device is said to be properly focused or in focus. *ex: Before the audience comes in, make sure that the projector is in focus.*

Focus Group [1654-00-00-0100] A group of individuals selected by a market research company for the purpose of studying responses to a marketing message or concept, a product, a service, or a creative work. *ex: Yesterday we convened a focus group to study the new advertising campaign.* **plural:** Focus Groups

For Position Only [1738-01-00-0100] See FPO *ex: The art director used one of our images for position only and the client decided to use it in the ad.*

Force Majeure [4990-00-00-0100] An unexpected or uncontrollable event. *info:* Used in a contract to make exceptions for performance when such events—such as a labor action, natural disaster, police action, terrorism or act of war—interfere. *ex: Our agreement to deliver by June 2 contains exceptions for force majeure. plural:* Forces Majeure

Foreground [3390-00-00-0100] The portions of an image or other visual presentation that appear to be closest to the viewer. *ex: We need to move that foreground onto this background. plural:* Foregrounds

Foreword [1582-00-00-0100] An introduction to a written work, usually by someone other than the author. *ex: The foreword begins on page three. plural:* Forewords

Format [1402-00-00-0100] The size, style or type of page, margins, printing requirements, and other specifications of a printed piece or a web page, or the act of preparing materials to meet those specifications. *ex: Their advertisement is prepared for a broadsheet vertical format. plural:* Formats

Four Color Process [2791-00-00-0100] Printing on a press using the standard four colors of cyan, magenta, yellow and black. *ex: The brochure will be reproduced using four color process printing.*

FPO [1738-00-00-0100] An image used on a layout or dummy as a placeholder, showing where and how a selected image might eventually be placed. *ex: The art director used one of our images as an FPO and the client decided to use it in the ad. plural:* FPOs *variation:* For Position Only

Frame

(1) Frame (Production) [4250-00-01-0100] A single photographic work. *info:* Different frames may appear similar, but each is treated separately, unless agreed to otherwise. A set up may include many frames. *ex: We wish to license only that particular frame from the set up. plural:* Frames

(2) Frame (Display) [4250-00-02-0100] A border around a work, especially one designed to hold and preserve it for viewing. *info:* A frame may be as simple as a digitally created border effect or as elaborate as hand-carved wood or stone. *ex: We need to have this image printed and put in a frame for the gallery show. plural:* Frames

Frame Rate [1404-00-00-0100] In film, video and animation, the number of frames continuously displayed per second of viewing time. *info:* There are three main international television standards that include frame rate parameters: NTSC system (30 frames, or 60 fields, per second), and PAL and SECAM (25 frames, or 50 fields, per second). Computer systems frequently use lower frame rates to simulate full-motion video display. The film projection standard is 24 frames per second, with higher and lower frame rates sometimes used for special effects, such as (respectively) time lapse and slow motion. Animation frame rates vary. *ex: Be sure the film is transferred at the proper frame rate. plural:* Frame Rates

Framed Art Print [2813-00-00-0100] An image rendered on paper or other material displayed within a constructed border (of materials such as metals, woods and plastics) or on a substrate, as a work of art or wall decor in a private or gallery setting. *info:* Does not include display within a frame for the express purpose of selling that frame (packaging). A framed art print is generally sold for private display without any license to reproduce. *ex: The framed art print will hang on the living room wall. plural:* Framed Art Prints

Framed Print [2811-00-00-0100] Display of an image within a constructed border (of materials such as metals, woods and plastics) or on a substrate as a work of art or wall decor in a corporate or commercial setting. *info:* Does not include display within a frame for the express purpose of selling that frame (packaging). Corporate and commercial use is often licensed for specific time limits, with any reproduction requiring an additional license. A print sold for private use is referred to as a framed art print. *ex: The framed print will hang in the outer reception area. plural:* Framed Prints

Free Standing Insert [1064-00-00-0100] Any magazine or newspaper insert that is included but not bound within a publication or its polybag. *info:* Examples include, but are not limited to, Blow In card, tip on and flyer. *ex: This ad will circulate next month as a free standing insert in four magazines. plural:* Free Standing Inserts *variation:* FSI, Freestanding Insert

Freebie [1021-01-00-0100] See Freemium [1021-00-00-0100] *ex: The client wants to use the image on a coffee mug to be sent as a freebie. plural:* Freebies

Freelance [1739-00-00-0100] Describes a self-employed professional available to work, rather than being committed to one employer, or the relationship between an independent contractor and a client. *info:* Freelance relationships are usually for a limited period. *ex: We hired a freelance designer to produce our annual report.*

Freelancer [5130-00-00-0100] A self-employed professional available to work, rather than being committed to one employer. *info:* Freelancers are usually hired for a limited period. *ex: We hired a freelancer to produce our annual report. **plural:** Freelancers*

Freemium [1021-00-00-0100] Merchandise given, not contingent on a purchase or payment, to a subscriber or prospect as an enticement. *ex: The client wants to use the image on a coffee mug to be sent as a freemium. **plural:** Freemiums **variation:** Freebie*

Freestanding Insert [1064-01-00-0100] See Free Standing Insert *ex: This ad will circulate next month as a freestanding insert in four magazines. **plural:** Freestanding Inserts **variation:** FSI*

Frequency

(1) **Frequency (Advertising)** [1022-00-01-0100] The number of times an audience might see a particular message. *ex: With all the pass-along readers, the frequency of that advertisement was high. **plural:** Frequencies*

(2) **Frequency (Magazine)** [1022-00-02-0100] The number of times in a year a publication is issued. *ex: Their magazine has a frequency of four times a year. **plural:** Frequencies*

(3) **Frequency (General)** [1022-00-03-0100] The number of times an event occurs over a given time unit. *info:* Applies to sound and radio waves, among other occurrences measured. *ex: The electrical power frequency in the U.S. is 60 hertz, or cycles per second. **plural:** Frequencies*

Front Cover [1405-00-00-0100] The front-facing outer wrapping of a book, periodical, annual report or other multi-page publication. *info:* Often used for promotion or for advertising the work. A model release and property release are usually required. Considered an advertising or packaging use. *ex: The front cover will include two photographs and type. **plural:** Front Covers*

Front Matter [1522-00-00-0100] Anything in a book that is before the main body of the work. *info:* Includes but is not limited to the table of contents, frontispiece, title page, foreword and preface. *ex: The front matter is 12 pages long.*

Frontispiece [2817-00-00-0100] An image that faces or appears immediately before the title of a book, book section or magazine. *ex: This illustration will appear as a frontispiece of her new book. **plural:** Frontispieces*

Frontlist [1588-00-00-0100] All of the books offered by a publisher in the current season and featured in the publisher's latest catalog. *ex: My book is on their frontlist, following its second printing. **plural:** Frontlists*

FSI [10640200-0100] Abbreviation for Free Standing Insert [1064-00-00-0100] *ex: This ad will circulate next month as an FSI in four magazines. **plural:** FSIs **variation:** Freestanding Insert*

FTP [1703-00-00-0100] An Internet communications protocol governing the transfer of files from one computer to another. *info:* FTP is relatively insecure but robust for large data transfers. *ex: Please upload those files to our FTP server. **variation:** File Transfer Protocol*

Fulfillment [1023-00-00-0100] The completion of certain specified obligations, or delivery of a product or service under contractually agreed terms and conditions. *ex: fulfillment will occur when the files are delivered to the client. **plural:** Fulfillments*

Full Page [2800-00-00-0100] A promotion, editorial or advertising piece that takes up one complete page. *info:* A full page license permits use of the image at any size up to the complete page. *ex: The ad will be a full page. **plural:** Full Pages*

Galley [1537-00-00-0100] A mid-production, unbound version of a work that is distributed for marketing, review and/or public relations purposes. *ex: Here is the galley of the new book. **plural:** Galleys*

Garment [1207-00-00-0100] An article of clothing. *ex: The four images licensed will comprise a new pattern for garment use. **plural:** Garments*

Gatefold [1408-00-00-0100] A foldout, especially one that opens to double or triple the normal page size. *info:* Both sides of a gatefold can fold out to form a four-page layout. *ex: The image will run as a background for a gatefold. **plural:** Gatefolds*

GB [4370-01-00-0100] Abbreviation for Gigabyte *ex: I think 1 GB of storage should be enough to store all the files from this small project.*

Generation [1767-00-00-0100] Each succeeding stage in reproduction from the original forward. *info:* Visual quality often degrades with each generation further removed from an original. When an original is digital, each successive generation, unless resized or edited in some fashion, has equal quality. Digital image files repeatedly opened and recompressed in the JPEG and similarly lossy compressed file formats are an exception. *ex: Here is the first generation original. **plural:** Generations*

Geographic Exclusive [2725-01-00-0100] See Geographic Exclusivity *ex: The client purchased a geographic exclusive for the image in Europe.* **plural:** Geographic Exclusives

Geographic Exclusivity [2725-00-00-0100] Describes a right that, when granted to a licensee, limits how the licensor (and other parties offering licenses of the work) may license rights in a work to a third party for use in a specified region of the world. *ex: The client purchased geographic exclusivity for the image in Europe.* **plural:** Geographic Exclusivities **variation:** Geographic Exclusive

Giclée Print [3570-00-00-0100] A term applied, primarily in fine art marketing and transactions, for high-quality output from systems that spray ink on paper and other substrates (such as canvas). *info:* Giclée (pronounced zhee-clay) is French for squirt or spray. Giclée appeared about 1989 as a marketing term for plateless reproductions of fine art on art-quality paper. At that time, they were produced with large format ink jet printers designed for making prepress proofs with watercolor inks. Since then, many other types of ink, printers and paper have been used to produce giclée prints, which tend to have vibrant color and fine detail, combined with the texture of the paper or other substrate used. This term, however, offers no firm standard of quality or print longevity. *ex: We will donate a Giclée Print of the image to the exhibit.* **plural:** Giclée Prints **preferred term:** Ink Jet Print **usability:** Caution

GIF [3480-00-00-0100] A very compact bitmap format that supports low-resolution transparency and animation, especially for website display. *info:* GIF is a legacy image file format from the early days of online communications. But because its files are very small, it's still used often for website display, especially for images with large expanses of flat colors, such as screen shots and logos. Capable of displaying continuous-tone photographs, but not very well. *ex: The designer wanted to use GIF image files on our home page, but we insisted that JPEGs would look better.* **plural:** GIFs **variation:** Graphics Interchange Format

Gift Certificate [1208-00-00-0100] A card purchased at a retail store to be given as a gift, redeemable for a specific amount of money that can then be spent at that store by the recipient. *info:* Frequently contains graphics and images. *ex: The gift certificate will include our logo and a stock image.* **plural:** Gift Certificates

Gift Wrap [1209-00-00-0100] Paper designed specifically for covering and decorating presents that are usually, but not always, related to specific holidays or special occasions. *info:* Usually includes an image or pattern design. *ex: The Christmas gift wrap will feature snow scenes from North Carolina.* **plural:** Gift Wraps

Gig [43700200-0100] See Gigabyte *ex: I think a gig should be enough to store all the files from this small project.* **plural:** Gigs

Gigabyte [4370-00-00-0100] A measure of file size and storage capacity referring to, depending on context, between 1,000,000,000 and 1,073,741,824, 8-bit data units or characters. *info:* Most software, memory chips and systems consider a kilobyte to be 1,024 (the binary quantity of 2 to the 10th power) bytes, a megabyte to be 1,024 such kilobytes, and a gigabyte to be 1,024 such megabytes or 1,073,741,824 bytes. However, some key standards groups state that 1,000 (10 to the 3rd power) bytes comprise a kilobyte, a megabyte is 1,000 kilobytes, and a gigabyte is 1,000 megabytes or one billion (10 to the 9th power) bytes. And many data storage manufacturers use this measurement to define their device sizes, meaning a computer may show less storage capacity on a drive than the drive's specified size suggests. *ex: A gigabyte of storage should be enough to store all the files from this small project.* **plural:** Gigabytes **variation:** GB, Gig

Giro [1615-00-00-0100] A payment system in which account holders direct financial institutions to transfer funds directly from their account to a creditor. *ex: Pay with your credit card, money order or use a giro to my bank.* **plural:** Giros

Glossary [1523-00-00-0100] A listing of terms and accompanying definitions, intended as a reference. *ex: Look up that term in the glossary.* **plural:** Glossaries

Graphic [1409-00-00-0100] A visual arrangement of artwork, either alone or in conjunction with other visual elements, live action or animated backgrounds. *info:* Includes individual letters, text, logos and other design elements displayed on a printed or web page, as well as in video, film and animated presentations. *ex: The graphic should be placed in the lower right corner of the page.* **plural:** Graphics

Graphic Use [1156-00-00-0100] An image used primarily for design purposes, rather than to depict subject matter. *ex: The client licensed this illustration for graphic use.* **plural:** Graphic Uses

Graphics Interchange Format [3480-01-00-0100] See GIF [3480-00-00-0100] *ex: The designer wanted to use graphics interchange format image files on our home page, but we insisted that JPEGS would look better.*

Grayscale Image

(1) Grayscale Image (Digital) [2790-00-01-0100] An image whose pixel data comprises only levels of luminance, without color data. *info:* Typically, a grayscale image has eight bits of luminance data per pixel and produces 256 shades of gray. More bits per pixel are possible and frequently yield smoother results, particularly when editing the image's tone and contrast. *ex: Your grayscale image will take one-third as long to download as a comparable RGB image would. plural:* Grayscale Images

(2) Grayscale Image (Photo) [2790-00-02-0100] A photograph that contains only white, black or shades of gray. *info:* May be recorded on black and white materials or electronic systems, or on color materials or systems that are converted to shades of gray during processing. May be printed on black and white or color materials, depending upon processing methods. *ex: We will ship a print of the grayscale image to you. plural:* Grayscale Images

(3) Grayscale Image (Print) [2790-00-03-0100] An image that is printed using only black ink. *info:* May be enhanced by adding one, two or three shades of gray ink (known as duotone, tri-tone or quadtone). Process color inks can also simulate the appearance of grayscale printing. *ex: Look at the grayscale image on page two of the brochure. plural:* Grayscale Images

Greeting Card [1210-00-00-0100] Inexpensive, printed piece on heavy stock, usually folded, and sold primarily in retail outlets and by mail order. Usually includes graphics and images. *info:* Used to express sentiment around holidays and special personal occasions, such as birthdays and anniversaries. *ex: Please send a greeting card on your father's birthday. plural:* Greeting Cards

Guide Print [5000-00-00-0100] An image output by a photographer to indicate for the printer and/or pre-press operator the colors, contrast and tonality the photographer would like to aim for on press. *info:* A guide print offers goals or targets, not confirmation that color or tones will be properly reproduced—or even reproducible. *ex: We will try to match the guide print, but we cannot guarantee the match will be exact. plural:* Guide Prints

Gutter [1411-00-00-0100] The center, vertical area where two facing pages in a magazine or book are bound together. *info:* Often considered unusable dead space, as content is not always visible in this area. *ex: Depending on the binding method for a piece, anything printed in the gutter may be difficult to see. plural:* Gutters

Half Page [1501-01-00-0100] See One Half Page *ex: The ad will be a half page. plural:* Half Pages

Halftone [1413-00-00-0100] The reproduction of a continuous tone image by translating the image into various-size dots. *info:* Originally produced optically using a mechanical screen and a regular dot pattern. Now almost always produced by software controlling digital scanners and imagesetters. Screen resolutions are described by lines per inch. *ex: That image made a beautiful halftone. plural:* Halftones

Hand Book [1157-01-00-0100] See Handbook *ex: We are publishing the definitive hand book on finding rare birds. plural:* Hand Books

Handbook [1157-00-00-0100] A printed and bound reference, sometimes in the form of a specialist directory or a specialist reference manual. *ex: We are publishing the definitive handbook on finding rare birds. plural:* Handbooks *variation:* Hand Book

Hang Tag [1211-00-00-0100] A dangling manufacturer's label or price card that may or may not describe merchandise. *ex: Her illustration appears as the background of the product hang tag. plural:* Hang Tags

Hardback Book [1158-00-00-0100] A published volume bound with heavy board, glue and stitching, usually covered with a material such as a printed sheet, linen or leather. *info:* Generally the first format in which a book is published. Subsequent formats: softcover, audio, large print, other languages. *ex: We have ordered the hardback book edition of that title for our library. plural:* Hardback Books

Hardbound [3620-00-00-0100] Describes a book whose pages are assembled within heavy board, glue and stitching, usually covered with a material, such as a printed sheet, linen or leather. *info:* Generally the first format in which a book is published. Subsequent formats: softcover, audio, large print, other languages. *ex: The hardbound edition will feature a four-color book jacket.*

Hardcover [1583-00-00-0100] A book bound with heavy board, glue and stitching, usually covered with a material, such as a printed sheet, linen or leather. *info:* Generally the first format in which a book is published. Subsequent formats: paper softcover, audio, large print, other languages. *ex: We have ordered the hardcover edition of that title from the bookstore. plural:* Hardcovers

Hero [5010-00-00-0100] The selected image or concept from a group of choices. *ex: That image clearly has the impact to be our hero to lead the layout. plural:* Heroes

Hero Card [1768-00-00-0100] A rectangular piece of printed paper stock used in sports for autographs. *ex: My photograph is being used on her hero card.* *plural:* Hero Cards

Hi-Lo Book [1591-00-00-0100] A book that combines a popular subject with less than challenging text. *ex: Here is the ad campaign for her next hi-lo book, which should have mass appeal.* *plural:* Hi-Lo Books

High Res [1650-01-00-0100] See High Resolution *ex: The client asked us to deliver a high res file.*

High Resolution [1650-00-00-0100] Refers to a relatively larger number of pixels per inch in a digital image or scan, which yields a larger digital file. *info:* Generally speaking, an image file that is larger than 10 megabytes (10MB) when opened in digital image viewing or editing software. Compression file formats can decrease the storage file size dramatically. *ex: The client asked us to deliver a high resolution file.* *plural:* High Resolutions *variation:* High Res

Highlight [1415-00-00-0100] The brightest part of an image, represented in a halftone or color separation by the smallest dots, or the absence of dots. *ex: We can just barely see the highlight detail.* *plural:* Highlights

Hold Harmless [1258-00-00-0100] A term often used in a contract; one party assumes the liability inherent in a situation, relieving the other party of responsibility. *ex: The contract includes a hold harmless term.*

Holding Fee [1641-00-00-0100] A charge for retaining material beyond an agreed-upon submission or license period. *ex: Please return within 30 days or you will be billed a holding fee.* *plural:* Holding Fees

Home Page [1416-00-00-0100] Refers to the first or opening page of a multipage website. *ex: The image will be displayed on their home page.* *plural:* Home Pages

Home Use [5020-00-00-0100] Denotes a license for personal, private display. *ex: Since the prints will be for home use, they will be much less expensive than those we licensed for public display.* *plural:* Home Uses

Horizontal [1417-00-00-0100] Parallel to the horizon—i.e., left to right. Wider than tall. *ex: The image will run as a horizontal on the page.* *plural:* Horizontals

Hour [1505-00-00-0100] A 60-minute time period. *ex: The project will take an additional hour to complete.* *plural:* Hours

HTML [1024-01-00-0100] Abbreviation for Hyper Text Markup Language *ex: Creating proper HTML code for a web site requires a computer specialist.*

Hue [1418-00-00-0100] The color reflecting from or transmitted through a material or object. *info:* Typically, a hue is named for its color, such red, green, blue or orange. Part of a useful method of representing color called the HSB model: hue, saturation and brightness. *ex: A hue shift will improve the appearance of that image.* *plural:* Hues

Hyper Text Markup Language [1024-00-00-0100] Computer code that, when rendered to a monitor by web browser software, controls how a web page appears. *info:* Includes text, formatting and layout instructions, font information, color specifications, coded instructions that allow interactivity, and coded instructions that link a web page to graphics, images (still and video) and dynamic content, and other web pages. *ex: Writing proper hyper text markup language code for a website requires a specialist.* *variation:* HTML

Hyperlink [1667-01-00-0100] See Link *ex: The web page contains a hyperlink back to the home page.* *plural:* Hyperlinks

ICC [1419-00-00-0100] An industry group responsible for setting technology standards that underlie color management systems for computer input and output devices, including monitors. *info:* International Color Consortium standards include the format for a color profile. *ex: Our images include ICC compliant color profiles to help ensure accurate color reproduction.* variation: **International Color Consortium**

Icon [1815-00-00-0100] A graphic symbol or small picture that represents a computer program, a data file, a command or a concept in a graphical user interface. *info:* Can include an image. *ex: The image-editing program icon contains a photograph.* *plural:* Icons

Illustrated Book [1159-00-00-0100] A book, often expensive, that features illustrations (often including photographs), to complement text. *info:* Not to be confused with a picture book that is composed mainly of images. *ex: The photograph will be used in an illustrated book.* *plural:* Illustrated Books

Illustration [1669-00-00-0100] A visual created or used to enhance, clarify, explain, decorate or add meaning to a text. Most often used to refer to drawings rendered in any medium. *ex: The client wants to use that illustration in their new book.* *plural:* Illustrations

Illustrator [3910-00-00-0100] Someone who conceives of or makes a visual created or used to enhance, clarify, explain, decorate or add meaning to a text. Most often refers to people who create drawings rendered in any medium. *ex: The illustrator painted a coral reef scene that included sharks, turtles, schools of fish and beautiful corals, an image almost impossible to capture with a camera. plural:* Illustrators

Image [1420-00-00-0100] A visual representation of one or more persons, places, things or ideas. Includes a photograph, illustration, collage, montage and/or composite, with or without text. *ex: Copies of the image are available in several sizes, depending on your reproduction needs. plural:* Images

Image Resolution [1421-00-00-0100] The amount of visual information stored in an image file, measured in pixels per inch (PPI) at a given physical size, or more simply, by the dimensions of the file in pixels. *info:* Much confusion surrounds PPI and image resolution. A PPI figure has little meaning without image dimensions in inches. A 2- by 3-inch image at 300 PPI contains the same visual information as a 6- by 9-inch image at 100 PPI. Both measure 600 pixels by 900 pixels and offer the same reproduction capabilities. *ex: The clients asked for the pictures at actual size for the layout with an image resolution of 300 PPI. plural:* Image Resolutions

Image Size

(1) Image Size (Print) [1422-00-01-0100] The size an image will appear in relation to the rest of the layout or page. *info:* May be expressed in inches, centimeters and/or picas. However, most licensing fees are based on the portion of a page an image occupies, such as full page, one half page or one quarter page—as well as the page size. *ex: The image size will be approximately one half page. plural:* Image Sizes

(2) Image Size (Digital) [1422-00-02-0100] The dimensions of a digital image, most clearly expressed in its pixel count, horizontally and vertically. Also may be expressed in PPI when paired with its size in inches. *info:* Much confusion surrounds image size, PPI and resolution. A PPI figure has little meaning without image dimensions in inches. A 2- by 3-inch image at 300 PPI contains the same visual information as a 6- by 9-inch image at 100 PPI. Both measure 600 pixels by 900 pixels and have the same reproduction capabilities. The size of an image file when stored on digital media is also a PPI measure for estimating actual image size, since bit depth, picture content, format and compression methods are all variables that affect stored file size. *ex: The

image size needed for page 23 is 2,000 by 3,500 pixels. plural:* Image Sizes

Imaging [5030-00-00-0100] A general term for the creation of photographs or copies by any means. *ex: The imaging industry addresses a wide variety of applications, from consumer photography, to x-rays, astrophysics and copiers.*

Immersive Imaging [1770-00-00-0100] Term for a broad array of virtual reality image capture and presentation technologies designed to help viewers sense more than they might from a two-dimensional picture. *info:* Includes photographic virtual reality, 3-D computer renderings, texture mapping, VR panoramas and object movies. *ex: The online campaign includes immersive imaging that will seemingly transport viewers to Hawaii.*

Implied Warranty [5200-00-00-0100] A legal obligation arising out of circumstances rather than a contract or other express promise. *ex: The implied warranty obligated the vendor to deliver in a timely manner. plural:* Implied Warranties

Impressions

(1) Impressions (Marketing) [1046-00-01-0100] The total number of all individuals or homes who see a marketing message (including duplicate exposures). *ex: That media buy gave us nearly a million impressions.*

(2) Impressions (Print) [1046-00-02-0100] The number of press sheets produced in a press run. *ex: The printer ran 10,000 impressions of the flyer.*

Imprint [1538-00-00-0100] Akin to a brand name: publishing companies use this term to describe different company names under which they publish different types, lines and/or genres of books. *ex: The publisher has created a separate imprint for these new books. plural:* Imprints

In Perpetuity [1260-00-00-0100] For an indefinite time period, without limits, forever. *ex: The images are licensed to the client in perpetuity. usability: Discouraged*

In Print [3790-00-00-0100] Describes a book that is available from its publisher's catalog. *info:* The publisher may or may not have plans to reprint the book. *ex: Our book remains in print, but its future is uncertain.*

In Store Date [2775-00-00-0100] The calendar day on which a product is made widely available. *ex: The in store date of the company's newest product, with our*

picture on the label, will be June 1. *plural:* In Store Dates *variation:* In-Store Date

In Store Marketing [2733-00-00-0100] Sales, marketing, advertising or other promotional piece placed at the location where a product or service is sold—on a retail counter, near a cash register or near the front door. *ex: This image will be used for in store marketing at a major chain store. variation:* ISM

In-Store Date [2775-01-00-0100] See In Store Date *ex: The in-store date of the company's newest product, with our picture on the label, will be June 1. plural:* In-Store Dates

Incorporation [1566-00-00-0100] The process of forming a legal entity for the purpose of doing business. *info:* A corporation separates the interests and operations of a business from those of its owners (who are shareholders in the corporation). U.S. corporations must be registered with state governments, are taxed separately and can sometimes provide a shield against personal liability arising out of contractual disputes or acts of the corporation. *ex: The incorporation of our business is almost complete. plural:* Incorporations

Indemnification [1261-00-00-0100] An agreement to remunerate for loss incurred or to protect from liability. *info:* When agreeing to indemnify, one accepts responsibility for actions and eventualities under one's control, implying—often stating—a warranty or guarantee. *ex: The contract includes an indemnification clause. plural:* Indemnifications *variation:* Indemnify

Indemnify [1261-01-00-0100] See Indemnification *ex: The contract includes a clause in which you indemnify us.*

Indemnity Clause [1567-00-00-0100] A part of an agreement or contract that specifies remuneration for loss incurred and protection from liability. *info:* When agreeing to endorse an indemnity clause, you are accepting responsibility for various actions and eventualities, preferably those you can control. Such responsibility often takes the form of a warranty or guarantee, implied or stated. *ex: The contract includes an indemnity clause. plural:* Indemnity Clauses

Independent Contractor [1568-00-00-0100] An individual or company that agrees to perform a certain task or project, for a given period of time, according to that person or company's own methods. *info:* Unless otherwise agreed, independent contractors own the copyright to work they produce and license usage of the work to the client. They work when they choose in order to meet certain specifications using equipment and/or premises they own or lease, but they do not receive employee benefits (e.g., matching retirement savings, health insurance, sick days, paid vacations, etc.). *ex: Please sign our independent contractor agreement before beginning the project. plural:* Independent Contractors

Index [3760-00-00-0100] A detailed, organized listing of terms, items and/or ideas included in a work or works—usually in alphabetical or numerical order. *info:* Usually published as back matter, but sometimes an index can fill a book or appear as an online guide with links. *ex: They licensed the image to also appear in the book's index. plural:* Indexes

Industry [1262-00-00-0100] The primary business area or segment of a product or service being sold, promoted or produced. *info:* The industry for an advertisement promoting a university would be education. For a magazine ad, the industry would be publishing—periodical. *ex: Our company is a part of the online publishing industry. plural:* Industries

Industry Exclusive [1263-01-00-0100] See Industry Exclusivity *ex: The client purchased an industry exclusive for automotive advertising. plural:* Industry Exclusives

Industry Exclusivity [1263-00-00-0100] A right that, when granted by a licensee, limits how the licensor (and other parties offering licenses of the work) may allow any third party to use the work in relation to a specified type or types of companies. *info:* Often combined with other types of exclusivity, such as duration and geographic. *ex: The client purchased industry exclusivity for automotive advertising. plural:* Industry Exclusivities *variation:* Industry Exclusive

Infringement [3780-00-00-0100] A violation or encroachment on a law or right. *info:* Copyright infringement takes place when a work is used without sufficient or with no license from the copyright holder. Infringement of rights to privacy, property (including trespass) and publicity are among other issues in picture licensing and use. *ex: Using that picture for an advertisement without a release and license would be an infringement on the rights of both the subject and the photographer. plural:* Infringements

Ink Jet Print [3880-00-00-0100] An image or document on paper or other material (such as a canvas or board) produced by a process that sprays dyes or pigments through tiny nozzles onto the material. *info:* Many sizes and types of printers produce ink jet prints, with various ink systems. Some printer systems emphasize speed, others color fidelity and/or print longevity.

*ex: The enclosed ink jet print is a guide print, but not a proof of the digital image. **plural:** Ink Jet Prints*

Insert [3800-00-00-0100] A printed piece, often a single sheet or blow in card, inserted into a multi-page publication. **info:** A newspaper insert can often be a full magazine, sales catalog or additional section. *ex: The Sunday insert project will include hundreds of pictures.* **plural:** Inserts

Insertion [2685-00-00-0100] A single instance of a work (including advertising, text, image, video etc.) appearing in any kind of commercial media. **info:** This term describes how many times an advertisement or other work appears. Each use in each issue of a named publication or other medium is a separate insertion. *ex: That advertising insertion will appear in next Thursday's issue.* **plural:** Insertions

Insertion Order [2686-00-00-0100] A document or other notification used to confirm the purchase of advertising in one or more media outlets, typically including details about the purchase. **info:** Identifies the advertising client and campaign, the specific publication(s) in which the ad(s) will appear, as well as the reproduction size(s), start date(s), end date(s), cost, and often, the CPM, applicable frequency discounts and other specifications. *ex: We received the company's insertion order yesterday, and we should get the ad in the next issue without a problem.* **plural:** Insertion Orders

Insertions [1280-00-00-0100] In a license, the number of times a work may appear in specified media. *ex: The client ordered three insertions of the advertisement, including our photograph.* **variation:** Number of Insertions

Inside Cover [1423-00-00-0100] A prominent page near the front of a book or magazine; typically the flip side of the front page that a reader sees before opening the work. **info:** The inside cover of a magazine is considered a prominent advertising placement, typically commanding a premium insertion fee from advertisers. *ex: Here is the image that we licensed for the inside cover.* **plural:** Inside Covers

Inside Page [3810-00-00-0100] One side of a sheet within a publication, other than its cover. **info:** With books, many consider inside pages as those that fall between the front matter and back matter. *ex: The inside pages of the book were filled with black and white images but the cover was in color.* **plural:** Inside Pages

Installment [3820-00-00-0100] A section or chapter of a book or article series that is preceded and/or followed by additional sections or chapters published at regular intervals. *ex: The next installment of the corruption series features our surveillance photographs.* **plural:** Installments

Institutional Sale [1547-00-00-0100] A transaction with a school, library, other large public organization or foundation, especially one dedicated to education. *ex: The book was produced specifically for institutional sale to university libraries.* **plural:** Institutional Sales

Intellectual Property [1264-00-00-0100] Refers generically to rights of ownership created through cognitive, creative and/or discovery efforts of a creator. **info:** Intellectual property rights can be protected under patent, trademark, copyright, trade secret, trade dress or other law. An intellectual property right is generally separate and distinct from any physical object and not transferred by mere sale of the object embodying the right. *ex: My writings and my photographs are my intellectual property.* **plural:** Intellectual Properties

Interactive Kiosk [1110-00-00-0100] A small, freestanding device that delivers content that varies based on user responses, such as a computer terminal, ATM or prepaid phone card dispenser. **info:** Often features printed or electronic advertisements. *ex: This image will appear on our interactive kiosk for one week.* **plural:** Interactive Kiosks

Interactive Use [5040-00-00-0100] A type of display that encourages and facilitates a viewer taking action to view more images, video, animation and/or text. **info:** Examples of interactive use include banners, buttons and other uses on websites, CD-ROMs, interactive kiosks and electronic gaming. *ex: The image is licensed for interactive use in a web advertisement.* **plural:** Interactive Uses

Interior Page

(1) Interior Page (Print) [1649-00-01-0100] In a book or magazine, a page between the front matter and back matter. *ex: The image will appear on an interior page.* **plural:** Interior Pages

(2) Interior Page (Online) [1649-00-02-0100] A web page other than the home page of a website, accessible usually (but not necessarily) via a link on the home page, a search engine, email or an external web page. *ex: The image will appear on an interior page of the corporate website.* **plural:** Interior Pages

International Color Consortium [1419-01-00-0100] See ICC *ex: Our images include embedded profiles compliant with International Color Consortium standards.*

International Distribution [1065-00-00-0100] When circulation of a service, product, message or usage occurs in a country or countries other than the country of origin. *ex: The Wall Street Journal has international distribution in Europe and Asia.*

International Rights [1265-00-00-0100] Permission to use a creative work within a specified territory or geographic region that is different from the country of origin (or in which the license agreement is made). *info:* Often confused with language rights. It is necessary to define international rights when licensing so the territory of distribution is clear. *ex: The client wants the license to include international rights for France.*

International Standard Book Number [1426-01-00-0100] See ISBN *ex: The International Standard Book Number symbol appears on the back of the book.* *plural:* International Standard Book Numbers

Internegative [1424-00-00-0100] In film-based photography—especially motion pictures—a duplicate negative conversion from a positive or interpositive. *info:* An intermediate production aid made with the same fine grain film used for making an interpositive, but instead made from a positive image yielding a negative image. *ex: We will make an internegative of that original.* *plural:* Internegatives

Internet [1109-00-00-0100] A global collection of largely public information and networks generally linked together with telecommunications hardware and software. *info:* At its core, the Internet comprises mainframe computers and heavy-duty servers connected via fiber-optic cable and large data routing devices communicating through several data protocols. At its edges, the Internet is personal computers connected via cable, copper telephone lines or wirelessly. All Internet communications are governed by protocols established by various standards bodies. *ex: The World Wide Web represents only one of several protocols on the Internet.*

Internet Service Provider [1701-01-00-0100] See ISP *ex: Our Internet service provider runs our web servers and email.* *plural:* Internet Service Providers

Interpolate [1266-01-00-0100] See Interpolation *ex: We will interpolate the image to increase its size.*

Interpolation [1266-00-00-0100] A digital imaging procedure used to enlarge or decrease digital image resolution. *info:* Specialized computer software (including most image-editing programs) calculates average values of adjacent pixels in an image, then adds the newly calculated pixels or replaces existing

pixels with fewer averaged pixels. May degrade visual image quality. *ex: We will use interpolation to increase the size of the image.* *plural:* Interpolations *variation:* Interpolate

Interpositive [1425-00-00-0100] In film-based photography—especially motion pictures—a duplicate negative made on very fine-grain film stock, part of a two-step procedure to produce an internegative. *info:* Copying a negative on negative film yields a positive. Copy that interpositive on negative film and get an internegative. Used in special effects, title super-impositions fades, dissolves and other visual effects, and as a step toward making projection prints. It is never projected and is only an intermediate step for making something else. *ex: We will make an interpositive of that original and from it, an internegative.* *plural:* Interpositives *variation:* IP

Intranet [1192-00-00-0100] A private computer network that uses the same kind of software and protocols as the Internet, but for use only within an organization. Not accessible to the public. *ex: The image appears on a web page that's available only on the client's intranet.* *plural:* Intranets

Introduction [3830-00-00-0100] A beginning section to a book, other publication or long article, usually written by the author or editor. *ex: The picture will run full page, opposite the book's introduction.* *plural:* Introductions

Invitation [1191-00-00-0100] A card, letter, email message, or sometimes far more elaborate piece that asks an individual or people to attend an event or gathering. *ex: The invitation will be mailed this afternoon.* *plural:* Invitations

Invoice [1569-00-00-0100] A billing document listing fees, expenses, charges, and descriptions of the work licensed, work created and/or goods delivered. *info:* Often lists any right licensed or transferred, payment terms, other applicable terms and conditions, and additional pertinent information. Issued by a licensor to a licensee, or more generally, by any seller to a buyer or client. *ex: Here is my invoice, detailing the project and its costs.* *plural:* Invoices

IP [1425-01-00-0100] Abbreviation for Interpositive *ex: We will make an IP of that original and from it, an internegative.* *plural:* IPs

IP Address [1699-00-00-0100] A set of numbers corresponding to a machine-readable Internet address of a server or domain. *info:* A special group of Internet servers translate the plain-language web address domain names into these numbers, so Internet-connected computers can locate each other. IP stands for Internet protocol. *ex: Please tell us the IP Address of your server. **plural:** IP Addresses*

ISBN [1426-00-00-0100] The unique identification number of a book that differentiates it from other titles. *info:* ISBN may or may not differentiate one book from a previous edition or revision. *ex: The ISBN symbol, a bar code, appears on the back of the book.* *variation:* International Standard Book Number

ISM [2733-01-00-0100] Abbreviation for In Store Marketing *ex: This image will be used for ISM at a major chain store.*

ISP [1701-00-00-0100] A supplier of Internet connections to business, education and/or the public. *info:* Typically offers such services as email, website hosting and off-location server hosting. *ex: Our ISP runs our web servers and email. **plural:** ISPs **variation:*** Internet Service Provider

Issue [1025-00-00-0100] All copies of a given magazine that are published on the date indicated on and inside the magazine. *info:* The date on the cover is not necessarily the same as the on sale date. *ex: The January issue went into the mail yesterday. **plural:** Issues*

Issue Date [1047-00-00-0100] The calendar day a magazine is actually distributed, often prior to the date printed on the cover. *ex: The issue date is March 1, although the cover date reads March 8. **plural:** Issue Dates*

Issue Life [1048-00-00-0100] The length of time it takes for an issue of a magazine to be read by the maximum measurable audience. *ex: The magazine's issue life is 45 days. **plural:** Issue Lives*

Jacket [1427-00-00-0100] A paper cover that folds over the bound cover of a book. *ex: The image will run on the jacket of the new book. **plural:** Jackets*

Jewel Case [1816-00-00-0100] A plastic container designed to store and transport one or two CD ROM or DVD discs, including those storing music, video, games, other software and computer data. *info:* Frequently includes liner notes with a printed listing of the disc contents, often along with images and other information. *ex: The jewel case will include liner notes featuring our pictures. **plural:** Jewel Cases*

Jigsaw Puzzle [1220-01-00-0100] See Puzzle *ex: The jigsaw puzzle that was made from our landscape image was popular because of its complex patterns.*

Job Change Order [5050-00-00-0100] A written notice that parameters, costs and/or requirements for a project have changed. *info:* A job change order is signed by both the contractor and the client to indicate their understanding that adjustments have been made and they will have costs associated with them. *ex: When we added several new scenes and poses, we documented them on a job change order. **plural:** Job Change Orders*

Journal [3840-00-00-0100] A printed collection of essays or articles. *info:* May be by one person or many, as in a scientific or literary journal. *ex: The illustration will dominate the cover of the journal, which focuses on molecular biology. **plural:** Journals*

JPEG [1428-00-00-0100] A file format featuring digital compression that reduces digital image file size, or an image file that has been so compressed. *info:* The common JPEG format deletes some image data when compressing a file. Application of a high compression ratio when saving JPEG files may cause undesirable visual artifacts. Repeatedly editing and saving a JPEG file will magnify such artifacts. However, when created with low compression (larger file sizes and higher-level settings), a JPEG image is almost indistinguishable from the original digital image from which it was generated. JPEG image file compression can be confusing, since most measures designate lower compression ratios with high numbers, intended to designate high quality. JPEG was originally an acronym for the Joint Photographic Experts Group, a standards group for still image compression, formed by the international organization for standardization (ISO) and the ITU telecommunication standardization sector (ITU-T). The popular JPEG image compression standards and the new JPEG 2000 file formats are the best known among this group's standards. *ex: She converted her image to a low res JPEG for Internet use. **plural:** JPEGs **variation:** JPG*

JPEG 2000 [3860-00-00-0100] An emerging standard for digital image encoding that uses compression techniques based on wavelet technology. *info:* The JPEG 2000 standards are broad, supporting a variety of applications using still photographs, motion pictures, publication files and more. JPEG 2000 includes compression formats that discard some image data, as well as those that are lossless. These formats promise to deliver smaller files of better quality than older JPEG implementations. *ex: Be sure the client can read a JPEG 2000 file before sending your image in that format. **plural:** JPEG 2000s*

JPG [1428-01-00-0100] Abbreviation for JPEG *ex: Email us a JPG of the image and we will optimize it in our editing software. **plural:** JPGs*

Jurisdiction [1267-00-00-0100] An area of judicial authority: the geographic region in which a court has power, or the types of cases it has power to hear. *ex: The court's jurisdiction includes civil cases in Mississippi. plural:* Jurisdictions

K [43500200-0100] Abbreviation for Kilobyte *ex: Every K of file size counts when you're transmitting files with a low-bandwidth connection.*

KB [4350-01-00-0100] Abbreviation for Kilobyte *ex: Every KB of file size counts when you're transmitting files with a low-bandwidth connection.*

Keyline [2809-00-00-0100] A preliminary representation of how a finished piece will appear in print, including outlined boxes where images will be placed, or a thin rule used to mark the finished borders of photographs, halftones or color separations. *ex: Here is the keyline for our new advertisement, with rough type in place and boxes representing artwork. plural:* Keylines

Keyword [5060-00-00-0100] A search term that describes some aspect of an image and can be used to locate it, or the act of developing a list of such search terms. *info:* A single image may be associated with many keywords. *ex: Give me the right keyword combination, and I'm sure I can locate the image you need in our DIM. plural:* Keywords

Kill [1610-00-00-0100] To remove, delete or cancel. *ex: The client is going to kill this project. plural:* Kills

Kill Fee [2796-00-00-0100] A payment that may be made (and may be called for by contract) to a creator when a client cancels a project. *ex: The amount of the kill fee is reasonable, considering the work that has been invested already. plural:* Kill Fees

Kilobyte [4350-00-00-0100] A measure of file size and storage capacity referring to 1,000 or 1,024, 8-bit data units or characters. *info:* Most software and systems consider a kilobyte to be 1,024 (the binary quantity of 2 to the 10th power) bytes. However, some key standards groups state that 1,000 (10 to the 3rd power) bytes comprise a kilobyte. And many data storage manufacturers use this measurement to define their device sizes, meaning a computer may show less storage capacity on a drive than the drive's specified size suggests. *ex: Every kilobyte of file size counts when you're transmitting files with a low bandwidth connection. plural:* Kilobytes *variation:* KB, K

Knock Out [4140-00-00-0100] A picture of a shape, person or object removed from its background and integrated into a page design. *info:* A knock out may be placed on a white background or on any other color or pattern, even another image. Sometimes a knock out is wrapped with text or headline type. Many pictures are made against white, green or other solid backgrounds, so that creating a knock out will be easy. *ex: The designer wants to use the picture of the girl as a knock out, wrapped with text. plural:* Knock Outs

Landscape

(1) Landscape (Design) [3080-00-01-0100] A horizontal image, one that is wider than it is tall. *info:* Commonly used term in software for word processing and printing. *ex: Page set up should be set to landscape if you want the comp to print correctly. preferred term*: Horizontal *usability:* Caution

(2) Landscape (Photo) [3080-00-02-0100] An image that depicts primarily natural scenery. *ex: As a landscape photographer, he focuses on huge fields of wildflowers.*

Language Exclusive [1709-01-00-0100] See Language Exclusivity *ex: The client purchased language exclusivity for Farsi. plural:* Language Exclusives

Language Exclusivity [1709-00-00-0100] Describes a right that, when granted to a licensee, limits how the licensor (and other parties offering licenses of the work) may license rights in a work to a third party for use accompanied by text in specified languages. *ex:* The client purchased language exclusivity for Farsi. plural: Language Exclusivities *variation: Language Exclusive*

Language Rights [1268-00-00-0100] A permission that specifies the languages in which a creative work may be used. *info:* Each separate language must be named in the license agreement. Often confused with international rights and territory rights, although it may be combined with such rights. *ex: The client is requesting specific language rights for Arabic and Hindi.*

Large Format [1429-00-00-0100] Refers to negative or transparency film that is 4 by 5 inches or larger, as well as the camera type that typically used such film, but may, instead or in addition, use a high-quality, high-resolution digital imaging system. *ex: Please produce that image with a large format camera since we will run it very large. plural:* Large Formats

Laser Print [3870-00-00-0100] Output of images and type on paper or other material (such as fabric or board) from an electrostatic- and light-based system that fuses toner to the paper or other material. *info:* Laser print systems are valued for their speed and/or comparatively low cost of output. They range widely in quality, capabilities and price—from inexpensive personal printers, to single-color, high-speed office and production printers, to advanced color printers that rival some ink jet print systems for quality. *ex: We'll use a laser print system for this short-run flyer.* **plural:** Laser Prints

Late Fee [1771-00-00-0100] A contract term that specifies an agreed fee if a balance due is in arrears. *ex: The parties agreed to a reasonable late fee.* **plural:** Late Fees

Launch Date [1036-00-00-0100] The specific calendar day (and in some cases, time) when a marketing, selling, mail, fax or email campaign is actually distributed and/or broadcast to the target audience. *ex: On the launch date, the advertisement will appear in five national magazines.* **plural:** Launch Dates

Layered File [3190-00-00-0100] A digital image or design document that is organized with virtual overlays, allowing a user to modify the appearance and attributes of visual data in the file and save those changes in the original file, while retaining its original unmodified attributes. *info:* Also allows users to reproduce only certain layers, something very handy for creating different versions of a piece or noting edits. *ex: Because the ad was designed as a layered file, exchanging its text without affecting the rest of the ad was a relatively easy step.* **plural:** Layered Files

Layout [1160-00-00-0100] A preliminary representation of an advertisement, page or other graphic work, or the act of assembling and arranging on a page or in design software the text and visual components of a piece intended for reproduction. *info:* Usually indicates the planned placement of photographs and/or illustrations and copy, along with examples of each. May have two stages—a rough outline called a mock up or visual, followed by the finished artwork (called a comp). *ex: The art director showed the layout, with all its components, to the client.* **plural:** Layouts

Leaflet [2781-00-00-0100] A pamphlet or single sheet, usually promotional or advertising in nature. *info:* Often folded, particularly in fourths. *ex: One side of the sheet that folds into the leaflet is printed in color and it forms the cover.* **plural:** Leaflets

Liability [1269-00-00-0100] Amount owed for items received, services rendered, expenses incurred, assets acquired, work performed, and amounts received but not as yet earned. It also results from a breach of contract, infringement, or contingent acts. *info:* The main thrust of this term in the industry is to potential liability as a result of alleged breach, or breach, of representations or warranties. *ex: The building mortgage is listed as a liability on the balance sheet.* **plural:** Liabilities

Libel [1270-00-00-0100] Defamation in the form of a writing that is the tort of making a false statement of fact that injures someone's reputation. *ex: Your calling him a liar in your newspaper column might be considered libel.* **plural:** Libels **variation:** Libelous

Libelous [1270-01-00-0100] See Libel [1270-00-00-0100] *ex: Your calling him a liar in your newspaper column might be considered libelous.*

Library Binding [1584-00-00-0100] A durable hardcover method of keeping the pages of a printed piece together, with cloth reinforcement and a robust sewing method. *ex: Our newest coffee table book uses library binding.* **plural:** Library Bindings

License [1271-00-00-0100] A legal agreement granting permission to exercise a specified right or rights to a work, often encompassed in an invoice, or the act of granting same. *ex:* We granted them a license to use the image in the magazine. plural: Licenses

License Fee [5070-00-00-0100] The price charged by a licensor to a licensee in exchange for a grant of rights permitting the use of one or more images in a manner prescribed in a license. *info:* A variety of factors, such as circulation, the size of reproduction and specific image qualities affect the determination of a particular license fee. *ex: The licensor paid the licensee a license fee for use of the image in the advertisement.* **plural:** License Fees

Licensee [1708-00-00-0100] One who is granted a license by a licensor. *ex: The photographer granted poster rights to his client, the licensee.* **plural:** Licensees

Licensor [1707-00-00-0100] One who gives or grants a license to a licensee. *ex: You must contact the licensor if you want to use that image.* **plural:** Licensors

Lightbox

(1) Lightbox (Digital) [1772-00-01-0100] An online web page designed to organize and/or store a selection of images. *ex: I have saved the selected images in my lightbox and you can access it to choose the one you like best.* **plural:** Lightboxes

Limitation of Liability [1272-00-00-0100] Agreement as to the maximum potential liability where there is no actual liability presently due. *ex: The contract includes a limitation of liability clause which limits the party's liability to a certain fee if it damages or loses an original transparency.*

Limited Edition [3200-00-00-0100] A pre-specified number of copies of a work that may be reproduced in a particular size or based on some other limiting factor. *info:* Historically, processes such as wood cuts or stone lithography could only produce a limited number of clean copies. Modern reproduction methods allow production of an unlimited number of identical copies, reducing the significance of some types of limited editions. However, limiting the number of copies produced can increase the value of each, and the tradition continues even with processes that have no practical limits. Care should be exercised in defining the limits of limited editions, with attention to ethical considerations and applicable laws. *ex: The artist produced a limited edition of twenty platinum prints. **plural:** Limited Editions **usability**: Caution*

Limited Rights [1633-00-00-0100] A license restricting use or other reproduction in a manner that must be described in the contract or agreement. *ex: The client accepted a limited rights license which meant he could use it for his internal newsletter only.*

Line Screen [3210-00-00-0100] The rate at which halftone dots are dispersed across a page, the printing plates and press components that print it, the graphic arts film (if any) from which the plate is made, and/or the digital file from which the halftone film or plate is generated. *info:* Typically expressed as lines per inch (LPI), referring to the number of lines in a screen that is used to optically produce halftones. Most halftones now come from digital output rather than from photographing artwork through a screen sandwiched with graphic arts film. LPI is not equivalent, however, to the DPI of a printer or image setter generating a halftone. A printer may use only one of its small dots for a highlight (or with a negative output, shadow) detail, while clustering many to produce a halftone dot in a shadow (or a highlight with negative output), all within a grid that matches the line screen's rate. Image pixel counts are another matter. As a rule of thumb a digital image destined for halftone reproduction should be sized to fit its place in a layout with a PPI rate of 1.5 to 2 times the line screen rate (LPI). *ex: Since they are printing that image on a 100 line screen, you will need to provide a file that is 200 PPI. **plural:** Line Screens*

Liner Notes [1773-00-00-0100] Explanatory words or commentary about a record album, cassette, or CD ROM included on the jacket or in the packaging. *ex: The liner notes on their new album explain the meaning behind their songs.*

Lines Per Inch [1434-00-00-0100] The unit of measurement used to describe the resolution of a black and white halftone or color separation. *ex: The image will be printed at 133 lines per inch. **plural:** Lines Per Inch **variation:** LPI*

Link [1667-00-00-0100] Text or an image on a web page or email message that, when clicked with a mouse, causes the user's web browser or email software to summon new content from the same or a different website. *ex: The web page contains a link back to the home page. **plural:** Links **variation:** Hyperlink*

Liquidated Damages [5080-00-00-0100] A sum of money agreed to in a license or contract, reasonably anticipating the amount of damage that would occur in the event of a breach. *info:* Typically specified for breaches such as damage or loss of original artwork, cancellation or delay of a production, or failure to publish a credit line. *ex: The agreement states liquidated damages should be paid if the original film is lost or damaged.*

List Price [1548-00-00-0100] Publishers and manufacturers set a suggested figure for a product or service. *info:* Many retail sales outlets often sell the product at below list price. *ex: The list price is printed on the tag. **plural:** List Prices*

Live Date [1026-00-00-0100] The specific time or day when a promotional piece or campaign is unveiled to its target audience. *ex: The live date for the campaign's release to the general public will be May 31. **plural:** Live Dates*

Live Image Area

(1) Live Image Area (Photo) [2696-00-01-0100] The area of a photograph that contains the actual image as opposed to the border area or frame around the image. *info:* In some cases, such as Polaroid frames showing in-camera borders or prints made from filed-out negative carriers, a border may be considered part of the live image area. *ex: Printing an image full frame does not remove or hide any of the live image area. **plural:** Live Image Areas*

(2) Live Image Area (Television) [2696-00-02-0100] The part of a television image that contains actual image as opposed to sync or other data (487 vertical lines for NTSC and 576 lines for PAL). *info:* The inactive area of the image is called blanking. *ex: If the TV set is properly tuned, viewers see only the live image area. **plural:** Live Image Areas*

Loan Fee [1273-00-00-0100] A fee charged for the retention of a creative work. *ex: Our delivery contract includes a loan fee provision that allows them to display the illustration in their lobby for six months. **plural:** Loan Fees*

Local [1431-00-00-0100] The area of a city and its closest surrounding suburbs, or some other small land area such as county, township, or other small region. *ex: The news of the traffic violation was only reported in the local newspaper.*

Local Distribution [1066-00-00-0100] When circulation of a product, message, or usage is limited to a single city, or otherwise limited geographic area. *info:* Several instances are spot distribution. The next larger distribution area is referred to as regional distribution. *ex: They started as a small local distribution magazine.* *plural:* Local Distributions

Location [5100-00-00-0100] A place, outside a studio, used for photographic productions. *ex: The school was used as a location for the photo shoot.* *plural:* Locations

Location Fee [5090-00-00-0100] The price paid for using and/or depicting a place in a production or finished work. *ex: The location fee covered both the cost of renting the property and of using the distinctive mansion in the background.* *plural:* Location Fees

Location Release [5110-00-00-0100] A document signed by the owner or controlling entity of property (a building, statue, or other object or area belonging to that owner or entity) that allows a photograph of it to be licensed for commercial use. *ex: The photographer has a location release on file allowing him to license pictures of the building.* *plural:* Location Releases

Logo [1193-01-00-0100] See Logotype *ex: Their logotype, a green rose, appears at the top of their stationery.* *plural:* Logos

Logotype [1193-00-00-0100] A special design, often accompanied by the name of a company or product, often used as a trademark in advertising. *ex: Their logotype, a green rose, appears at the top of their stationery.* *plural:* Logotypes *preferred term:* Logo *usability:* Caution *variation:* Logo

Loss Fee [1806-00-00-0100] A stipulated damages clause wherein the party to a contract agrees to what the damages will be in the event of a breach of the agreement, including damage to or failure to return original or duplicate slides or negatives. *info:* A common contract clause with respect to the delivery of photographs and duplicates. Damages at the time a contract is made can be difficult to ascertain. They must bear a reasonable relationship to the actual loss. *ex: The loss fee charged for the damage of the artwork was set at an amount agreeable to both parties.* *plural:* Loss Fees *variation:* Lost Image Fee

Lost Image Fee [1806-01-00-0100] See Loss Fee *ex: The lost image fee charged for the damage of the artwork was set at an amount agreeable to both parties.* *Plural:* Lost Image Fees

Low Contrast Print [1432-00-00-0100] A paper stock used especially for transfer to videotape. *ex: When the image was reproduced on a low contrast print, it lost some of its impact, but it looked great after it was transferred to videotape.* *plural:* Low Contrast Prints

Low Res [1433-01-00-0100] Abbreviation for Low Resolution *ex: Send the client a low res file for presentation use.*

Low Resolution [1433-00-00-0100] An image file that is under one megabyte (1,048.576KB) in size (based on a full page) when opened in digital image viewing or editing software. *info:* Useful for presentation purposes but generally insufficient for high quality printed reproduction except at very small size. Low resolution reproduced less than a full page would translate into a lower KB size, i.e. 500KB or less. *ex: Send the client a low resolution file for presentation use.* *plural:* Low Resolutions *variation:* Low Res

LPI [1434-01-00-0100] Abbreviation for Lines Per Inch. *ex: The image will be printed at 133 LPI.* *plural:* LPIs

Macro [3220-00-00-0100] An image produced at a ratio of 1:1 or higher magnification than the subject on the film or sensor. *info:* Macro photography typically deals with magnifications between 1:1 and 50:1. *ex: His macro photo of the bee revealed its intricate pattern in a way never before seen.* *plural:* macros

Magalog [1027-00-00-0100] Part magazine, part catalog, a direct mail piece with two or more pages. *info:* Typically resembles a magazine, with content, a pitch to potential subscribers and some means for subscribers to order. *ex: The magalog is being shipped to our mailing list today.* *plural:* Magalogs

Magazine [1161-00-00-0100] A periodical that may be targeted to the general public or to a limited group such as a trade or profession, or for a captive audience. *info:* May be sold or given away to readers. *ex: The magazine contained articles on Caribbean travel via sailboat.* *plural:* Magazines

Magazine Print Advertising [1112-00-00-0100] Attracting public attention to a product, idea or business using announcements printed in a periodical. *info:* This is typically a paid placement, unless provided pro bono to a nonprofit by the publisher. *ex: Magazine print advertising is the preferred method for many advertisers wanting to reach people who do not frequent the Internet.*

Mainline [1616-00-00-0100] A large magazine rack or reading center in the aisle of a supermarket, store or other retail outlet. *ex: Our book will be featured on the mainline in all their stores and every person who shops there will see it. plural:* mainlines

Make Good [1028-020-0-0100] See Makegood *ex: Because our ad was mistakenly left out, the magazine will run a make good next month.*

Make-Good [1028-01-00-0100] See Makegood *ex: Because our ad was mistakenly left out, the magazine will run a make-good next month.*

Makegood [1028-00-00-0100] Running an ad again at no additional cost to the advertiser when the initial advertisement distribution in a magazine or other media is lower than promised, or when the initial ad is omitted or reproduced poorly. *info:* Terms are usually negotiable and can include fee reduction or a refund. *ex: Because our ad was mistakenly left out, the magazine will run a makegood next month. plural:* Makegoods *variation:* Make Good, Make-Good

Manipulate [1774-00-00-0100] To change an image by digital imaging or optical processes. *ex: You can manipulate that image in the darkroom or on your computer. plural:* Manipulates

Manual [3170-00-00-0100] A reference source giving instructions, rules, and procedures for performing certain tasks. *info:* May be an independent title or an ancillary associated with a textbook or product. *ex: The lab manual used a sequence of photos to show how the experiment described in the textbook should be carried out. plural:* Manuals

Manufacturer's Suggested Retail Price [3230-00-00-0100] Recommended selling price for a product or service. *ex: The price I ultimately paid was far below the manufacturer's suggested retail price. plural:* Manufacturer's Suggested Retail Prices *variation:* MSRP

Marketing [1513-00-00-0100] The direct application of advertising and public relations in order to promote and sell products to the buying public. *ex: The marketing plan included an extensive advertising campaign and speaking tour.*

Mask [1860-00-00-0100] Used in compositing and digital imaging. A high contrast black and white image version used to select (or protect) areas of the image during editing. *info:* Advanced digital masking tools permit low contrast edges for more seamless blending between one image element and another. *ex: We will produce a mask for that image*

so that any alterations we apply will not permanently change it until we are ready to do so. *plural:* Masks

Mass Market Paperback [1524-00-00-0100] A small softbound book printed on lower quality paper, typically meant for general consumer purchase. *info:* Typically sold at retail locations such as supermarkets and airports. *ex: I can always depend on a mass market paperback to keep me occupied during a long airplane flight. plural:* Mass Market Paperbacks

Masthead [1049-00-00-0100] A listing in a magazine, newspaper, newsletter or other periodical of its official title, postal and email addresses, telephone number, owner and publisher names and sometimes those of editors and staff. *ex: According to the magazine's masthead, she is no longer the editorial director. plural:* Mastheads

Mat Ad [2805-00-00-0100] An already designed and ready-to-go printed advertising template distributed to franchises, distributors, dealers and area product representatives for placement at their discretion. *info:* Contains a blank area for the local distributor to insert its address, telephone number, etc. No instruction regarding distribution or placement is furnished to the licensor. *ex: The mat ad that headquarters sent saved us from having to hire our own designer for the advertising campaign. plural:* Mat Ads

Match Print [4420-00-00-0100] A high-quality outputted sample that is used as a comp for a customer and a guide for when a piece goes to press. *ex: We could tell from the match print that the image was going to appear too red so we substituted it for a different one at the last minute. plural:* Match prints *preferred term:* Contract Proof *usability:* Discouraged *variation:* Matchprint

Matchprint [4420-01-00-0100] See Match Print *ex: We could tell from the matchprint that the image was going to appear too red so we substituted it for a different one at the last minute. Plural:* Matchprints *preferred term:* Contract Proof *usability:* Discouraged

Matte

(1) Matte [1436-00-01-0100] (Production Used in compositing and digital imaging. A high contrast black and white image version that blocks or cuts a hole in a background image. *info:* The hole allows the image that the matte was made from to seamlessly merge into the background. *ex: A matte will allow us to isolate the animal from its background. plural:* mattes

(2) Matte [1436-00-02-0100] (Print A non-glossy surface, with or without notice653able texture. *ex: This type of image will look better on a matte paper.*

MB [4360-01-00-0100] Abbreviation for Megabyte *ex: That image should compress down to a file size under 1 MB.*

Mechanical [1437-00-00-0100] An industry standard term standing for the combination of three things: laser hardcopy representing a press ready layout; a disk containing all layout and graphic files used to create that hardcopy as well as all necessary fonts; and a disk transmittal form that provides information about the job. *ex: Because the mechanical was missing the specialized fonts used for the job, the piece was on hold until the fonts could be procured. **plural:** Mechanicals **variation:** Digital Mechanical*

Media

(1) Media (Journalism) [1678-00-01-0100] The various forms of mass communication including print (e.g., newspapers, magazines, brochures), electronic (e.g., radio and television), and online (e.g., World Wide Web and email). *info:* Singular form is medium. *ex: It's such an interesting story that we are seeing it appear in all types of media.*

(2) Media (Digital) [1678-00-02-0100] Digital objects or devices on which digital data is stored. *info:* The singular form is medium. *ex: Our images are stored on hard disks and tape media.*

Media Buy [1681-00-00-0100] A license or contract to purchase selected space or time in specified media. Or, the total cost of all specific media purchases for a particular advertisement or campaign. *info:* Usually described in terms of total number of insertions in particular publications and/or the total dollar cost for an entire campaign. *ex: The media buy for a year's worth of advertising in five different national publications plus will be $6 million. **plural:** Media Buys*

Media Exclusive [1825-01-00-0100] See Media Exclusivity *ex: He could not grant a license to use that image for a newspaper ad campaign because it was already media exclusive to another client. **plural:** Media Exclusives*

Media Exclusivity [1825-00-00-0100] A right that, when granted by a licensor to a licensee, limits the right of the licensor (and other parties offering licenses of the work) to license the right to any third party to use the work in specified media. *ex: He could not grant a license to use that image for a newspaper*

ad campaign because he had already granted media exclusivity of that image to another client. ***plural:*** Media Exclusivities ***variation:*** Media Exclusive

Media Kit [1814-00-00-0100] A folder or bundle of promotional and/or editorial materials used to announce or promote something. *info:* Usually distributed to representatives of trade or consumer publications and other news outlets. *ex: The media kit contained two samples of the product and an advertising rate sheet. **plural:** Media Kits*

Media Rights [1680-00-00-0100] The listing of particular means of mass communication included in a given license. *ex: The media rights include print advertising and broadcast, but not online use.*

Media Usage [1679-00-00-0100] The use of a work in media. In a license agreement or contract, the listing of particular forms of mass communications media permitted under the given license. *ex: Permitted media usage, noted on the invoice, includes magazines, billboards, and bus shelters. **plural:** Media Usages*

Medium Format [1438-00-00-0100] A negative or transparency film size that is larger than 35mm but smaller than four-by-five, and the type of camera body used with these film types. *ex: Many professional photographers believe that medium format cameras allow for more detail in their images and prefer using it over a 35mm format.*

Medium Resolution [1775-00-00-0100] An intermediate number of pixels per inch in a digital image or scan. *info:* Generally speaking, an image file that is larger than one megabyte (1MB) but smaller than five megabytes (5MB) when open in image editing software. Compression can decrease the storage file size dramatically. *ex: A medium resolution copy of the image will be suitable for our printing needs. **plural:** Medium Resolutions*

Megabyte [4360-00-00-0100] A measure of file size and storage capacity referring, depending on context, to between 1,000,000 and 1,048,576, 8-bit data units or characters. *info:* Most software, memory chips and systems consider a kilobyte to be 1,024 bytes (the binary quantity of 2 to the 10th power) and a megabyte to be 1,024 such kilobytes or 1,048,576 bytes. However, some key standards groups state that 1,000 (10 to the 3rd power) bytes comprise a kilobyte, and a megabyte (the mega prefix means million or 10 to the 6th power) is 1,000 kilobytes. And many data storage manufacturers use this measurement to define their device sizes, meaning a computer may show less storage capacity on a drive than the drive's specified size suggests. *ex: That image should com-*

press down to a file size under one megabyte. **plural:** Megabytes **variation:** MB

Menu

(1) Menu (Software) [1212-00-01-0100] An ordered list of linked content, activities, or additional areas of interest within a website or a software program, or of controls for an electronic device. **ex:** *Depending upon whether you want to edit or view your work, you can make your choice from the menu.* **plural:** Menus

(2) Menu (Print) [1212-00-02-0100] A printed list of what a restaurant or other establishment offers, often with prices. **info:** May include images. **ex:** *Our image appeared as background for the restaurant's menu.* **plural:** Menus

Menu Board [1213-00-00-0100] A large display listing offerings of a restaurant or other establishment, often with a price list. **ex:** *This image will be used as a background on their menu board.* **plural:** Menu Boards **variation:** Menuboard

Menuboard [1213-01-00-0100] See Menu Board [1213-00-00-0100] **ex:** *This image will be used as a background on their menuboard.* **plural:** Menuboards **preferred term:** Menu Board **usability:** Discouraged

Merchandising [1691-00-00-0100] Promotion of goods or services by coordinating marketing, production, advertising, display and sales strategies. **ex:** *The merchandising program includes giveaway T-shirts with our logo printed on the front.*

Meta Data [3240-01-00-0100] See Metadata *[3240-00-00-0100]* **ex:** *I* looked in the image meta data to find the contact information for the copyright holder. **preferred term:** Metadata [3240-00-00-0100] **usability:** Discouraged **variation:** Meta-data

Meta-Data [3240-03-00-0100] See Metadata [3240-00-00-0100] **ex:** *I looked in the image meta-data to find the contact information for the copyright holder.* **preferred term:** Metadata **usability:** Discouraged **variation:** Meta data

Metadata [3240-00-00-0100] Data embedded or stored within a digital image file that provides information about copyright, credit, restrictions, captions, keywords, or other quality characteristics, etc. **info:** There are several forms of image metadata, the oldest form is that popularized by the international press telecommunications council or IPTC. The IPTC image resource block (IRB) schema is the older version, while the newer is called IPTC core and is designed

to work with newer XMP compatible applications. EXIF or exchangeable image file format, is another form of metadata that is used by digital cameras and provides information such as the make/model of camera, as well as apertures and shutter-speeds, etc. **ex:** *I looked in the image metadata to find the contact information for the copyright holder.* **variation:** Meta data, Meta-data

Metropolitan [1274-00-00-0100] Of or constituting a large city or urban region including adjacent suburbs and towns. **ex:** *The usage will include the New York metropolitan area.*

Middle Reader [1592-00-00-0100] A book geared for readers aged nine to eleven. **ex:** *A child who has a basic ability to read can usually handle a middle reader book.* **plural:** Middle Readers

Midlist [1540-00-00-0100] Books that are expected to enjoy a moderate amount of success but not be best sellers. **ex:** *The majority of books never make it past midlist status, but their authors still get reasonable royalties.*

Minor Release [3250-00-00-0100] A document signed by a subject's guardian of an image or series of images that allows that image or series of images to be published for advertising or other commercial purpose. **ex:** *Because the subject was only seven years old, a minor release, signed by his legal guardian, was needed by the advertising agency before they would consider using the photographer's image.* **plural:** Minor Releases **variation:** Release

Mobile [3920-00-00-0100] A device that responds as a normal telephone while being transported over a wide area. It allows connections to be made to a telephone network by dialing the other party's number on a built-in keypad. **info:** It uses a combination of radio wave transmission and conventional telephone circuit switching. Some use packet switching for Internet access and other wireless applications. **ex:** *The image was licensed for use on mobile devices as a screensaver.* **plural:** Mobiles **variation:** Mobile Phone

Mobile Phone [3920-01-00-0100] See Mobile [3920-00-00-0100] **ex:** *The image was licensed for use on mobile phone devices as a screensaver.*

Mock Up [1440-00-00-0100] An early form of an advertisement or other graphical piece used during creative and production processes. **ex:** *We will produce a mock up of the advertisement so that everyone will know how we envision the campaign.* **plural:** Mock Ups **variation:** Mockup

Mockup [1440-01-00-0100] See Mock Up [1440-00-00-0100] *ex: We will produce a mockup of the advertisement so that everyone will know how we envision the campaign.* *plural:* Mockups *preferred term:* Mock Up *usability:* Discouraged

Model

(1) Model (Photo) [1617-00-01-0100] A person depicted in an image or who poses for an artist or image-maker, or an individual who displays merchandise (i.e., fashion model). *ex: The client told us which model they wanted to use, based on the look they wanted to depict in their ads.* *plural:* Models

(2) Model (Design) [1617-00-02-0100] A representation of an object, or a plan or schematic diagram of an object, problem or process. *ex: This model gives you a sense of what the final piece will look like.* *plural:* Models

Model Release [1275-00-00-0100] A document signed by the subject (or, if under age, the subject's guardian) to permit use of their likeness, voice or name for advertising or commercial purposes. *ex: Before the advertising agency will consider using the image, they need to know if the photographer has a model release on file.* *plural:* Model Releases *variation:* Talent Release, Release, MR

Monochrome [1442-00-00-0100] Reproduction in black, gradations of gray, and white, or, in a single tint such as blue or green. *ex: We will reproduce the image in monochrome, which will allow us to avoid a four-color print job.* *plural:* Monochromes

Monograph [1577-00-00-0100] A scholarly piece of writing of essay or book length, with or without images, focusing on a specific, often limited subject. *info:* Often book length. *ex: Interested in anything to do with gravity, he purchased a recently written monograph on the subject.* *plural:* Monographs

Montage [1162-00-00-0100] The art, style or process of making one pictorial composition from many images or designs closely arranged or superimposed on one another. *ex: They used several images to create a montage of a coral reef scene.* *plural:* Montages

Month [1506-00-00-0100] Four weeks or about thirty days. One of 12 periods into which the year is divided. *info:* In licensing terms usually the period between a date in one month and the same date in the next month. *ex: The duration of the agreement is one month, a relatively short time for an ad campaign.* *plural:* Months

Monthly [3260-00-00-0100] A publication with a unique title that is issued once a month *ex: Because it is a monthly, the twelve-issues-a-year magazine must schedule tight deadlines in order to stay on schedule.* *plural:* monthlies

Moral Rights [1276-00-00-0100] The right of authors to have their works correctly attributed, published anonymously or pseudonymously, and to prevent unauthorized alterations. Moral rights may also refer to not having work subjected to derogatory treatment, not having work falsely attributed and in some cases may include the right of privacy. *info:* Moral rights are not fully recognized in the United States. For still photography, the Visual Artists Rights act of 1990 limits moral rights to works of visual art (works created for exhibition only) produced in editions of two hundred or less, consecutively numbered, and signed by the artist. *ex: Moral rights vary from country to country and protection for artists is not guaranteed.*

Motion Picture [3310-00-00-0100] An audiovisual media that enacts a story by a sequence of images, usually accompanied by audio. *info:* When a motion picture includes a still image, that usage is identified as a film still. *ex: The motion picture was being shown in 2500 movie theatres.* *plural:* Motion Pictures

Mouse Over [1695-00-00-0100] When a computer cursor moves over a portion of interactive digital content and the content changes visual appearance to indicate the presence of an underlying link to other content or activity. *ex: If you mouse over this image, its description appears on the screen.* *plural:* Mouse Overs *variation:* Mouse-Over, Roll-over

Mouse Pad [1214-00-00-0100] A soft protective material for use with a computer pointing device that makes the device work better. *ex: The mouse pad by his computer was the same color as the mouse on top of it and made it hard to find the mouse.* *plural:* Mouse Pads *variation:* Mousepad

Mouse-Over [1695-01-00-0100] See Mouse Over *preferred term:* Mouse Over *usability:* Discouraged

Mousepad [1214-01-00-0100] See Mouse Pad *ex: A computer mousepad is a natural place to put an image.* *plural:* Mousepads *preferred term:* Mouse Pad *usability:* Discouraged

Movie [2689-00-00-0100] An audiovisual media that enacts a story by a sequence of images, usually accompanied by audio. *info:* When a movie includes a still image, that usage is identified as a film still. *ex: The movie was about the life and times of Charlie Chaplin.* *plural:* Movies

Movie Poster [1114-00-00-0100] A stand-alone printed advertisement for a film or other theatrical release that is meant for display. *ex: An image from the movie's wedding scene will appear on the movie poster.* *plural:* Movie Posters

Movie Still [3410-00-00-0100] An image produced by a motion picture company to publicize a movie. *info:* Usually distributed in large quantities to garner maximum publicity in the printed media. *ex: The movie still taken of the actor in the movie was later modified so much that he looked ten years younger than he did in the actual movie.* *plural:* movie stills

Movie Trailer [1115-00-00-0100] A short audiovisual advertisement for a movie, film or other theatrical release, often containing selected scenes from such. *ex: The movie trailer was so exciting that I could not wait to see the whole movie.* *plural:* Movie Trailers

MR [1275-03-00-0100] Abbreviation for Model Release *ex: Before the advertising agency will consider using the image, they need to know if the photographer has an MR on file.*

MSRP [3230-01-00-0100] Abbreviation for Manufacturer's Suggested Retail Price *ex: The price I ultimately paid was far below the MSRP.*

Multi-Media [1194-01-00-0100] See Multimedia *ex: The multi-media presentation on the fourth of July included canon shots, fireworks, orchestral music, and holographic images.* *preferred term:* Multimedia *usability:* Discouraged

Multimedia [1194-00-00-0100] Information presented using multiple simultaneous formats, such as text, still or moving images and audio. *ex: The multimedia presentation on the 4th of July included canon shots, fireworks, orchestral music, and holographic images.* *variation:* Multi-Media

Multiple Rights [1277-00-00-0100] Permission that allows more than one usage for the same image. *ex: The client wants the license to include multiple rights such as book, poster, and calendar usage.*

Multiple Use [1278-00-00-0100] A usage that includes more than one medium. *ex: They purchased a multiple use license and were covered for video, CD, and DVD usage.* *plural:* Multiple Uses

Mural [1163-00-00-0100] A large work of art, often painted or placed directly on a wall or side of a building. *info:* Photographs of murals (and/or artwork depicted in a photograph by third parties) often require separate permission from the mural artist(s)

before licensing. *ex: The mural of the summer scene will be installed on the wall of our building's lobby this afternoon.* *plural:* Murals

Museum Display [1164-00-00-0100] Educational information or work exhibited for groups of people to view, generally but not always publicly, often large, placed inside a depository for collecting and displaying objects having scientific, historic or artistic value as part of an exhibit. *ex: The museum display on indigenous peoples contained photos of their lifestyles, illustrations, and samples of their artistic endeavors.* *plural:* Museum Displays

Music Packaging [1215-00-00-0100] The container or wrapper used for consumer music, including CD ROM discs, tapes or records. *ex: The music packaging for their latest album consisted of a montage of images suggested by the included songs.*

National [3430-00-00-0100] Of, relating to, or belonging to the whole of one specific country, which serves to distinguish it from local or regional rights. *info:* National typically refers to the same country in which the license is being given unless otherwise noted. *ex: Since the billboard was national, it was seen by motorists from coast to coast.*

National Distribution [1067-00-00-0100] The process or act of moving goods or services, such as a piece, advertisement, other print form, or message within one specific country. *info:* Usage may cross state and regional lines but not international borders. *ex: Because the product had a national distribution, it was seen from coast to coast.*

NDA [3470-01-00-0100] Abbreviation for Non-Disclosure Agreement *ex: We could not brag that our image was scheduled to appear on the ads for the new computer screen because of the NDA we had signed.*

Negative [1443-00-00-0100] Fixation of an image on film emulsion in which tonal values of the originally photographed subject are inverted. Usually (but not always) refers to a camera original. *info:* Light objects appear dark, dark objects appear light, and colors are represented by their complementary color (e.g., a red flower will appear green). Black and white film images are usually (but not always) on negative film. *ex: She has the original negative in her library and can produce more prints whenever her client needs them.* *plural:* Negatives

Negotiate [1593-00-00-0100] To confer with others in order to reach an agreement on definitions, terms and conditions, including any obligations, liabilities and or responsibilities. *info:* Other types of things that may be negotiated include fees, expenses covered and license granted. *ex: To negotiate an agreement that will endure, both sides have to believe it is fair and written in good faith. plural:* Negotiates

Net Paid Circulation [1052-00-00-0100] The total number of magazines sold as single copies at retail locations and by subscription. *ex: They print two million one hundred thousand copies but their net paid circulation is two million. plural:* Net Paid Circulations

New Use [3960-00-00-0100] An additional use of content previously used. This is a nonspecific term denoting the reproduction of a work. May be qualified or restricted by specific terms of a license or contract agreement as to media, territory, duration, or other parameters. *info:* Typically applied when a licensee returns to a licensor to license uses not previously granted. *ex: We previously licensed annual report rights for the image, but now need to license new use for point of purchase advertising. plural:* New Uses

Newsletter [1195-00-00-0100] A small publication distributed publicly to convey information about an organization to stockholders, clients, vendors or suppliers, among others, or, an internal publication for similar purposes but distributed only to members or employees of the organization. *ex: The company newsletter showed images from their recent picnic and included a profile on their new president. plural:* Newsletters

Newspaper [1165-00-00-0100] Collected journalistic content (images and text) within a periodical news publication that is distributed every day, week, month, etc. Often includes paid advertising. *info:* Can be local, regional, national or international, for sale or distributed free. *ex: We read about the latest political campaign in our local newspaper. plural:* Newspapers

Newspaper Print Advertising [1116-00-00-0100] Print advertising within a periodical news publication containing collected journalistic content (images and text). *info:* May be distributed daily, weekly, monthly, bi-weekly or -monthly, etc. Distribution can be local or within a given region, national or international, free or for sale. *ex: The ad campaign included newspaper print advertising so that it would reach commuters who read on the train each morning.*

Niche Marketing [1578-00-00-0100] Marketing and promoting a product or service to a small, targeted group of buyers, such as people in a certain geographical region, or with a specific hobby or interest. *ex: Our niche marketing effort is aimed only at 45-year-old right-handed men.*

Non-Disclosure Agreement [3470-00-00-0100] A contract stipulating that the party receiving information which is confidential and proprietary shall not disclose this information further during the time that the providing party has not publicly disclosed that information, and for which penalties for the receiving party's disclosure are outlined. *info:* Software developers, reporters, and sometimes beta testers are often required to sign these before they are given access to either information about upcoming products or the product itself. *ex: We could not brag that our image was scheduled to appear on the ads for the new computer screen because of the non-disclosure agreement we had signed. plural:* Non-Disclosure Agreements *variation:* NDA

Non-Exclusive License [2723-00-00-0100] A grant of rights issued by a licensor to a licensee that does not preclude the licensor from granting the same rights to other licensees. *info:* Unless otherwise negotiated, licenses are non-exclusive. *ex: The stock agency granted a non-exclusive license to two different clients. plural:* Non-Exclusive Licenses

Non-Exclusive Right [1279-00-00-0100] A legal claim, title, or privilege granted by a licensor to a licensee giving official permission that does not preclude the licensor from transferring to other licensees the same permission within the same scope. *ex: The stock agency granted a non-exclusive right to two different customers. plural:* Non-Exclusive Rights

Non-Exclusive Use [2724-00-00-0100] A right to use, granted by a licensor to a licensee. It does not preclude the licensor from transferring to other licensees the same permission within the same scope. The ability to issue this is covered under copyright and trademark law. *info:* A purchase option that must be negotiated. *ex: The client's license includes a non-exclusive use in brochures and catalogs so others may be using the same image on similar products. plural:* Non-Exclusive Uses

Non-Exclusivity [2722-00-00-0100] A type of right granted by the copyright owner. The licensor (and other parties offering licenses of the work) may license similar, related or identical rights to another licensee at any time. *info:* A purchase option that must be negotiated. Unless the right of exclusivity is expressly granted by a licensor to a licensee, any other rights granted under a license are non-exclusive by default. *ex: A competing magazine was able to use the same image on the cover because they had only negotiated for non-exclusivity of the photo. plural:* Non-Exclusivities

Non-Profit Organization [4450-00-00-0100] An incorporated establishment which exists for educational, political, charitable or business league reasons, and from which its shareholders or trustees do not benefit financially. *ex: The images were used on the non-profit organization's promotional materials in order to raise money.* **plural:** Non-profit Organizations **variation:** Not-for-Profit Organization

Non-Transferable [1634-00-00-0100] When the conveyance of rights from one party to another is specifically prohibited. *ex: You cannot sell the license we granted you since all our licenses are non-transferable.*

Not-for-Profit Organization [4450-01-00-0100] See Non-Profit Organization *ex: The images were used on the not-for-profit organization's promotional materials in order to raise money.* **plural:** Not-for-Profit Organizations

Novelty Book [1552-00-00-0100] Designed with interactive features and construction not usually associated with books, e.g. sliders, inserts, noisemakers and pop outs. *ex: Their new novelty book includes seven different types of fabrics with varying textures.* **plural:** Novelty Books

Number of Insertions [1280-02-00-0100] See Insertions *ex: The number of insertions of the advertisement with our picture should be listed as three.*

Object Movie [1776-00-00-0100] Interactive digital media which allows the viewer to see an object from any angle. *info:* Created with sequential views from different angles surrounding the object. *ex: The object movie will be displayed in the showroom.* **plural:** Object Movies

OE [1031-01-00-0100] Abbreviation for Outer *ex: The OE is brown Kraft paper.* **plural:** OEs **usability:** Discouraged

Off Sale Date [1029-00-00-0100] The specific time or day when a given magazine issue is supposed to be removed from retail distribution. *ex: On the off sale date of May 31, the June issue will replace the may issue on the rack.* **plural:** Off Sale Dates **variation:** Off-Sale Date

Off-Sale Date [1029-01-00-0100] See Off Sale Date *ex: On the off-sale date of May 31, the June issue will replace the may issue on the rack.* **plural:** Off-Sale Dates **preferred term:** Off Sale Date **usability:** Discouraged

On Sale Date [1539-00-00-0100] The specific time or day on which a product is made widely available. *ex: The on sale date of the newest product of the company will be June 1, 2006.* **plural:** On Sale Dates **variation:** On-Sale Date

On-sale Date [1539-02-00-0100] See On Sale Date *ex: The on-sale date of the newest product of the company will be June 1, 2006.* **plural:** On-Sale Dates **usability:** Discouraged

One Eighth Page [1807-00-00-0100] A promotion, editorial or advertising piece that takes up an eighth of a page. *info:* A one eighth page image usage license permits use of the image at any size up to one eighth page. *ex: The small ad will be only one eighth page which will allow for up to seven other ads on the same page.* **plural:** One Eighth Pages **variation:** One-Eighth Page

One Half Page [1501-00-00-0100] A promotion, editorial or advertising piece that takes up one half of a page. *info:* A one half page image usage license permits use of the image at any size up to one half page. *ex: The ad will be one half page.* **plural:** One Half Pages **variation:** Half Page, One-Half Page

One Page [1499-00-00-0100] A promotion, editorial or advertising piece that takes up one complete page. *info:* A one page image usage license permits use of the image at any size up to the complete page. *ex: The ad will be one page.* **preferred term:** Full Page [2800-00-00-0100] **usability:** Discouraged

One Quarter Page [1808-00-00-0100] A promotion, editorial or advertising piece that takes up a quarter of the page. *info:* A one quarter page image usage license permits use of the image at any size up to one quarter page. *ex: The ad will be one quarter page, which will allow three other ads to fit on the page.* **plural:** One Quarter Pages **variation:** One-Quarter Page

One Sheet [2757-00-00-0100] A single page advertisement meant to stand alone or be inserted into a publication. *ex: We ordered five thousand copies of the one sheet so we could send it out to all our clients.* **plural:** One Sheets

One Sixteenth Page [1500-00-00-0100] A promotion, editorial or advertising piece that takes up one sixteenth of a page. *info:* A one sixteenth page image usage license permits use of the image at any size up to one sixteenth page. *ex: The ad will be one sixteenth page which will allow for up to 15 other ads on the same page.* **plural:** One Sixteenth Pages **variation:** One-Sixteenth Page

One Time Use [1281-00-00-0100] The limited right to reproduce an image or other work only one time in a manner specifically set forth in a license or contract agreement. *ex: The image is licensed for one time use in an advertisement in the January issue of their magazine.* **plural:** One Time Uses *variation:* One-Time Use

One-Eighth Page [1807-01-00-0100] See One Eighth Page *ex: The small ad will be only one-eighth page.* **plural:** One-Eighth Pages **preferred term:** One Eighth Page **usability:** Discouraged

One-Half Page [1501-02-00-0100] See One Half Page *ex: The ad will be one-half page.* **plural:** One-Half Pages **preferred term:** One Half Page **usability:** Discouraged

One-Quarter Page [1808-01-00-0100] See One Quarter Page *ex: The ad will be one-quarter page.* **plural:** One-Quarter Pages **preferred term:** One Quarter Page **usability:** Discouraged

One-Sixteenth Page [1500-01-00-0100] See One Sixteenth Page *ex: The ad will be one-sixteenth page.* **plural:** One-Sixteenth Pages **preferred term:** One Sixteenth Page **usability:** Discouraged

One-Time Use [1281-02-00-0100] See One Time Use *ex: The image is licensed for one-time use in an advertisement in the January issue of their magazine.*

Online

(1) Online (General) [1857-00-01-0100] When two or more computers are connected via a digital network. *ex: Since our data center is online the whole company can access it.*

(2) Online (Media) [1857-00-02-0100] Media, information or digital data that exist on a computer or network of computers. **info:** This is specifically used to describe use on the Internet or World Wide Web. *ex: Many people prefer to read the newspaper online rather than in print.*

Onsert [2709-00-00-0100] An advertising page or card in a polybag along with the periodical that is being enclosed by the polybag. **info:** Like a cover wrap but not attached and most typically associated with a magazine. *ex: The onsert is orange, to attract attention and make sure it is seen through the polybag that encloses the new magazine.* **plural:** Onserts

Option [1627-00-00-0100] Defines a future right and guarantees that the right will be available, usually for a fee. **info:** May be limited by duration. Fees may be specified when an option right is requested or granted, or may be negotiated at a future date. *ex:*

The client wants an option to extend the license past the initial two year term if necessary. **plural:** Options

Option Clause [1822-00-00-0100] A clause in a license agreement giving the buyer the right to acquire additional rights, typically at a predetermined fee. **info:** May be limited by duration or other factors. *ex: There is an option clause in the agreement which will allow them to extend the license by one year.* **plural:** Option Clauses

Original [1444-00-00-0100] First or master version of a digital or analog image. **info:** It has come to be used when referring to an original transparency or digital image, to differentiate it from a duplicate or scan. *ex: The original transparencies are stored away and they only send out duplicates to their clients.* **plural:** Originals

Out

(1) Out (Rights) [4480-00-01-0100] A shorthand way to refer to a class of license usage that is not available or is restricted. *ex: He was able to use the image in Good Housekeeping magazine, but since the usage license said newsmagazines out, he couldn't include it in Newsweek.* **variation:** Out Take, Outtake

(2) Out (Photo) [4480-00-02-0100] Alternate versions of the final work. Usually not used in the final job production. *ex: He licensed one of his assignment outs for use in a textbook.* **variation:** Out Take, Outtake

Out of Home [1118-00-00-0100] Media that deliver advertising messages to consumer audiences outside of their home, whether delivered outdoors or indoors. **info:** Includes (but is not limited to) billboard, transit advertising, movie theater advertising, and point of purchase. *ex: The image will be used in an extensive out of home campaign, targeting shoppers in that mall.*

Out of Print [1541-00-00-0100] When no copies of a printed work are available and the publisher has no plans to reprint the material. *ex: The book is out of print and only available in used bookstores.*

Out of Stock [1542-00-00-0100] When no copies of a work are available, but the publisher plans to reprint the material at some later time. **info:** This is also used in a retail context when an item is not available at that outlet but can be re-ordered from the publisher or producer. *ex: We are temporarily out of stock but should have some new copies available soon.*

Out Take [4480-03-00-0100] See Out *ex: He licensed an out take from one of his assignments for use in a textbook. **plural:** Out Takes*

Outdoor [1721-00-00-0100] Media that deliver advertising messages in public areas, usually outside. *info:* Examples include billboard and transit advertising. *ex: The ad campaign will include a strong outdoor component to attract daily commuters.* **plural:** Outdoors

Outer [1031-00-00-0100] A direct mail envelope or wrapper. *ex: The outer is brown Kraft paper.* **plural:** Outers **variation:** OE

Outsert [1032-00-00-0100] An advertising page or card in a magazine polybag. *info:* Like a cover wrap but not attached. *ex: The outsert is orange, so it attracts attention.* **plural:** Outserts

Outtake [44800200-0100] See Out [4480-00-00-0100] *ex: He licensed an outtake from one of his assignments for use in a textbook.* **variation:** Out Take

Overhead [2756-00-00-0100] The sum of money required to open a business and, over time, keep it running and solvent. *info:* Includes rent, utilities, labor, taxes and other costs that are not part of the cost of goods sold. Generally expressed as dollars per day. *ex: The assignment costs included fees for models, film, processing, and props as well as a customary overhead fee.*

Overrun [1448-00-00-0100] In print production, the copies that are printed in excess of the specified quantity. *ex: The overrun from the printer gave us enough extra copies of the calendar that we had no problem donating them to the entire first grade class.* **plural:** Overruns

Owner [2693-00-00-0100] The person or entity who owns the copyright to a work. *info:* May or may not be the author of the work, and may or may not be the designated licensor. *ex: I am the owner of that portrait and have the right to negotiate a usage price.* **plural:** Owners

P.O. [4620-01-00-0100] Abbreviation for Purchase Order *ex: The agency needed a signed P.O. before they would remit payment.*

Packaging

(1) Packaging (Products) [1196-00-01-0100] A product's container or wrapping. *info:* Often includes images. *ex: The stiff white paperboard packaging protects the fragile product within it.*

(2) Packaging (Business) [1196-00-02-0100] Assembling a proposition or offer that bundles several different items together. *ex: My agent is good at packaging several usages together into one license.*

Page

(1) Page (Print) [1656-00-01-0100] A leaf or one side of a leaf in a book, letter, magazine, newspaper, or manuscript. *ex: One page of the book will contain the table of contents while the majority will be filled with art.* **plural:** Pages

(2) Page (Online) [1656-00-02-0100] Audio or visual information appearing on a single screen (or able to be seen by scrolling) without having to link to information on another part of a website or a file on a web server that collects various bits of data and presents it to a browser. *ex: The image will be used on a minor page of the website and will only be accessible if someone clicks the correct link.* **plural:** Pages

Page Rate [2799-00-00-0100] A compensation method based on the area in a publication occupied by an advertisement, an image or other work. *info:* Calculated as a portion of the size of the page, and/or the size, position, or prominence of the page (e.g., one quarter page, front cover, interior page, etc.) and whether or not the ad or image is color or black and white. *ex: Their page rate is lower for images used less than a full page.* **plural:** Page Rates

Page Size [1449-00-00-0100] The total area on a page that is occupied by content, expressed in inches or centimeters. Includes the page margin and gutter. *info:* Portions of a page are expressed as one quarter page, one half page, etc. *ex: The page size in the magazine is a standard 8 1/2 x 11.* **plural:** Page Sizes

Paid Circulation [1282-00-00-0100] The total number of copies of a publication which are sold. *info:* Independent companies audit these figures and make them available to advertisers and other interested parties. *ex: Their paid circulation is in excess of two million, and they send out 5000 free copies.* **plural:** Paid Circulations

Pamphlet [1119-00-00-0100] A small printed booklet advertising or giving information about a product or service. *info:* Usually distributed by hand or placed in kiosks and other high traffic areas. *ex: You can pick up a descriptive pamphlet at the door.* **plural:** Pamphlets

Panorama [1450-01-00-0100] See Panoramic *ex: We will use a panorama image that will start on the back and end on the front cover.* **plural:** Panoramas **preferred term:** Panoramic **usability:** Discouraged

Panoramic [1450-00-00-0100] An image or series of images representing a wide or tall continuous scene. *info:* Produced by a special type of camera with a height-width ratio of 1:3 or greater, or by stitching together several frames using computer software or special darkroom techniques. *ex: We will use a panoramic image that will start on the back and end on the front cover. plural:* Panoramics *variation:* Panorama

Panoramic Movie [1777-00-00-0100] Interactive digital media that allows the viewer to pan with a 360-degree view on a computer monitor, with the ability to look up, down and zoom in or out for detail. *info:* Usually created from a series of images (all shot from the same position but facing different directions), which are digitally stitched or assembled into a single seamless panorama file. *ex: By viewing the panoramic movie they took of the sunken ship, we were able to get a clear picture of all the life growing around it. plural:* Panoramic Movies

Pantone [1778-00-00-0100] An ink color matching system designed to ensure that color output will be the color intended whether on-screen or in output from a printer. *info:* The dominant color matching system used in North America. *ex: The color in my Pantone book was much greener than it appeared on my monitor and this confirmed that my monitor had not been properly calibrated.*

Paperback [4400-00-00-0100] A volume bound in a light-weight flexible paper. *info:* Unlike a hardbound book, paperbacks are often printed on a lesser grade of paper, with a lighter weight and flexible cover. They are often perfect bound rather than having signatures stitched and bound. *ex: The paperback version of the bestseller, outsold its hardbound counterpart and became a bestseller at major airports. plural:* Paperbacks

Part Opener [2768-00-00-0100] Special prominent use of an image to designate a new portion of a work. *info:* Often treated as a special design element. *ex: The image of the giant tomato will be used as a part opener for the section on spaghetti sauce. plural:* Part Openers

Partwork [1167-00-00-0100] Sections of a book or encyclopedia that appear at intervals in separate issues and can be collected and bound together to form a whole book or encyclopedia. *ex: Because each section of the book will only be available as partwork, we'll have to wait a year until we can find out what happens at the end. plural:* Partworks

Party [1624-00-00-0100] Particular persons, groups, or legal entities that are identified and defined in a contract, agreement or other legal writing. *ex: One party agrees to make a payment to another. plural:* Parties

Paternity Fee [1283-00-00-0100] A fee for failure to properly attribute authorship of a creative work. *ex: A missing credit line might trigger the paternity fee clause. plural:* Paternity Fees

Pay-per-Download [4520-00-00-0100] Used to describe content that can only be purchased on an individual basis, as opposed to a subscription basis. Licensing model by which products (e.g. images, footage, CDs of either) are purchased on an individual basis. *info:* The term can also be used to describe the website on which these products can be purchased individually. *ex: Because the book was available online at a pay-per-download rate, he was able to tell how many people had downloaded it more than once.*

PDA [3510-01-00-0100] Abbreviation for Personal Digital Assistant *ex: The image was used on the welcome screen of a popular PDA.*

Perfect Binding [1779-00-00-0100] A method in which all the pages of a book are cut into single sheets, held in a clamp and attached to the cover's spine with adhesive. *ex: A book with a perfect binding might have its individual pages fall out if it is bent backwards. plural:* Perfect Bindings

Period [1706-00-00-0100] A specified interval of time with a beginning and an end. *ex: This license is only good for a period of one month. plural:* Periods

Periodic Exclusivity [4540-00-00-0100] A right that, when granted by a licensor to a licensee, limits the right of the licensor (and other parties offering licenses of the work) to license the right to any third party to use the work during a specific period of time. *ex: Because of the periodic exclusivity licensed for the image, it could only be used March 1 through March 31, 2006. plural:* Periodic Exclusivities

Periodical [1672-00-00-0100] A publication with a unique title that is issued at regular intervals greater than one day. *ex: I subscribe to a weekly periodical that allows me seven days to read it before the next one is delivered. plural:* Periodicals

Permission [1576-00-00-0100] An agreement or license from copyright holders that grants the right to someone else to reproduce their work. *ex: They have permission to use the image for the cover of their album as long as they do not print more than one million copies. plural:* Permissions

Personal Digital Assistant [3510-00-00-0100] A handheld device whose functions may or may not include computing, telephone/fax, Internet and networking features. *ex: The image was used on the welcome screen of a popular personal digital assistant.* **plural:** Personal Digital Assistants **variation:** PDA

Personal Print [1168-00-00-0100] A single copy of an image or illustration, meant for noncommercial use. **info:** Usually printed on higher quality photo paper. *ex: I sold him a personal print that is now framed and hanging in his living room.* **plural:** Personal Prints

Personal Use [1169-00-00-0100] Only for private purposes and not related to business or commerce. No reproduction rights granted. *ex: She purchased a print for personal use and will hang it in her office.* **plural:** Personal Uses

Phone Card [1216-00-00-0100] A rectangular piece of stiff plastic, sometimes decorated with images, that either indicates prepayment or is used as a credit card for making telephone calls. *ex: He used a phone card to pay for the call.* **plural:** Phone Cards

Photo [1673-01-00-0100] Abbreviation for Photograph *ex: The photo of the play's curtain call included all the members of the cast plus the backstage crew.* **plural:** Photos **usability:** Discouraged

Photo Composite [1657-01-00-0100] See Composite *ex: A colleague has licensed one of my images for use in a photo composite.* **plural:** Photo Composites

Photo Credit [1244-00-00-0100] A line of text identifying the copyright holder (and, optionally, date of the copyright). Usually located near an image, at the bottom or side of a page or screen on which the image appears, or in a separate area of the publication. **info:** Licenses issued by stock photo agencies require a credit line that includes their name as well as the photographer's *ex: If I had not seen his name in the photo credit, I would never have realized he took that image.* **plural:** Photo Credits

Photo Illustration [1683-00-00-0100] A photograph created or used to enhance, clarify, explain, decorate or add meaning to a text. **info:** Often includes illustration elements, and can stand alone or be the basis of an advertisement, poster, etc. *ex: The client wants us to create a photo illustration to show the stages of photosynthesis.* **plural:** Photo Illustrations **variation:** Photo-Illustration

Photo Research [4550-00-00-0100] To investigate, acquire and edit images found through stock agencies, photographers, libraries, museums, governmental agencies, educators, video, film and digital media producers. Skill set includes varying levels of knowledge about art, history, social and physical sciences, photography, imaging, Internet, copyright, permissions procedures, data and image management. *ex: He performed extensive photo research to illustrate the encyclopedia.* **variation:** Picture Research

Photo-Illustration [1683-01-00-0100] See Photo Illustration *ex: The client wants us to create a photo-illustration to show the stages of photosynthesis.* **plural:** Photo-Illustrations **preferred term:** Photo Illustration **usability:** Discouraged

Photograph [1673-00-00-0100] An image recorded by a film or digital camera. **info:** A reproduction of a photograph is also called a photograph. *ex: The photograph of the play's curtain call included all the members of the cast plus the backstage crew.* **plural:** Photographs **variation:** Photo

Photographer [3900-00-00-0100] Someone who takes an image recorded by a film or digital camera, especially as a profession. **info:** A good photographer might be a combination of artist, craftsman, and scientist. *ex: The photographer for the magazine said he would wait until the light was right before taking the photo.* **plural:** photographers

Photographic [1674-00-00-0100] An image (printed or otherwise) that consists of a photograph, or exhibits similar visual appearance. *ex: The client wants an illustrator to create a photographic look in their new ads.*

Photography

(1) Photography (Digital) [3520-00-01-0100] The process or technique of rendering images using electronic sensors to record images as pieces of electronic data. *ex: By using digital photography he was able to download the images directly onto his computer shortly after taking them.*

(2) Photography (Film) [3520-00-02-0100] The process or technique of rendering an image of an object or objects by the chemical action of light and other forms of radiant energy on photosensitive surfaces. *ex: The type of photography he did required a special combination of chemicals in the film's processing to bring out the desired results.*

Photomatic [1068-00-00-0100] A storyboard for television, film or other commercial production that uses photos as the primary visual element. **info:** Usually produced for testing, presentation, concept and editorial review prior to full-scale production. Photomatic usage does not include an actual broadcast. *ex: The photomatic clearly indicates that the* *director intends to have the main characters running, swimming, and bicycling during the half hour show.* **plural:** Photomatics

Pica [1451-00-00-0100] Printer's unit of measurement used primarily in typesetting. One pica equals approximately one-sixth of an inch. **ex:** *The 72 pica type size on the advertisement nearly blotted out the image below it.* **plural:** Picas

Pick-Up Use [1468-00-00-0100] To re-use an image in a different title, project or program produced by the same end user or someone granted ownership of the work by the previous end user. **ex:** *Sometimes it is difficult to locate the copyright owner to get permission to use an image for pick-up use.* **plural:** Pick-Up Uses **variation:** Pickup Use

Pickup Use [1468-01-00-0100] See Pick-Up Use **ex:** *Sometimes it is difficult to locate the copyright owner to get permission to use an image for pickup use.* **plural:** Pickup Uses **preferred term:** Pick-up Use **usability:** Discouraged

Picture

(1) **Picture (Digital)** [3590-00-01-0100] A visual recording of objects, scenes and/or people that is encoded into a digital file. **info:** Can result from a digital scan, digital capture, original input of artwork on a computer or combinations of several sources. **ex:** *We can email you a digital picture from our most recent trip.* **plural:** Pictures

(2) **Picture (Display)** [3590-00-02-0100] A printed copy of an image, intended for viewing by an audience, usually in a public place, rather than reproduction. **info:** Does not include a picture within a frame for the express purpose of selling that frame (packaging) or for fine art. **ex:** *The picture will be mounted in a train station kiosk.* **plural:** Pictures preferred term: Print [2700-00-00-0100] usability: Discouraged

(3) **Picture** [3590-00-03-0100] (Film An image reproduced in black and white or color on paper stock. **ex:** *They took a long time to decide where to hang the picture in the new office.* **plural:** pictures preferred term: Print **usability:** Discouraged

Picture Book [1170-00-00-0100] A brief book targeted at toddlers and very young children, usually including numerous images or illustrations and minimal easy-to-read text. **ex:** *Her illustrations of pigs and cows will be used in a picture book on farm animals.* **plural:** Picture Books

Picture Element [1453-01-00-0100] See Pixel **ex:** *Every picture element in that underwater scenic represents different shades and colors.*

Picture Frame Insert [1218-00-00-0100] An image used to promote the sale of picture frames, typically appearing within the frame and printed on a very light stock of paper. **ex:** *The picture of brightly colored balloons on the picture frame insert attracted the most attention in the store display.* **plural:** Picture Frame Inserts

Picture Research [4550-01-00-0100] See Photo Research **ex:** *He was charged a picture research fee after he decided not to use any of the images sent to him for review.*

Piece [1844-00-00-0100] An example of artistic creativity or workmanship, such as a photo or illustration. **ex:** *The advertising piece includes text and one of our images.* **plural:** Pieces

Pixel [1453-00-00-0100] The basic unit from which a video or digital image is comprised. **info:** The unit of measurement for image resolution. **ex:** *Every pixel in that underwater scenic represents different shades and colors.* **plural:** Pixels **variation:** Picture Element

Pixelated [1454-00-00-0100] An image in which the pixels are visible as squares or jagged edges. Usually recognized by large blocks of color lacking any definition. **info:** Sometimes desired by art directors or designers as a kind of visual look. **ex:** *The image is so pixelated that I cannot make out its subject.*

Pixels Per Inch [1456-01-00-0100] See PPI [1456-00-00-0100] **ex:** *The resolution of that image is seventy-two pixels per inch, which is satisfactory for the web, but given its size of 2 x 3 inches, would not produce a high quality print on press.* **preferred term:** PPI **usability:** Discouraged

Placemat [1120-00-00-0100] A (usually) printed piece placed on a table underneath a place setting, sometimes containing images, advertising or other information. **ex:** *The restaurant licensed this image for use on their new placemat.* **plural:** Placemats

Placement [1821-00-00-0100] The positioning and location of an image within a publication. **info:** Usually refers to image use in a prominent way which marks or enhances content (e.g., cover, back cover, frontispiece or chapter opener). **ex:** *They switched the placement of the image from the table of contents page to the chapter opener.* **plural:** Placements

Playing Card [1217-00-00-0100] One of a set, typically printed on heavier paper stock and used in playing various games. *info:* Usually all playing cards in a given game feature the same image or design on one side. *ex: Each playing card in the deck will feature a photo of an animal.* *plural:* Playing Cards

Point of Purchase [1034-00-00-0100] Sales, marketing, advertising, or other promotional piece placed at the location where a product or service is sold, often on a retail counter, near a cash register or front door. *ex: The point of purchase use he had in mind included printing the image on a counter card for placement by the cash register.* *plural:* Points of Purchase *variation:* POP

Point of Sale [2735-00-00-0100] Sales, marketing, advertising, or other promotional piece placed at the location where a product or service is sold on a retail counter, near a cash register or front door. *ex: The point of sale use he had in mind included printing the image on a counter card for placement by the cash register.* *plural:* Points of Sale *variation:* POS

Polybag [1033-00-00-0100] A (usually) sealed plastic envelope or sleeve containing a magazine and possibly additional advertisements. *ex: The polybag will hold the magazine, a brochure, and four business reply cards.* *plural:* Polybags

POP [1034-01-00-0100] Abbreviation for Point of Purchase *ex: The POP use he had in mind included printing the image on a counter card for placement by the cash register.* *usability:* Discouraged

Pop Under [2701-00-00-0100] A web browser window with no navigation buttons or toolbar that opens underneath or behind the main browser window containing marketing or promotional messages. *info:* May open automatically or when the user clicks a particular link on a web page. *ex: We use a pop under window to thank our users for visiting our site.* *plural:* Pop Unders *variation:* Popunder

Pop Up

(1) Pop Up (Web) [1780-00-01-0100] A web browser window with no navigation buttons or toolbar that opens on top of the main browser window. May open automatically or when the user clicks a particular link on a web page. *ex: The instructions will appear in a pop up window.* *plural:* Pop Ups variation: Popup

(2) Pop Up (Book) [1780-00-02-0100] A page in a book that becomes three-dimensional when the spread is opened or the book that contains these pages. *ex: The images will be used in a children's pop up book on farm animals.* *plural:* Pop Ups variation: Popup

Popunder [2701-01-00-0100] See Pop Under [2701-00-00-0100] *ex: We use a popunder window to thank the user when they leave our site.* *plural:* Popunders *preferred term:* POP Under *usability:* Discouraged

Popup [1780-01-00-0100] See Pop Up *ex: The instructions will appear in a popup window.* *plural:* Popups *preferred term:* POP Up *usability:* Discouraged

Portal [1702-00-00-0100] A website considered as an entry point to other websites or online content. *info:* Usually provides a search engine. *ex: Their home page is a corporate portal to all their subsidiary websites.* *plural:* Portals

Portfolio [4560-00-00-0100] Collected materials (digital or print) that are representative of an artist's work. *ex: The photographer's portfolio included 20 covers from prominent magazines.* *plural:* Portfolios

Portrait

(1) Portrait (Design) [2789-00-01-0100] Perpendicular to the horizon, running up and down, and taller than wide. *ex: The image will appear in portrait orientation on the page.* *plural:* Portraits

(2) Portrait (Photo) [2789-00-02-0100] A pictorial representation of a person, usually showing the face. *info:* Subject is typically looking directly at the camera. *ex: He took a portrait of the writer for use on the back cover of her new book.* *plural:* Portraits

POS [2735-01-00-0100] Abbreviation for Point of Sale *ex: The point of sale use he had in mind included printing the image on a counter card for placement by the cash register.* *usability:* Discouraged

Positive [1828-00-00-0100] A photographic image in which the values of light and shade of the original photographed subject are represented as they appear to the eye. *ex: That color transparency is a positive so it is very easy to get an idea of its colors by simply holding it up to a light.* *plural:* Positives

Post Production [3600-00-00-0100] Everything that happens to a visual work after production, typically after images (either still or moving) have been recorded to film or digital media. *info:* Post production might include editing, color correction, etc. *ex: The color imbalance of the original image was corrected in post production.* *variation:* Post-production

Post-Production [3600-01-00-0100] See Post production *ex: The color imbalance of the original image was corrected in post-production.*

Postal Giro [4300-00-00-0100] A payment system in which money can be transferred through postal systems between those who hold postal accounts. *ex: The Japanese agency can accept payment by postal giro. plural:* Postal Giros

Postcard [1219-00-00-0100] A two-sided printed piece on heavy paper stock, sold at retail, intended for a personal message and postal delivery. *info:* Frequently used by corporations as direct mail. *ex: A promotional postcard is a low-cost way of advertising individual images. plural:* Postcards

Poster [1121-00-00-0100] A large-sized printed image usage usually meant for display. *info:* Examples might include wall decor, transit poster, or a display banner, and the usage might include advertising, marketing or promotion. Does not include billboard usage. *ex: The poster of that image was framed and hung in her son's room. plural:* Posters

Postponement Fee [1781-00-00-0100] A fee applicable when previously scheduled production of a work or works is delayed or rescheduled by a commissioning party. *info:* Postponement fee may vary based on the date/time that notice is given by the commissioning party. *ex: Please send us an invoice for the postponement fee, since the production of the assignment will not take place for at least six months. plural:* Postponement Fees

Power Point [4570-01-00-0100] See PowerPoint *ex: The images were used in the speaker's Power Point presentation at the sales meeting.*

PowerPoint [4570-00-00-0100] A Microsoft graphic application for creating presentations, speeches, slides, etc *ex: The images were used in the speaker's PowerPoint presentation at the sales meeting.* variation: *Power Point*

PPI [1456-00-00-0100] Pixels per inch, a measure of the resolution of an instance of a digital image at a specific size. Often confused with DPI. *info:* Usually given as a pair of figures, width x height and PPI. *ex: The resolution of that image is seventy-two PPI, which is satisfactory for the web, but given its size of 2 x 3 inches, would not produce a high quality print on press. variation:* Pixels Per Inch

PR

(1) PR (Legal) [1284-02-00-0100] Abbreviation for Property Release *ex: The photographer has a PR on file and so has the right to license the use of this image of a house.*

(2) PR (Marketing) [1784-01-00-0100] Abbreviation for Public Relations *ex: The PR campaign includes several news releases and photos, and videotaped interview with the chairman. usability:* Discouraged

PR Use [1636-02-00-0100] See Promotional Use [1636-00-00-0100] *ex: The image is being licensed for PR Use for the life of the product. preferred term:* Promotional Use *usability:* Strongly Discouraged

Pre-Press [1528-01-00-0100] See Prepress *ex: That problem was fixed during pre-press and so the actual press run went very smoothly. usability:* Discouraged

Pre-Production [1070-01-00-0100] See Preproduction *ex: Many phone calls will be made during pre-production so that the assignment runs smoothly. preferred term:* Preproduction *usability:* Discouraged

Pre-Publication [1589-01-00-0100] See Prepublication *ex: During the pre-publication period we made so many subscription sales that we had to increase our print run. preferred term:* Prepublication *usability:* Discouraged

Preface [1585-00-00-0100] Introductory section of a book or magazine article, usually written by the author or editor. *info:* Also may be written by an expert on the subject of the work. *ex: The preface described the research the author undertook in writing the book. plural:* Prefaces

Premium

(1) Premium (Marketing) [1035-00-01-0100] Something given away as an incentive or sweetener to an advertising or merchandising promotion. *ex: When I bought the car, I was given this wristwatch as a premium. plural:* Premiums

(2) Premium (Photo Technical) [1035-00-02-0100] A term used to differentiate a high quality product, e.g., a premium image. *ex: Our premium brand products are typically more expensive. plural:* Premiums

Prepress [1528-00-00-0100] All preproduction and preparation steps required before a work can actually be printed. *info:* This might include conversion of the digital file from an RGB color space to a specific CMYK color space, or the sizing, and sharpening of the high resolution image to the specific size needed in the publication. *ex: That problem was fixed during prepress and so the actual press run went very smoothly. variation:* Pre-Press

Preproduction [1070-00-00-0100] Work on a project or job that is related to preliminary preparations. *info:* Includes all planning and the making of any arrangements necessary to enable or facilitate final production. Typically billed as time plus any costs expended. *ex: Many phone calls will be made during preproduction so that the assignment runs smoothly.* *variation:* Pre-Production

Prepublication [1589-00-00-0100] The period of time prior to actual or contemplated publication and distribution of a product or work. *ex: During the prepublication period we made so many subscription sales that we had to increase our print run.* *variation:* Pre-Publication

Presentation [1171-00-00-0100] An audiovisual or printed display used to convey information, often as a companion to a speech or meeting. *ex: They showed the ad campaign they envisioned at the client presentation.* *plural:* Presentations

Presentation Use

(1) Presentation Use (Production) [1071-00-01-0100] Use in one or a very few copies of an entire layout or dummy that shows headlines, images, type and text. *info:* License often includes the term for internal viewing only. *ex: The image license is for presentation use and a separate license will be negotiated if they choose to use it in their campaign.* *plural:* Presentation Uses

(2) Presentation Use (Audiovisual) [1071-00-02-0100] Use as a part of an audiovisual program, such as PowerPoint or a slide show, with a speech. Can be part of an internal (within a company) or external meeting (to outside parties). *ex: The image was licensed for presentation use as part of his lecture on the ecosystems of Costa Rica.* *plural:* Presentation Uses

Press Kit [2764-00-00-0100] A folder or group of promotional and/or editorial materials used to announce or promote something. May be in printed or digital form. *info:* Usually distributed to representatives of trade or consumer publications and other news outlets. *ex: The press kit included short bios on each of the officers of the organization as well as their mission statement.* *plural:* Press Kits

Press Release [1197-00-00-0100] Information sent to the press to promote a product, event or person. Typically one or two pages of text, often accompanied by images. *info:* Sometimes supplied as digital text and image files on a CD-ROM disc, or downloadable from a website. *ex: The press release focuses on the benefits of our new product.* *plural:* Press Releases

Press Run [1457-00-00-0100] The actual operation of the printing device or the specific number of copies printed or supposed to be printed during a continuous operation of a printing press. *ex: Because the book will be so popular, we anticipate having to make more than one press run.* *plural:* Press Runs *variation:* Pressrun

Pressrun [1457-01-00-0100] See Press Run *ex: Because the book will be so popular, we anticipate having to make more than one pressrun.* *plural:* Pressruns *preferred term:* Press Run *usability:* Discouraged

Preview

(1) Preview (Web) [3610-00-01-0100] A web page that is accessed by clicking on a thumbnail version of an image or product. *info:* The preview will frequently contain additional information about the image or product that is otherwise not displayed and may provide links to additional functionality such as ecommerce or download access for the image or product being displayed. May also apply to the larger on-screen version of an image, the next size up from a thumbnail, but smaller than a comp or FPO. *ex: Just click on the thumbnail to see the preview sized image.* *plural:* previews variation: Preview Page

Preview Page [3610-01-00-0100] See Preview *ex: Just click on the thumbnail to see the preview page's sized image.*

Price Sticker [2740-00-00-0100] Small printed or plastic tags attached to a product, used to show price and product information. *ex: The price sticker was so large that it was able to include an image in addition to the product specifications and price.* *plural:* Price Stickers

Price Tag [1122-00-00-0100] Small printed or plastic tags attached to a product, used to show price and product information. *ex: The price tag includes the item number, the cost, and the sale price as well as a photo of someone wearing the item.* *plural:* Price Tags

Primary Rights [3980-00-00-0100] The use of artistic work for its first (intended) reproduction. An example might include primary rights for a hardbound book and then secondary rights for a lesser-quality book club edition. *info:* Secondary rights use the same content in lower quality and lower value, such as photocopies. *ex: The primary rights he sought in the usage license included use in a coffee table book, though he intended to relicense the work for companion notecards at a later date.* *preferred term:* First Rights *usability:* Discouraged

Print

(1) Print (Production) [2700-00-01-0100] A manufacturing process for reproducing copies of texts and images using ink, toner or colorants on paper. *ex: We will print one thousand copies of the poster.* **plural:** Prints

(2) Print (Media) [2700-00-02-0100] Collectively, all media that utilize paper and ink to convey information to an audience. *ex: The print campaign they designed will include advertising in major magazines sold at retail outlets.*

(3) Print (Film) [2700-00-03-0100] A copy of a movie produced on film or a type of photographic film that, when developed, turns into a negative with the colors (or black and white values, in black and white film) inversed. *info:* This type of film must be printed onto photographic paper in order to be viewed as intended. *ex: When the lab developed their print film, they always gave them two copies of each image.* **plural:** Prints

(4) Print (Products) [2700-00-04-0100] A photographic black and white or color image that is reproduced on paper using either film-based or digital methods. *ex: This print is from the original film negative.* **plural:** Prints

Print on Demand [1458-00-00-0100] Publisher's right (by permission or license) to electronically reproduce or license a work when it is requested by end users. *ex: The book will be produced using the latest print on demand technology.*

Print Run [2774-00-00-0100] The specific number of copies made or requested during the continuous operation of a printing press. *ex: The first print run was 5000 but we expect to need another print run in a few months.* **plural:** Print Runs **variation:** Printrun

Printed Matter [3630-00-00-0100] Any published document from government publications to annual reports, books and magazines. Can also include brochures, pamphlets, and more. *ex: By granting a license for all printed matter, he gave them the right to use his image in calendars, greeting cards, books, and magazines.* **preferred term:** Print **usability:** Caution

Printer's Error [1529-00-00-0100] Faults in a printed piece that occur during the actual press reproduction process. *info:* Examples include mis-registration of colors, ink spots, holes, smudges, splotches, or smears. *ex: Because of a printer's error the piece had to be reprinted.* **plural:** Printer's Errors

Printing Resolution [1463-00-00-0100] The LPI of a reproduced image, or the DPI of an output device, it determines how much detail the press (and the paper) can hold. *ex: A higher printing resolution usually produces more pleasing results.* **plural:** Printing Resolutions **variation:** Resolution of Print

Printrun [2774-01-00-0100] See Print Run *ex: The first printrun is almost finished.* **plural:** Printruns **preferred term:** Print Run **usability:** Discouraged

Process Color [1459-00-00-0100] The four pigments (cyan, magenta, yellow, and black) used in full-color offset printing. *ex: The brochure will be printed with black and one other process color.* **plural:** Process Colors

Product Exclusive [1711-01-00-0100] See Product Exclusivity *ex: The client decided to purchase a product exclusive so he could avoid having the same image usage by his competitor.* **plural:** Product Exclusives **preferred term:** Product Exclusivity **usability:** Discouraged

Product Exclusivity [1711-00-00-0100] A right that, when granted by a licensor to a licensee, limits the right of the licensor (and other parties offering licenses of the work) to license the right to any third party to use the work in relation to a specified product category. *ex: The client decided to purchase product exclusivity so he could avoid having the same image usage by his competitor.* **plural:** Product Exclusivities **variation:** Product Exclusive

Production Fee [1635-00-00-0100] A charge related to the preparation, planning, setup, props and styling, gaffers, grips and assistants. After production, it is related to post-processing and delivery. *ex: The production fee for the complicated assignment exceeded the budget by a great deal.* **plural:** Production Fees

Profit [1596-00-00-0100] Gross revenue less all expenses and cost of goods sold. *info:* The notion of profit can be nuanced in ways that affect the dollar amounts that might be due under an agreement or contract. *ex: We will make a nice profit on this job after all our expenses are paid out.* **plural:** Profits

Program Advertising [1783-00-00-0100] Marketing or promotional message in a printed piece, often small, that contains the order of performance and/or other information about the performance, public event or social function. *ex: The campaign includes opera program advertising.*

Promotion [1834-00-00-0100] A general marketing and advertising catch-all that may include various forms of merchandising, collateral, brand extension, public relations, direct mail, etc., singly or together.

This term is overly broad and ambiguous and should not be used in licenses or contracts. *ex: The image used in their promotion was so popular that they made it into a T-shirt. **plural:** Promotions **usability***: Strongly Discouraged

Promotional Envelope [1123-00-00-0100] A flat paper container on which a message may be written or printed. Usually holds promotional or advertising information inside. *info:* May include images. *ex: The promotional envelope that will hold all the advertising coupons will be printed tomorrow. **plural:** Promotional Envelopes

Promotional Postcard [1124-00-00-0100] A two-sided printed piece on heavy paper stock, on which a message may be written or printed, intended for mailing without an envelope. The sender must affix a stamp for direct mailing. *ex: A promotional postcard is a low-cost way to advertise the product. **plural:** Promotional Postcards

Promotional Rights [1636-01-00-0100] See Promotional Use *info:* This term is overly broad and ambiguous and should not be used in licenses or contracts. *ex: The image is being licensed for promotional rights for the life of the product. **usability**:* Strongly Discouraged

Promotional Use [1636-00-00-0100] Use of a work in the context of any type or kind of promotion. This term is overly broad and ambiguous and should not be used in licenses or contracts. *info:* Use specific usage or media descriptions instead. *ex: The image is being licensed for promotional use for the life of the product. **plural:** Promotional Uses **preferred term:** Publicity Use **usability***: Discouraged **variation:** Promotional Rights, PR Use

Proof [1530-00-00-0100] A final review copy of a work sent to the author, creator or client for quality check prior to production. *info:* Proofs may be presented in many forms, clients may view contract or inkjet proofs on paper, or electronic proofs on a computer screen. *ex: Please review the electronic proof and report any errors. **plural:** Proofs

Prop [1172-01-00-0100] See Prop Decor *ex: The image will be used on a prop.*

Prop Decor [1172-00-00-0100] Any object or image that appears on the stage or screen during a television show, theatrical performance, film or photo shoot. *info:* Does not include costumes or scenery. *ex: The image will be used as a prop decor. **plural:** Prop Decors **usability**:* Discouraged **variation:** Prop

Property Release [1284-00-00-0100] A document signed by the owner or controlling entity of property (a building, statue, or other object or area belonging to that owner or entity) that allows a photograph of that property to be published in advertising or other commercial use. *ex: The photographer has a property release on file and so has the right to license the use of its image. **plural:** Property Releases **variation:** PR, Release

Proprietary Information [1745-00-00-0100] Confidential information and documentation, usually related to technology that, if released publicly or to the wrong party, could be damaging to the interests of a company or entity that owns or developed it. *info:* Often specified in contracts and non-disclosure agreements (NDAS) between visual authors and their clients, and may affect the subsequent ability of the author to license his or her work to third parties. *ex: That is proprietary information, so please keep it confidential.*

Protective Cover [1460-00-00-0100] Wrap around overlay that prevents damage to the cover of a book, magazine or product—meant to be removed and discarded. *ex: The protective cover on the book is a thin translucent plastic. **plural:** Protective Covers

Prototype [1620-00-00-0100] An original type, form or instance of a thing that serves as a model for subsequent products or projects. *ex: We ran a test with the prototype and found that it still needed a great deal of work before it could be mass produced. **plural:** Prototypes

Pub Date [1543-01-00-0100] Abbreviation for Publication Date *ex: The pub date for the next magazine issue is June 1st.*

Public Domain [1286-00-00-0100] When a work is not considered to be the intellectual property of any copyright owner, for example when copyright has been lost or has expired. Copyright protection expires in the U.S and Europe after the life of the author plus 70 years. In Australia and Canada it expires after the life of the author plus 50 years. *info:* Works in the public domain can be freely reproduced, distributed or sold without obtaining permission of the creator. Works created before copyright laws came into effect are generally part of the public domain. *ex: Those images are in the public domain and can be used without authorization. **plural:** Public Domains

Public Relations [1784-00-00-0100] Organized efforts to establish or maintain a media presence and public awareness of a client's products, services or ideas. License for such use would include gratis editorial insertions but would exclude paid advertising insertions. *info:* Specialty public relations areas include crisis, reputation and issue management, investor relations, and word-of-mouth public relations. *ex: The public relations campaign includes several news releases and photos, and a videotaped interview with the chairman. variation:* PR

Publication [1287-00-00-0100] A work that is distributed to the public by sale, rental, or lease or the offering to distribute work to a group of persons for purposes of further distribution, public performance, or public display. A public performance or display of a work does not of itself constitute publication. *info:* Includes but is not limited to print, broadcast, and online. In the U.S., refer to the U.S. Copyright Act (17 USC 101) for a legal definition of publication. *ex: Our illustrations will appear in the organization's publication, which is sent to each of its members. plural:* Publications

Publication Date [1543-00-00-0100] The date on which a work is distributed to the public by sale, rental, or lease or the offering to distribute work to a group of persons for purposes of further distribution, public performance, or public display. A public performance or display of a work does not of itself constitute publication. *info:* In the U.S., refer to the U.S. Copyright Act (17 USC 101) for a legal definition of publication. *ex: The publication date for the next magazine issue is June 1st. plural:* Publication Dates *variation:* Pub Date

Publicity Use [1643-00-00-0100] Use of a work in a press release, media kit or other public relations piece distributed for gratis editorial insertion in publications. Excludes use in advertising, advertorials and other media involving paid or bartered insertions. *ex: The image was licensed for publicity use in addition to its use on the record album cover. plural:* Publicity Uses

Publish [1685-00-00-0100] To prepare or cause a work to enter public distribution or be placed on sale. *info:* In the U.S., refer to the U.S. Copyright Act (17 USC 101) for a legal definition of publication. *ex: They will publish the book next week and it will appear in the bookstores within the month. plural:* Publishes

Purchase Order [4620-00-00-0100] A document generated by a licensor, often describing the works to be created or licensed and the license requested in association with the works. Typically specifies an approved budget for a project and/or license, a reference number for use in billing, and terms and conditions. *info:* Licensors and licensees should ensure that the descriptions and terms of the purchase order

are consistent with terms negotiated by the parties, as memorialized in the licensor's estimate, invoice and other related documents. *ex: The agency needed a signed purchase order before they would remit payment. plural:* Purchase Orders *variation:* P.O.

Push Date [2737-00-00-0100] The specific time or day when a marketing, sales, mail, fax or email campaign is actually distributed to the target audience. *ex: On the day after the push date, they expect their sales will increase dramatically. plural:* Push Dates

Puzzle [1220-00-00-0100] A set of small irregularly shaped pieces that form a picture or design when fitted together. *ex: The puzzle that was made from our landscape image was popular because of its complex patterns. plural:* Puzzles *variation:* Jigsaw Puzzle

QTVR [1785-01-00-0100] Abbreviation for QuickTime VR *ex: You can take a virtual tour of my new house by viewing the QTVR on my website. usability:* Discouraged

Quantity [2713-00-00-0100] The number or amount of reproductions made, displayed or distributed. *info:* Related but not synonymous to frequency. While frequency might be used to refer to the number of insertions in a magazine (or, whether the insertions are monthly, bimonthly, etc.), quantity indicates the circulation for the magazine. *ex: We need to publish a quantity of ten thousand books to meet the anticipated demand. plural:* Quantities

Quicktime VR [1785-00-00-0100] Apple's popular media technology that allows for display of virtual reality imagery. *info:* There are two types, panorama and object movie. *ex: You can take a virtual tour of my new house by viewing the Quicktime*(TM) *VR on my website. plural:* QuickTime(TM) VRs *variation:* QTVR

Quote [3640-00-00-0100] A pre-production document formulated by a licensor based on a project description provided by the licensee, describing work to be produced and/or licensed, the scope of the license, any terms and conditions applicable to the transaction, and the fees and costs for the project and/or license. *ex: We could not begin the assignment until he agreed to our quote. plural:* Quotes *preferred term:* Estimate [1063-00-00-0100] *usability:* Caution

Raster [2732-00-00-0100] An image composed of a rectangular grid of pixels. Each pixel contains a defined value about its color, size, and location in the image. *info:* If the pixels are bi-level (pure black or white with no shades of gray), the image can be represented with one bit per pixel (e.g., a fax image). *ex: The resolution of a raster image is determined by how many pixels it contains. plural:* Rasters

Rate Card [3650-00-00-0100] A listing provided by magazines to advertisers and potential advertisers that show specifications and costs for ads based on the area in a publication that will be occupied by an advertisement, image or other work. *ex: The magazine's rate card gave a choice of only full or half page ads at roughly the same cost as their major competitor. **plural:** Rate Cards*

RAW file [1826-00-00-0100] A digital camera file format akin to a film original. Similar to a digital negative but may include manufacturer-specific information or technology. *info:* Typical of more expensive digital cameras, a RAW file requires post-processing before it can be used. Capable of containing more information and delivering more color, dynamic range and resolution than a TIFF or JPEG digital image file, it also is a much larger file than a TIFF or JPEG. *ex: We put the RAW file on a CD ROM because it took up too much space on our limited hard drive. **plural:** RAW Files*

Re-License [4440-00-00-0100] The renewal of a legal written agreement granting permission to exercise a specified right or rights to a work, often encompassed in an invoice, or the act of granting same. *ex: We granted them a re-license to use the image in the next edition of the book. **plural:** Re-Licenses **variation:** Relicense*

Re-Shoot [4470-01-00-0100] See Reshoot *ex: A reshoot was scheduled because the initial images were underexposed.*

Re-Use [1296-00-00-0100] Subsequent utilization of a work by the same publisher in the same or related publication, advertising or marketing venue. *info:* Some licensors grant a small discount for re-use, though this is not necessarily an industry-wide practice. Some clients expect a discount. *ex: We are licensing this image to you for re-use in the abridged version of the textbook. **plural:** Re-Uses **variation:** Reuse*

Record

(1) Record (Digital) [2754-00-01-0100] One single collected unit of data fields in a database containing many such units. *ex: You are currently viewing one record of glossary data. **plural:** Records*

(2) Record (Music) [2754-00-02-0100] A flat vinyl disk etched with spiral grooves that contains audio: music or spoken words. *info:* Usually packaged in an album sleeve. *ex: We are listening to an old record. **plural:** Records*

Red Green Blue [1471-01-00-0100] See RGB *ex: Computer monitors project light in red, green, blue.*

Redress [3740-00-00-0100] To set right, rectify or remedy, often by making compensation for a wrong or grievance. *ex: A kill fee was the type of redress offered by the client who cancelled the assignment.*

Reference

(1) Reference (General) [3750-00-01-0100] A source of information such as a dictionary, encyclopedia or directory, that contains specific facts, data, or other bits of information. *info:* Can be in book format or electronic. *ex: She consulted a reference book to find out the population of that country 20 years ago. **plural:** References*

(2) Reference (Design) [3750-00-02-0100] A photo or illustration that a creator may refer to for inspiration. *info:* Be very clear on how much the end product may look like the original image. *ex: His cat photo was used as reference for the artist's sculpture. **plural:** references*

Region [1289-00-00-0100] An area of a country, usually more than one state, often denoted by its geographical location. *ex: The advertisement will run in the New England region. **plural:** Regions **variation:** Regional*

Regional [1289-01-00-0100] See Region *ex: The advertisement will run in the New England regional edition. **plural:** Regionals **preferred term:** Region **usability:** Discouraged*

Regional Distribution [1290-00-00-0100] Limited distribution of an advertisement, piece, or other message form, in one specific regional area such as tri-state, northeast, or southwest. *ex: That newspaper has regional distribution. **plural:** Regional Distributions*

Regional Exclusive [2727-01-00-0100] See Regional Exclusivity *ex: The client purchased a regional exclusive. **plural:** Regional Exclusives*

Regional Exclusivity [2727-00-00-0100] A right that, when granted by a licensor to a licensee, limits the right of the licensor (and other parties offering licenses of the work) to license the right to any third party to use the work in specified geographic regions. *ex: Because this client purchased regional exclusivity, we cannot offer the same region to another client. **plural:** Regional Exclusivities **variation:** Regional Exclusive*

Register Card [1221-00-00-0100] A small rectangular piece of stiff paper or plastic, generally containing advertising, typically displayed in retail stores near a cash register. *ex: The register card includes images of the items on sale.* **plural:** Register Cards

Release

(1) Release (People) [1275-02-00-0100] See Model Release *ex: Before the advertising agency will consider using the image, they need to know if the photographer has a release on file.*

(2) Release (Property) [1284-01-00-0100] See Property Release *ex: The photographer has a release on file and so has the right to license the use of this image of a house.*

(3) Release (Minor) [3250-01-00-0100] See Minor Release *ex: Because the subject was only seven years old, a release, signed by his legal guardian, was needed by the advertising agency before they would consider using the photographer's image.*

Relicense [4440-01-00-0100] See Re-license *ex: We granted them a relicense to use the image in the next edition of the book.* **plural:** Relicenses

Remainder Copy [1549-00-00-0100] Extra reproductions or leftover versions of a book. *info:* Typically offered for sale at discounted prices. *ex: You may still find a remainder copy.* **plural:** Remainder Copies **preferred term:** Remaindered **usability:** Discouraged

Remaindered [3770-00-00-0100] A book that has been taken out of a publisher's catalog, declared out of print, and then sold as remaining inventory. *ex: You may still find a copy of this book, which has been remaindered, on the bargain racks of a few select stores.*

Remit [1037-00-00-0100] When one party makes payment to another as compensation for goods or services. *ex: Kindly remit the full amount.* **plural:** Remits **variation:** Remittance

Remittance [1037-01-00-0100] See Remit *ex: Kindly remit the full amount.* **plural:** Remittances

Renewal Rights [1291-00-00-0100] Permission to renew an existing license for use of a creative work. May or may not be included in the original license agreement. *ex: The client wants to include renewal rights in our agreement.*

Rep [3670-01-00-0100] Abbreviation for Representative *ex: He had to call the rep to go over the details of the assignment since the photographer was out of town.*

Repeat Use [1469-00-00-0100] Multiple placements of the same image within one edition of a single title, project, or program. *ex: They requested repeat use for the anthology.* **plural:** Repeat Uses

Representation

(1) Representation (Legal) [1292-00-01-0100] A statement of fact made to induce another to enter into a contract or agreement. *ex: They made a representation that they could indeed pay the licensing fee.* **plural:** Representations

(2) Representation (General Business) [1292-00-02-0100] Having an official delegate, spokesperson, or agent. *ex: Yesterday we acquired representation.* **plural:** Representations

Representative [3670-00-00-0100] A party authorized to act or speak for another. *info:* A representative can be—but isn't necessarily—an agent. *ex: The client called the representative to go over the details of the assignment since the photographer was out of town.* **plural:** Representatives **variation:** Rep

Reprint [1461-00-00-0100] A reproduction substantially resembling a previous reproduction. Or, the act of creating reproduction(s) substantially resembling previous reproduction(s). *info:* Characteristics, quantity, distribution, timing, and other factors are often subject to the specifications of a license granting use of any incorporated images. *ex: The reprint was sent to new subscribers as a bonus.* **plural:** Reprints

Repro Print [2814-01-00-0100] Abbreviation for Reproduction Print *ex: We are making a repro print for scanning purposes.* **plural:** Repro Prints

Reproduction [4460-00-00-0100] The act of copying or the condition or process of being copied. *ex: They purchased rights to reproduction of the image as an art print.* **plural:** Reproductions

Reproduction License [2710-00-00-0100] A legal contract or permission outlining the parameters under which a copyrighted work may be used. *ex: Refer to the reproduction license to double check the number of copies we can reproduce.* **plural:** Reproduction Licenses

Reproduction Print [2814-00-00-0100] A print of an image which is especially made so as to provide optimal quality when reproduced. *info:* Reproduction prints are typically made with lower contrast—the whites are not as bright, and the blacks (shadow areas) are made to show more detail. This is to compensate for the increase in contrast that occurs naturally as part of the reproduction process, or from generational loss due to dot gain and other factors. *ex: We are making a reproduction print for scanning purposes. **plural:** Reproduction Prints **variation:** Repro Print

Resample [1462-00-00-0100] To change image resolution through interpolation, making calculations using already known values. **info:** Resampling a digital image downwards discards pixel information; resampling upwards requires creating pixel information based on the adjacent values. *ex: We will resample the image to your specification. **plural:** Resamples

Research Fee [3680-00-00-0100] A charge made by an agency, photographer, illustrator, or professional image researcher for investigative efforts to locate appropriate images on behalf of a client. *ex: Our research fee does not include copyright clearance services. **plural:** research fees

Research Use [1644-00-00-0100] The application of an image for scholarly or art reference. No reproduction or redistribution rights are included. *ex: We licensed that image for research use. **plural:** Research Uses

Reseller [1293-00-00-0100] One who buys (or receives on consignment) goods or other products from suppliers, and in turn trades or sells them to consumers. **info:** Some resellers add value to their transaction by testing various applications, devices, etc. and recommending specific sets of items that are known to work well together. *ex: For product pricing information, please contact our reseller. **plural:** Resellers

Reshoot [4470-00-00-0100] Rephotographing a job due to the initial results being unsatisfactory. *ex: A reshoot was scheduled because the initial images were underexposed. **plural:** Reshoots **variation:** Re-shoot

Residual [3690-00-00-0100] A fee paid for repeated broadcast of a film after original presentation or period of its use. *ex: He was paid a residual every time the commercial that contained his image was aired. **plural:** Residuals

Residual Rights [4500-00-00-0100] Rights that have remained with the copyright owner of the work after some rights have been granted to another party. *ex: The client purchased first rights, but the artist retained the residual rights.*

Resolution of Print [1463-01-00-0100] See Printing Resolution *ex: A higher resolution of print value usually produces more pleasing results. **preferred term:** Printing Resolution **usability:** Discouraged

Restriction [1294-00-00-0100] Any limitation on a right available for licensing or in a given license or other agreement. **info:** May include industries, products, services, and/or subject matter excluded from the licensed use. *ex: The license includes a restriction on usage in the financial services sector. **plural:** Restrictions

Retail [1786-00-00-0100] The sale of goods or services directly to consumers. **info:** Typically all sales made in department stores or supermarkets are retail sales. *ex: That magazine is available at retail outlets. **plural:** Retails

Retention Fee [1295-00-00-0100] A charge made for the extension of the period that a client is permitted to hold a creative work. *ex: If the images are not returned this week, a retention fee will be charged. **plural:** Retention Fees

Retouch [1840-01-00-0100] See Digitally Retouch [1840-00-00-0100] *ex: We will retouch the image to remove the scar from CEO's nose. **Plural:** Retouches

Return [1038-00-00-0100] A product distributed at retail but not sold. **info:** A return usually goes back to a wholesaler or distributor who sometimes issues a credit to the retailer. *ex: Last month we did not have one single return. **plural:** Returns

Reuse [1296-01-00-0100] See Re-Use *ex: We are licensing this image to you for reuse in the abridged version of the textbook. **plural:** Reuses

Revenue [1597-00-00-0100] The total (gross) income. *ex: Some deductions must be made from the revenue before your percentage can be calculated. **plural:** Revenues

Reverse Out [1464-00-00-0100] When an image or text inverts from (shows through) a background or image. **info:** Can be either positive to negative or negative to positive. *ex: We will reverse out the client's logo against the black background. **plural:** Reverse Outs

Revised Edition [1465-01-00-0100] See Revision *ex: This new advertisement is a revised edition of the previous ad. **plural:** Revised Editions **preferred term:** Revision **usability:** Discouraged

Revision

(1) Revision (General) [1465-00-00-0100] An updated or modified version of a previously existing work. *ex: This new advertisement is a revision of the previous ad. **plural:** Revisions **variation:** Revised edition

(2) Revision (Major) [1466-00-00-0100] Changes that typically amount to more than 10 percent of the total work (words and images). *info:* More inclusive in scope and broader than revision (minor). *ex: This new advertisement is a revision (major) of the previous ad. plural:* Revisions (Major)

(3) Revision (Minor) [1467-00-00-0100] Changes typically amounting to less than 10 percent of the total work (words and images). *info:* Less broad or inclusive in scope than revision (major). *ex: This new advertisement is a revision (minor) of the previous ad. plural:* Revisions (Minor)

(4) Revision (Re-use) [1470-00-00-0100] To repeat a usage in a subsequent advertisement, book, magazine, or other publication, project, or program edition. *ex: The image in this new advertisement is a revision (re-use) from the previous ad. plural:* Revisions (Re-Use)

Revision Use [1645-00-00-0100] Usage within the same title, project, or program but in a new edition thereof. *ex: The photo on the cover of the book's second edition qualifies as a revision use. plural:* Revision Uses

Revocation [1297-00-00-0100] The withdrawal of an offer under a contract or license by the offeror or the power to recall or make void an offer. *ex: Our agreement includes a revocation clause. plural:* Revocations

RF [1304-06-00-0100] See Royalty Free *ex: We licensed an RF image.*

RGB [1471-00-00-0100] A method of displaying color that uses the three primary colors of red, green, blue. *ex: Computer monitors project light in RGB. variation:* Red Green Blue

Right [1647-00-00-0100] A legal claim, title or privilege. *ex: You have the right to use this image. plural:* Rights

Right of Privacy [1298-00-00-0100] The privilege to be left alone, free from unwarranted publicity, and to live without unwarranted interference by the public in matters with which the public is not necessarily concerned. *ex: The publisher is requiring the author to represent that the literary work does not violate any living person's right of privacy. plural:* Rights of Privacy

Right of Publicity [1299-00-00-0100] The right of a person to control the use of his or her image, voice, and likeness for commercial purposes. *info:* The law varies from state to state and may or may not survive the individual's death depending on the law that

governs. *ex: Using the starlet's picture in an ad without her permission may violate her right of publicity. plural:* Rights of Publicity

Right to Assign [1598-00-00-0100] A contract term allowing a licensee to pass or convey rights in a work to a third party or third parties without further permissions or fees. *info:* A contract may specify or limit the third parties to which rights may be assigned. *ex: The publisher has the right to assign the images from the shoot. plural:* Rights to Assign

Right to Transfer or Sell [2714-00-00-0100] A contract term allowing a licensee to pass or convey rights in a work to a third party or third parties without further permissions or fees. *info:* A contract may limit or specify the third parties to which rights may be transferred or sold. *ex: The publisher has the right to transfer or sell the images from the shoot. plural:* Rights To Transfer Or Sell

Rights Control [1300-00-00-0100] Prior to licensing a creative work, the process of checking all previous licenses to ensure that they do not duplicate, contradict, or overlap with the contemplated license. *ex: Stock photo agencies use rights control procedures to track image usage history. plural:* Rights Controls

Rights Exclusivity [2719-00-00-0100] A right that, when granted by a licensor to a licensee, limits the right of the licensor (and other parties offering licenses of the work) to license rights in a work to a third party. *info:* An exclusive may be broad or specific. The rights grant may provide the licensee with exclusive rights to use a work singly or in any combination of: a specified media, industry, territory, or language, or for a specific time period, product, or other specific right negotiated by the licensor and licensee. *ex: The advertising agency wants to license rights exclusivity for TV for a year. plural:* Rights Exclusivities

Rights Managed [1303-00-00-0100] A licensing model in which the rights to a creative work are carefully controlled by a licensor through use of exact and limiting wording of each successive grant of usage rights. *ex: Let's ask the stock agency if anyone else has licensed this rights managed image in the past year. variation:* RM

Rights Management [1746-00-00-0100] The processes associated with active control and management of the licensing history of a work. *info:* Exact and carefully limited wording of each successive grant of usage rights is a central concept. *ex: Be sure to check with the agency's rights management division about the past history of that image.*

Rights Package [1599-00-00-0100] A bundle of rights allowing multiple uses of one or more images for a single fee. *info:* The fee for a rights package is typically less than the total fees for each use if licensed separately. *ex: The client wants to purchase a rights package to use the image in three separate promotions for a new product.* *plural:* Rights Packages

Rights Protected [1302-00-00-0100] A creative work whose licensing is carefully controlled through use of exact and limiting wording of each successive grant of usage rights. *info:* While it is possible to restrict the use of a work by others, no restrictions on the use by other buyers or competitors is guaranteed unless specific limitations on other uses are negotiated and agreed to. Works are normally licensed for one-time, non-exclusive use. *ex: Some portals include rights protected images.*

Rights Protection [1856-00-00-0100] The purchase by a licensee of an exclusive right from the licensor which guarantees that the work under license will not be made available to a third party for one or any combination of the following: similar usage, use in the same media, in the same industry, within the same territory, within a given time period or in a given language. *info:* The extent of rights protection must be negotiated. *ex: In addition to the basic license, the client wants rights protection for similar usage in the same industry for a full year.*

RM [1303-01-00-0100] See Rights Managed *ex: Let's ask the stock agency if anyone else has licensed this RM image in the past year.*

Roll Over [2778-00-00-0100] When a computer cursor moves over a portion of interactive digital content and the content changes visual appearance to indicate the presence of an underlying link to other content or activity. *ex: If you roll over the image, you'll see directions to go to the member page.* *plural:* Roll Overs *variation:* Roll-Over

Roll-Over [2778-01-00-0100] See Roll Over *ex: If you roll-over the image, you'll see a link to the member page.* *plural:* Roll-Overs

Roughs [4580-00-00-0100] Rudimentary sketches used to explain or describe how to illustrate a concept. *ex: Use the roughs to relay our ideas to the illustrator.*

Royalty [1511-00-00-0100] A percentage-based portion of revenue that is paid by an agent or publisher or user to the creator of a work. *ex: Your royalty check is in the mail.* *plural:* Royalties

Royalty Free [1304-00-00-0100] Denotes a broad or almost unlimited use of an image or group of images by a licensee for a single licensee fee. License agreement typically specifies some limitations (e.g., resale of the image to a third party is usually prohibited). *info:* The terms of royalty free license agreements vary and often include warnings or disclaimers regarding liability in connection with model-released imagery. *ex: Royalty free licensing emerged in the early 1990s, consisting entirely of image collections on CD-ROM.* *variation:* RF, Royalty-Free

Royalty-Free [1304-01-00-0100] See Royalty Free *ex: Royalty-free licensing emerged in the early 1990s, consisting entirely of image collections on CD-ROM.*

Saddle Stitch [1787-00-00-0100] A binding process that uses metal staples through the middle fold line to secure the pages of a book or magazine. *ex: The magazine has a saddle stitch binding.*

Salary [1600-00-00-0100] Fixed compensation paid by an employer to an employee that is irrespective of the number of hours worked. *info:* Paid weekly, bi-weekly or monthly with social security and other deductions and may include health and other benefits. *ex: My new job pays a better salary than my previous one.* *plural:* Salaries

Sale of Original Artwork [4590-00-00-0100] The transferring of a work from the artist to a second party usually involving the exchange of currency. *ex: The sale of original artwork was made at the same time it was accepted for publication in the magazine.* *plural:* Sales of Original Artwork

Sales Kit [1125-00-00-0100] Items supplied to personnel as presentation aids to persuade customers to purchase products or services. *info:* The components can be as varied as brochures, videos, product information sheets, folders, post cards, cassettes, and more. *ex: Our sales kit comes in a spiral binder.* *plural:* Sales Kits

Sales Sheet [1126-00-00-0100] A single page with a product description printed on one side; mailed to clients, distributed at a point of sale or demonstration, or included in a sales kit. *ex: The sales sheet has a picture of the product and descriptive text.* *plural:* Sales Sheets

Sample [1039-00-00-0100] In electronic media, a small portion of a work that is reused as part of another work. *ex: A sample of the cover image was used on the contents page.* *plural:* Samples

Sample Print [1472-00-00-0100] An image reproduction made by the image user to show to a client, frequently to help decide whether the image is appropriate for a specific project. *ex: The art director asked for a sample print to show the client.* **plural:** Sample Prints

Sampling Error [1053-00-00-0100] In audience research reporting, the estimated or expected error percentage (usually expressed as plus or minus) when only a part of an audience is researched rather than the entire audience). *ex: The survey results are subject to a sampling error of plus or minus five percent.* **plural:** Sampling Errors

Sanctioning Body [1788-00-00-0100] An organization (or a group within an organization) that sets rules and procedures and gives approval. *info:* Many sports sanctioning bodies require copies of public relations and marketing images. *ex: We will send the event photographs to the sanctioning body.* **plural:** Sanctioning Bodies

Saturation [1658-00-00-0100] The attribute of a color image that determines or describes its apparent colorfulness. *ex: The image has the correct level of saturation.*

Scan [1473-00-00-0100] The acquisition of visual information with a device that passes light through (or bounces it off) an analog original and captures its brightness and color information with a light-sensitive sensor. *info:* The resulting information is typically sent to an attached computer where it is stored as a digital image. Scans can be made using analog drum scanners, or digital film or flatbed scanners. *ex: We are sending the image out for a scan.* **plural:** Scans

School Book [2743-01-00-0100] See Schoolbook *ex: This school book is for sixth graders.* **plural:** School Books **preferred term:** Textbook **usability:** Discouraged

Schoolbook [2743-00-00-0100] A volume in printed or electronic form containing information on one or more subjects used in a real or virtual classroom by students and teachers. *info:* Usually includes images. Ancillaries, which require specific licenses, might include other edition(s), such as instructor handbooks, a student edition, an edition in another language or an electronic edition. *ex: This schoolbook is for sixth graders.* **plural:** Schoolbooks **preferred term:** Textbook **usability:** Discouraged **variation:** School Book

Screen [3420-00-00-0100] The portion of a presentation on a television, projection, or computer monitor that is visible at a given moment. *info:* Applies to television, computer software (including games), online presentations, projected presentations, etc. *ex: We licensed the image to appear on the first screen of the website.* **plural:** Screens

Screen Resolution

(1) Screen Resolution (Digital) [1474-00-01-0100] The number of addressable pixels of a monitor or television. *info:* Traditionally, 640 x 480, or 1,024 x 768 at 72 or 96 pixels per inch (PPI), though much higher-resolution displays of 1920 x 1440 at 140 PPI are becoming commonplace. *ex: A high screen resolution display is usually more expensive.* **plural:** Screen Resolutions

(2) Screen Resolution (Print) [1474-00-02-0100] The lines per inch (LPI) of a mechanical screen used to create a color-separated image. *info:* Eighty-five lines per inch (LPI) is common for newspapers, 133 LPI for magazines, and up to 250 LPI for highest-quality sheet-fed lithography). *ex: A higher screen resolution on coated paper makes for a more pleasing visual appearance.* **plural:** Screen Resolutions

Screen Saver [1175-00-00-0100] A moving or animated design or presentation that appears on a computer screen when there has been no input or activity for a period of time. *info:* Often includes scrolling text, moving images and/or graphics. Prevents monitor damage that occurs when the same areas of light and dark are displayed too long. *ex: My screen saver is programmed to turn on after five minutes of inactivity.* **plural:** Screen Savers

Screenshot [4600-00-00-0100] Display from a computer screen used to show people what a layout or website looks like without sending them the layout file or a web address. *ex: We send the client a screenshot before we finalize a layout.* **plural:** Screenshots

Search Fee [1305-00-00-0100] A charge made by an agency, photographer, illustrator, or professional image researcher for investigative efforts such as locating appropriate images on behalf of a client. *info:* Includes time to research the request and search out the images needed. *ex: Our search fee does not include copyright clearance services.* **plural:** Search Fees **preferred term:** Research Fee **usability:** Discouraged

Season [1747-00-00-0100] A recurrent period measured by a schedule (including the calendar) and characterized by certain occurrences. *info:* Used in sports, television, fashion, etc. *ex: The usage will occur in the spring season only.* **plural:** Seasons

Seat License [1306-00-00-0100] Allows a licensee of a technology, product, or content to copy and use it throughout a defined premise of operations. Often used for computer software or royalty free licensing. *info:* May include the copyright holder's limitation of the number of concurrent users or computers that are entitled to access and use the given licensed work. *ex: You may buy a seat license for our software.* **plural:** Seat Licenses

Second Cover [1475-00-00-0100] First inside full page that stands apart from any text and is used primarily for design. *ex: The image will run on the second cover.* **plural:** Second Covers

Second Serial Rights [1307-00-00-0100] Post-publication of selected parts of a book (or other work), including images in a magazine or periodical. *ex: Second serial rights for a chapter in the book were purchased by a national magazine.*

Secondary Page [2795-00-00-0100] A section of a website that is accessible only via a link from the home page, a link from a different website, or a link in an email message. *ex: The image will be used on a secondary page.* **plural:** Secondary Pages

Secondary Rights [1308-00-00-0100] In the copyright environment, rights to use content in applications of lower quality and lower value, such as photocopying of text. Content typically would appear in very small circulations or lesser media. *info:* Any usage fee is usually collected through blanket licensing by collecting societies. Digital technology is eliminating the quality distinction, and current practice bases value on size of the audience and type of media, making this term irrelevant. *ex: If you photocopy and distribute the book chapter at your meeting, you may be responsible for payment for secondary rights.* **usability:** Discouraged

Secondary Use [1309-00-00-0100] In publishing, an alternative, often lesser, product or use for the same image; in the stock business, any use after the initial use for which the work was created and used. *info:* An example would be an interior page use in a magazine in addition to usage on the cover. *ex: The image assigned and used on their magazine cover also had a secondary use in their public relations campaign.* **plural:** Secondary Uses **preferred term:** Re-Use **usability:** Caution

Secondary Web Page [1790-00-00-0100] A section of an Internet site that is accessible only via a link from the home page, a link from a different Internet site, or a

link in an email message. *ex: The image will be used on a secondary web page.* **plural:** Secondary Web Pages

Seconds [4610-00-00-0100] Images produced but not selected or used for a given assignment or purpose. *ex: These seconds were deselected from the assignment take.* **preferred term:** Out **usability:** Discouraged

Self Mailer [1662-00-00-0100] Promotional postal item not enclosed in an envelope, designed so that a portion can be used for a reply. *ex: The self mailer will be in the July issue.* **plural:** Self Mailers **variation:** Self-Mailer

Self-Mailer [1662-01-00-0100] See Self Mailer *ex: The self-mailer will be in the July issue.* **plural:** Self-Mailers **preferred term:** Self Mailer

Sensitive Issue [1310-00-00-0100] A topic that, when depicted visually, may be considered offensive to a person's sensibilities. *info:* A sensitive issue is a nuanced concept and its definition may vary. Includes but is not necessarily limited to sexuality, sexually transmitted diseases, contraception, alcohol, tobacco, abortion, substance abuse, physical or mental diseases, plastic surgery, mental or physical abuse, aging, political affiliation, and matters of race or religion. Images depicting or being used in conjunction with such topics may warrant obtaining a usage-specific release from the model. *ex: The client requested a sensitive issue release from the model.* **plural:** Sensitive Issues

Sepia Tone [1791-00-00-0100] A brownish shade on a print produced by a darkroom chemical process. Especially prevalent in older photographs. *info:* Can be produced through digital imaging techniques. *ex: The client chose the image with a sepia tone.* **plural:** Sepia Tones

Series Similar [1480-01-00-0100] See Similar *ex: The image used in the computer ad is a series similar to the one used in the photographer's promotional piece.* **plural:** Series Similars

Server [1693-00-00-0100] A heavy-duty computer system or computer program, which provides some service to other programs or computers connected to it via a network, or which processes requests from other computers. *info:* There are many servers associated with the Internet, such as those for web services, email services, FTP, or domain name services. Requests may be for a digital file such as an HTML web page or digital image, music or video, or for data to be used by other computer software. A server might also perform procedures on groups of digital files (e.g., image printing). *ex: When the server broke down, work came to a standstill.* **plural:** Servers

Service Provider [1700-00-00-0100] Work performed by a company or individual as an occupation or business. *ex: Our website is hosted by a service provider. plural:* Service Providers *variation:* SP

Set Decor [2749-00-00-0100] Any object or image that appears on the stage or screen during a television show, theatrical performance, film, or photo shoot. *info:* Does not include costumes or scenery. *ex: The framed photograph will be used as set decor. variation:* Set Decoration

Set Decoration [2749-01-00-0100] See Set Decor *ex: The framed photograph will be used for set decoration.*

Set Up [4260-00-00-0100] A single scene in a particular locale, photographed using a particular set of techniques and equipment, from a single angle and perspective. *info:* A set up includes: minor changes in cropping, composition and/or poses; interchanging models and/or products; wardrobe changes; and, subtle lighting adjustments. A new set up exists after a significant change in camera position, major relighting of the scene, a changed background, or moving to a new locale—nearby or distant. *ex: We can choose up to ten shots from that set up. plural:* Set Ups *variation:* Set-Up

Set-Up [4260-01-00-0100] See Set Up *ex: We can choose up to ten shots from that set-up. plural:* Set-Ups

Shade [1476-00-00-0100] A color or tone that has been mixed with black or from which some portion of luminance has been removed. *ex: That's exactly the right shade of red. plural:* Shades

Shadow [1477-00-00-0100] The darker parts of an image, represented in a halftone or color separation by larger or more numerous ink dots. *info:* In the deepest shadow portions of an image, these dots usually merge to form a solid area of ink. *ex: We can barely see the shadow detail. plural:* Shadows

Sharpening [1675-00-00-0100] A digital imaging process that increases contrast, usually at the edges of tonal transitions, and adds apparent acuity or clarity to a digital image. *info:* The most common method is called unsharp masking, but there are others. *ex: We will need to apply some sharpening to counteract the softening effect of the halftone screen.*

Sharpness [1478-00-00-0100] The degree of clarity or acuity (especially at edges) in an image. *ex: The client has a very high standard for sharpness.*

Shelf Life [4090-00-00-0100] The period of time a product remains for sale. *ex: The shelf life of this book is expected to be six months. plural:* Shelf Lives

Shelf Talker [1222-00-00-0100] An advertising piece on a display case of a retail outlet designed to attract buyer attention to one or several products. *ex: The shelf talker has an adhesive strip along one edge so it can be easily fastened to the shelves in the store. plural:* Shelf Talkers

Shoot [4640-00-00-0100] The actual production during the making of a photograph. *ex: The shoot is scheduled for Saturday morning. plural:* Shoots

Shot [4270-00-00-0100] Slang for a single photographic work. *info:* Different shots may appear similar, but each is treated separately. There may be many shots in a set up. *ex: We wish to license only one shot from the set up. plural:* Shots

Shrink [1041-00-00-0100] The quantity of unsold magazine copies that are returned and destroyed. *ex: The shrink on the January issue was very low. plural:* Shrinks

Silhouette [1479-00-00-0100] An image cross-faded into an empty background with either an abrupt or a soft-edged transition. *info:* In the design world an image that has been silhouetted, or could easily be removed from its background and made into a silhouette. *ex: Make the silhouette against a plain white background. plural:* Silhouettes

Similar [1480-00-00-0100] An image recorded at the same time or on the same assignment as an image chosen by a publisher or an image that has the same or similar characteristics, such as subject, action, or appearance, to another image chosen for a particular usage. *info:* If viewed side by side, it is obvious that similars are from the same set, of the same subject, and recorded at the same time. *ex: The image used in the computer ad is a similar to the one used in the photographer's promotional piece. plural:* Similars *variation:* Series Similar

Single [1311-00-00-0100] A license which grants the right to a specified solitary reproduction of a work. *ex: We licensed a single to the show organizers for the event display poster. plural:* Singles

Single Page [2802-00-00-0100] A promotion, editorial, or advertising piece that takes up one complete leaf in a publication or presentation. *info:* A one page image usage license permits use of an image at any size up to a complete page. *ex: The ad will be a single page. plural:* Single Pages

Single Sheet Mailer [1127-00-00-0100] A one page sales piece usually for promotional or advertising use, that is sent to consumers through the postal system. *ex: The single sheet mailer will be printed tomorrow. plural:* Single Sheet Mailers

Site License [1642-00-00-0100] Allows a licensee of a technology, product, or content to copy and use that technology, product, or content throughout a defined premise of operations. *info:* Common with computer software, allowing a single license to support use by an unlimited number of employees or associates at the location. Also applicable to picture licensing. *ex: Our company purchased a site license to use the software at our headquarters in Miami. plural:* Site Licenses

Sketch [4630-00-00-0100] Concepts illustrated in a simple and often rudimentary way. *ex: The sketch will illustrate an article in the magazine. plural:* Sketches

Slander [4040-00-00-0100] A false statement spoken to a person or persons, harming the reputation of another. Or, the act of making such a statement. *ex: Not only words, but even sounds and gestures can be interpreted as slander.*

Slide [3450-00-00-0100] A mounted 35mm original or duplicate transparency. *ex: Please scan the slide for delivery online. plural:* Slides

Slide Show [1174-00-00-0100] The display of a series of analog photographs through a projector or digital images on a computer. *info:* Often designed to convey information or to reinforce a specific idea or message. *ex: They put together a slide show of my images on the website. plural:* Slide Shows

Slim Jim [5170-00-00-0100] A brochure, typically 4 to 6 panels, that is folded to fit in a no. 10 envelope; typically used together with a sales letter. *info:* Contains supporting materials that may include product photos, diagrams, graphs, specifications, features, background on the company, testimonials, a customer list, and more. *ex: The letter sells, the slim Jim tells. plural:* Slim Jims

Slip Case [1481-00-00-0100] A box or container for one or a set of books or magazines. *ex: This image will appear on their slip case. plural:* Slip Cases

Softback Book [1176-00-00-0100] A volume bound in light-weight flexible paper. *info:* Unlike a hardbound book, softbound books are often printed on a lesser grade of paper, with a lighter weight, flexible cover, and they are often perfect bound rather than having signatures stitched and bound. *ex: Here is the softback book you ordered. plural:* Softback Books *preferred term:* Paperback Book *usability:* Discouraged

Softbound [3730-00-00-0100] A volume bound in a light-weight flexible paper cover that is usually a heavier paper than its inside pages. *info:* A softbound edition is often, but certainly not always, published after a hardbound edition. Increasingly, first editions of books are softbound. *ex: The image will appear on the cover of the softbound edition only. plural:* Softbounds

Softcover [3660-00-00-0100] A volume bound in light-weight flexible paper. *info:* Unlike a hardbound book, softcovers are often printed on a lesser grade of paper, with a lighter weight, flexible cover, and are often perfect bound rather than having signatures stitched and bound. *ex: The softcover came out two years after the hardcover. plural:* Softcovers *preferred term:* Paperback Book usability: Discouraged

Software Packaging [1223-00-00-0100] The container or wrapping enclosing new computer software. *info:* Often includes images. *ex: They will use the image for their software packaging.*

Souvenir [1224-00-00-0100] Small trinkets or mementos from a particular place, attraction, or event, usually sold to tourists or attendees. Can include the use of images. *ex: This souvenir from the trade show has your image on it. plural:* Souvenirs

SP [1700-01-00-0100] Abbreviation for Service Provider [1700-00-00-0100] *ex: Our website is hosted by an SP. plural:* SPs

Space Rate [1601-00-00-0100] A compensation method based on the area in a publication occupied by an advertisement, an image, or other work. *info:* Calculated as a portion of the size of the page, and/or the size, position, or prominence of the page (e.g. one quarter page, front cover, interior page, etc.). *ex: Please tell us your space rate for an inside front cover. plural:* Space Rates

Spec [1602-00-00-0100] Creating work according to specific client directions without a contract, written agreement, or formal guarantee of payment. Abbreviation for speculation. *ex: The images the artist made on spec were used by the client several times. variation:* Speculation

Special Term [1312-00-00-0100] Any unusual condition or usage specified in a license, contract, or agreement. *ex: At your request, we added a special term to the license that addresses additional future uses for a year. plural:* Special Terms

Speculation [1602-01-00-0100] See Spec *ex: The photographer shot images on speculation for the textbook editor.*

Spin-Off [2699-00-00-0100] Special magazine issues, books, trade shows, merchandise, or electronic products (CDs or websites) that carry a brand name and deal with topics that are related to the brand. *info:* Publishers or manufacturers often use spin-offs to increase revenues and awareness of a brand. *ex: The magazine celebrated its tenth anniversary with a spin-off, which was a special edition showcasing the best images from past issues.* **plural:** Spin-Offs

Spine [1792-00-00-0100] The vertical back of a book cover or an LP record album sleeve, usually printed with the title and the name of the author or performer. *ex: The type on the spine will use a gold metallic ink.* **plural:** Spines

Splash Page [1692-00-00-0100] The initial screen displayed when a user opens a computer software package, computer presentation or a website. *ex: They licensed this image for use on their website splash page.* **plural:** Splash Pages

Split Run [1054-00-00-0100] Two different versions of an advertisement appear in one issue, and each reader receives one issue with one of the two versions of the advertisement. *ex: We will schedule these advertisements as a split run.* **plural:** Split Runs

Spoilage [1531-00-00-0100] Expected paper waste as a result of the printing process. *ex: The printer ordered extra paper in anticipation of spoilage.*

Spot

(1) Spot (Usage) [1072-00-01-0100] When an image is reproduced in print at less than one quarter page. *info:* Some publishing situations consider spot reproduction as one eighth page or less or even one sixteenth page or less. *ex: One of the five images submitted was selected to run as a spot.* **plural:** Spots

(2) Spot (Distribution) [1072-00-02-0100] When circulation includes only one or two local or regional areas. *ex: The spot distribution will be in Manhattan only.* **plural:** Spots

(3) Spot (Print) [1072-00-03-0100] A special non-process color added to an image or graphic during printing that enhances its appearance or makes it stand out on the page. *info:* Spot colors are typically special Pantone colors used to match a specific logo color, or for special treatments like metallic inks, or

even a gloss or matte varnish. *ex: The printer added a fifth spot color.* **plural:** Spots

Spot Exclusive [1313-01-00-0100] Abbreviation for Spot Exclusivity *ex: The client purchased spot exclusivity in the northwest region for three months.* **plural:** Spot Exclusives

Spot Exclusivity [1313-00-00-0100] A right that, when granted by a licensor to a licensee, limits the right of the licensor (and other party or parties offering any license of the work) to license expressly specified rights to any third party. *info:* A narrow form of exclusivity, but can include exclusivity (singly or in any combination) in specified media, time periods, territories, industries, products, languages, or other specific exclusive rights negotiated by the licensor and licensee. *ex: The client purchased spot exclusivity in the northwest region for three months.* **plural:** Spot Exclusivities *variation:* Spot Exclusive

Spread [1482-00-00-0100] Two facing pages in a book, magazine, or newspaper. *ex: The article will run as a spread.* **plural:** Spreads

Start Date [1314-00-00-0100] The specific time—day, month, year—upon which a contract or the period of use of a piece begins. *ex: The start date of our agreement is May 1, 2006.* **plural:** Start Dates

State-Specific Edition [4080-00-00-0100] A variation of a book tailored for the needs of a particular state. *info:* Educational book publishers who have to meet state educational board requirements for a particular state may request image rates for state use rather than national use. *ex: A state-specific edition was published for Kansas.* **plural:** State-Specific Editions

Stationery [1128-00-00-0100] Paper and envelopes with a corporate or promotional logo, images and/or designs. Includes letterhead and envelopes used for correspondence. *ex: The photographer's stationery included one of his iconic images.*

Statutory Damages [1315-00-00-0100] Damages resulting from statutorily created causes of actions, as opposed to actions at common law. Under section 504 of the Federal Copyright Act, a registered copyright owner has the right to elect statutory damages in lieu of actual damages for copyright infringement. (The copyright registration must be made prior to an infringement or within three months of first publication of the work.) *info:* Statutory damages range from $750 to $30,000 and can be increased up to $150,000 if the infringement is willful. The amount is discretionary with the court. *ex: We sued for statutory damages.*

Still for TV [2716-00-00-0100] A still image used in a TV production as editorial or advertising content. *ex: The image will be used as a still for TV. plural:* Stills For TV

Still Life [3460-00-00-0100] An image consisting predominantly of inanimate objects. *info:* Objects could be books, candles, cooking utensils, musical instruments, fruit, flowers, and more. *ex: The still life contained the old man's most treasured possessions. plural:* Still Lifes

Still Photography [5180-00-00-0100] The process or technique of rendering images either using electronic sensors to record images as pieces of electronic data or by the chemical action of light and other forms of radiant energy on photosensitive surfaces. *ex: The director of the motion picture asked to see the still photography from the early scenes so he could formulate ideas for the promotional poster.*

Stipulated Damages [1316-00-00-0100] A sum agreed to in a license or contract, reasonably anticipating the amount of damage that would occur in the event of a breach. *info:* Typically specified for breaches such as damage or loss of original artwork, cancellation or delay of a production, or failure to publish a credit line. *ex: The artist and client agreed upon stipulated damages to be paid by the client in the event that the artist's original work should be lost or damaged.*

Stock [1638-02-00-0100] See Stock Photograph *ex: The client wants to license stock.*

Stock Agency [4210-00-00-0100] A company authorized to market and license existing photography for another company or individual. *ex: My stock agency markets my pictures for a percentage of the license fees. plural:* Stock Agencies

Stock Agent [4220-00-00-0100] A party authorized to market and license existing photography for another. *ex: His stock agent can provide more caption information on the images you chose. plural:* Stock Agents

Stock Photo [16380300-0100] See Stock Photograph *ex: The client wants to license a stock photo. plural:* Stock Photos

Stock Photograph [1638-00-00-0100] An image that is available for licensing. *info:* Protected by copyright from the moment of creation when the image becomes fixed, be it on film or digital media. *ex: The client wants to license a stock photograph. plural:* Stock Photographs *variation:* Stock Photography, Stock, Stock Photo

Stock Photography [1638-01-00-0100] See Stock Photograph *ex: The client wants to license stock photography.*

Stock Sale [1603-00-00-0100] The licensing of an image from a pre-existing collection of images. *ex: The picture agency made a stock sale to the textbook publisher. plural:* Stock Sales

Store Card [1225-00-00-0100] A credit card that authorizes the holder to buy goods or services on credit at a specific retail business. *ex: The store card includes the retailer's corporate logo. plural:* Store Cards

Store Display [1129-00-00-0100] Advertising placed in a retail establishment that promotes a particular product, special sale, or the shop itself. *ex: The department store promoted its Founder's Day sale in a store display. plural:* Store Displays

Storyboard [3490-00-00-0100] A panel or series of panels on which a set of images is arranged depicting consecutively the important changes of scene and action in a series of shots (as for a film, television show, or commercial). *info:* Storyboards are sometimes drawn on a telepad, which is a preprinted page with the appropriate aspect ratio for the broadcast media. They are used by directors and producers to envision creative concepts and to evaluate a concept's visual qualities and continuity. Production coordinators, production designers, and directors of photography use storyboards to plan the production schedule, choose locations, construct scenery, and determine lighting and camera shots for each scene. *ex: We need to make a storyboard of this commercial for the producer. plural:* Storyboards

Street Furniture [1722-00-00-0100] Objects such as bus stop or subway platform benches that are installed near roads, streets, and thoroughfares. Can carry advertising or promotion messages. *ex: Their promotion campaign includes street furniture ads on the bus stop benches.*

Stripping [1532-00-00-0100] A print production process, where individual page elements are mounted onto large press pages that are printed together and later cut apart for binding. *info:* Virtually obsolete in today's digital publication environment. *ex: The catalog is in the stripping process. usability:* Retired

Student Course Book [1793-01-00-0100] See Student Edition *ex: The student course book will have a special cover. preferred term:* Student Edition *usability:* Discouraged

Student Edition [1793-00-00-0100] Version of a book or magazine prepared especially for school scholars or pupils. *info:* Usually includes exercises in which students answer questions by writing in the book itself. This is reportedly a growing category of usage with specific needs and pricing issues. *ex: The student edition will have a special cover.* *plural:* Student Editions *variation:* Student Course Book

Sub-Agent [4110-00-00-0100] A company hired by an agency to store, market, and license goods or services to a specific market or markets. *info:* Sub-agents typically receive a percentage of the fees collected in each transaction. *ex: The artist's stock distributor has a sub-agent in France to handle image requests in that country.* *plural:* Sub-Agents *variation:* Subagent

Sub-Distributor [4100-00-00-0100] A company hired by an allocator to store, market, sell, and/or license the same product or service as the original company. *info:* Generally requires additional payments beyond the distributor's fees. Must have permission of a copyright holder to use and bill for the sub-distributor's services. *ex: The artist recommended a sub-distributor on the west coast.* *plural:* Sub-Distributors *variation:* Subdistributor

Sub-License [4680-01-00-0100] See Sublicense [4680-00-00-0100] *ex: The poster company was granted a sub-license.* *plural:* Sub-licenses

Sub-Licensee [4670-00-00-0100] A person granted the rights of production or marketing of products or services to a person or company; not the primary holder of such rights. *ex: The artist granted poster rights to a sub-licensee.* *plural:* Sub-licensees *variation:* Sublicensee

Sub-Licensor [4660-00-00-0100] The person granting the rights of production or marketing of products or services to another (a sub-licensee). *ex: Contact the sub-licensor if you want to use that image on wallpaper.* *plural:* Sub-Licensors *variation:* Sublicensor

Subagent [4110-01-00-0100] See Sub-Agent *ex: The artist's stock distributor has a sub-agent in France to handle image requests in that country.* *plural:* Subagents

Subdistributor [4100-02-00-0100] See Sub-Distributor *ex: The artist recommended a subdistributor on the west coast.* *plural:* Subdistributors

Sublicense [4680-00-00-0100] A contract or agreement allowing a party who does not own rights to a product or service to produce and/or market that product or service. *ex: The poster company was

granted a sublicense.* *plural:* Sublicenses *variation:* Sub-License

Sublicensee [4670-01-00-0100] See Sub-Licensee *ex: The photographer granted poster rights to the sublicensee.* *plural:* Sublicensees

Sublicensor [4660-01-00-0100] See Sub-Licensor *ex: Contact the sublicensor if you want to use that image on wallpaper.* *plural:* Sublicensors

Submission [1571-00-00-0100] An offering of creative works to a potential user or agent often delivered with a memo of understanding or delivery contract, subject to the terms and conditions of a subsequent license or agreement. *ex: Yesterday I shipped a submission of 100 images from my latest shoot to my agent in New York.* *plural:* Submissions

Subscriber [1055-00-00-0100] Someone who pays and is authorized to receive or access a print publication or other information resources for a set period of time. *info:* Authorization can be for an individual, a home, a company, or a seat. *ex: The public relations company is a subscriber to our magazines.* *plural:* Subscribers

Subscription Imagery [2759-00-00-0100] A collection of royalty-free products licensed in a way that grants access and usage rights by payment of a predetermined fee. *info:* Typically accessed via the World Wide Web. May be limited by duration or by the number or size of files accessible. The extent of access and rights granted under this business model varies by supplier. In all cases, the license granted is limited to the terms of the agency's royalty free license terms, which sometimes places limitations on print runs and, in most instances, types of use. For example, most RF licenses specifically exclude the rights to use RF imagery as logos. *ex: We purchased access to their subscription imagery collection.*

Subscription License [1318-00-00-0100] An agreement or contract granting access and usage rights to a collection of royalty-free products by payment of a predetermined fee. *info:* Typically accessed via the World Wide Web. May be limited by duration or by the number or size of files accessible. The extent of access and rights granted under this business model varies by supplier. In all cases, the license granted is limited to the terms of the agency's royalty free license terms, which sometimes places limitations on print runs and, in most instances, types of use. For example, most RF licenses specifically exclude the rights to use RF imagery as logos. *ex: We purchased a subscription license to their collection of images.* *plural:* Subscription Licenses

Subscription Stock [2758-00-00-0100] A collection of royalty-free products licensed in a way that grants access and usage rights by payment of a predetermined fee. *info:* Typically accessed via the World Wide Web. May be limited by duration or by the number or size of files accessible. The extent of access and rights granted under this business model varies by supplier. In all cases, the license granted is limited to the terms of the agency's royalty free license terms, which sometimes places limitations on print runs and, in most instances, types of use. For example, most RF licenses specifically exclude the rights to use RF imagery as logos. *ex: We purchased access to their subscription stock collection for six months.*

Subsidiary Rights [1319-00-00-0100] Permission granted beyond the initial grant to publish a literary work in book form. *info:* Includes electronic rights, film and television rights, audio book rights, audiovisual rights, merchandising rights as well as dramatic or performance rights. *ex: The client wants the license to include subsidiary rights.*

Subtractive Color [4310-00-00-0100] A system of reproducing hues, shades, and tones based on the primaries of reflected light: cyan, magenta, and yellow. *info:* The CMY colors, respectively, are direct complements to red, green, and blue. *ex: Most labs make traditional color prints using subtractive color enlargers. **plural:** Subtractive Colors*

Subway Advertising [1849-00-00-0100] A marketing or promotional piece, usually poster-sized or larger, displayed on the interior or exterior of a public transportation vehicle. *info:* May be printed or displayed on monitors or other digital devices. *ex: The campaign includes subway advertising.*

Subway Stop Advertising [1845-01-00-0100] See Subway Terminal Advertising *ex: The campaign includes subway stop advertising.*

Subway Terminal Advertising [1845-00-00-0100] A promotional piece, usually poster-sized or larger, placed on the structure of a public subway stop, station, platform or terminal. *info:* May be printed or displayed on monitors or other digital devices. *ex: The campaign includes subway terminal advertising. **variation:** Subway Stop Advertising*

Sunday Supplement [1794-00-00-0100] A magazine or other periodical inserted into newspapers on Sunday. *info:* Can be for regional distribution or national distribution. *ex: The advertorial appeared in the Sunday supplement to the city newspaper. **plural:** Sunday Supplements*

Supplementary Work [1717-00-00-0100] A legal term referring to a piece prepared for a publication as a secondary adjunct to a work by another author for the purpose of introducing, concluding, illustrating, explaining, revising, commenting upon, or assisting in the use of the other work. *info:* Examples include forewords, afterwords, pictorial illustrations, maps, charts, tables, editorial notes, musical arrangements, answer material for tests, bibliographies, appendixes, and indexes. *ex: My illustration was licensed as a supplementary work in their new book. **plural:** Supplementary Works*

Survival [1320-01-00-0100] See Survive *ex: Make certain you read the survival clause in our agreement.*

Survive [1320-00-00-0100] To continue to exist in force or operation beyond the expiration or termination of a contract or agreement. *ex: This clause will survive the contract term. **plural:** Survives **variation:** Survival*

T and I [1750-01-00-0100] Abbreviation for Team and Individual *info:* Slang for team and individual. *ex: Next week we will produce a two-day T and I shoot.*

T-Shirt [1227-00-00-0100] A short-sleeved, collarless pullover, often with a printed image, illustration or graphic. Can include advertising or promotion messages. *info:* Frequently used as a marketing or merchandising product by corporations. *ex: The client licensed our image for use on a T-Shirt. **plural:** T-Shirts*

Table of Contents [1525-00-00-0100] A listing, usually at the beginning of a work, of the titles and/or short descriptions of chapters or sections or articles within. *info:* Often includes a repeat use of images. *ex: The image appeared in the article and on the table of contents. **plural:** Tables of Contents **variation:** TOC*

Table Tent [2782-00-00-0100] A small printed promotional piece placed where a product is sold. *ex: The table tent is printed on bright orange paper to attract attention. **plural:** Table Tents*

Tabloid [3710-00-00-0100] A newspaper format in which pages are folded a single time and inserted into one another to produce a piece that is manageable to read in confined spaces; typically the finished size is that of a broadsheet folded in half. *info: Sometimes includes additional sections, printed in broadsheet format, and inserted inside the centerfold of the tabloid outer section. **Several** standard web widths exist, with corresponding standard advertising sizes. *ex: The New York post has a tabloid format. plural: Tabloids*

Tag [4070-00-00-0100] A hanging label on a product. *info:* Standard U.K. Term. *ex: Was a photograph purchased for the tag?* *plural:* Tags

Talent [4830-00-00-0100] Subjects, usually paid models or actors, of a photographic, film, video, or illustration project. *ex: Make sure we have signed model releases from all of the talent.*

Talent Release [1275-01-00-0100] See Model Release *ex: Before the advertising agency will consider using the image, they need to know if the photographer has a talent release on file. plural:* Talent Releases

Target Audience [1579-00-00-0100] A specific group of consumers likely to be interested in a particular product or project. *ex: Our target audience is the eighteen to thirty-four year-old professional. plural:* Target Audiences

Taxi Advertising [1853-00-00-0100] A promotional piece, usually poster-sized or larger, displayed on the interior or exterior of a public transportation vehicle. *info:* May be printed or displayed on monitors or other digital devices. *ex: The campaign includes taxi advertising.*

TB [4380-01-00-0100] Abbreviation for Terabyte *ex: With a growing imaging library, we're approaching 1 TB of storage. plural:* TBs

Teachers' Edition [1751-00-00-0100] Version of an educational book with additional instructional material. *info:* Usually reprints verbatim enlarged pages of a student (pupil) edition with side notes. *ex: The image will only be used in the teachers' edition. plural:* Teachers' Editions

Team and Individual [1750-00-00-0100] Photographs taken at the beginning of a sports season that show all members together and each player by him or herself. *ex: Next week we will produce a two-day team and individual shoot. plural:* Teams and Individuals *variation:* T and I

Tear Sheet [1796-00-00-0100] Page or portion of a page clipped from a printed publication and sent to advertisers to verify that the ad was correctly run. *info:* Increasingly, newspapers and other print publishers are emailing PDF files as electronic tear sheets. Editors sometimes send tear sheets to a publication's editorial contributors to show them how their work was used. Photographers, illustrators, and models often use tear sheets in their portfolios. *ex: A tear sheet of the ad was sent to the client. plural:* Tear Sheets

Television [1130-00-00-0100] A mass communication medium that operates through the transmission of images and sounds and carries editorial and advertising content. *ex: Rights are being negotiated to use his images of Chicago in a television documentary. plural:* Televisions *variation:* TV

Television Still [2715-01-00-0100] See TV Still *ex: This image is being licensed as a television still. plural:* Television Stills

Template [4690-00-00-0100] A model or framework used as the basis for creating a work. *info:* As in a web or email template, or a template license (granted to permit the use of copyrighted work in a template). *ex: Two images are used in the template. plural:* Templates

Terabyte [4380-00-00-0100] A measure of file size and storage capacity referring to, depending on context, between 1,000,000,000,000 and 1,099,511,627,776, 8-bit data units or characters. *info:* Most software, memory chips, and systems consider a kilobyte to be 1,024 bytes (the binary quantity of 2 to the 10th power), a megabyte to be 1,024 such kilobytes a gigabyte to be 1,024 such megabytes, and terabyte to be 1,024 such gigabytes or 1,099,511,627,776 bytes. However, some key standards groups state that 1,000 (10 to the 3rd power) bytes comprise a kilobyte, a megabyte is 1,000 kilobytes, a gigabyte is 1,000 megabytes or one billion bytes, and a terabyte is one trillion (10 to the 12th power) bytes. And many data storage manufacturers use this measurement to define their device sizes, meaning a computer may show less storage capacity on a drive than the drive's specified size suggests. *ex: With a growing imaging library, we're approaching one terabyte of storage. plural:* Terabytes *variation:* TB

Term

(1) Term (Legal) [1725-00-01-0100] A word, phrase or expression. In a contract, a stipulation. *ex: One term in the contract is about maintaining confidentiality. plural:* Terms

(2) Term (Duration) [1725-00-02-0100] The period during which contractual stipulations remain in force. *ex: The agreement has a two year term. plural:* Terms

Termination [1321-00-00-0100] An end, usually before the completion of a license or contract. *info:* Sometimes by mutual consent or as a remedy by one party due to the default of the other party. *ex: Our contract includes a termination clause. plural:* Terminations

Terms and Conditions [1604-00-00-0100] The collected operative statements in a contract or agreement that are not part of the rights, privileges, or compensations set out by the agreement. ***info:*** Many standard contracts or agreements will have a boilerplate of terms and conditions on the reverse of the printed document. ***ex:*** *The terms and conditions are on the last page of the agreement.*

Territorial Exclusive [1640-05-00-0100] See Territory Exclusivity ***ex:*** *The client purchased territorial exclusive rights.* ***plural:*** Territorial Exclusives

Territorial Exclusivity [1640-01-00-0100] See Territory Exclusivity ***ex:*** *The client purchased territorial exclusivity.* ***plural:*** Territorial Exclusivities

Territory [1322-00-00-0100] An area of land or a district or a region where a work will be distributed or broadcast. ***info:*** Territorial rights are often combined with or further defined by language rights within a license. ***ex:*** *The territory for that license will include the northeast.* ***plural:*** Territories

Territory Exclusive [1640-04-00-0100] See Territory Exclusivity ***ex:*** *The client purchased territory exclusivity.* ***plural:*** Territory Exclusives

Territory Exclusivity [1640-00-00-0100] A right that, when granted by a licensor to a licensee, limits the right of the licensor (and other parties offering licenses of the work) to license the right to any third party to use the work in specified geographic regions. ***ex:*** *The client purchased territory exclusivity.* ***plural:*** Territory Exclusivities ***variation:*** Territorial Exclusivity, Territory Exclusive, Territorial Exclusive

Test [1752-00-00-0100] A series of questions or problems designed to determine knowledge, intelligence, or ability. ***info:*** May be an ancillary product to other educational products. ***ex:*** *The image will be used on their test materials.* ***plural:*** Tests

Test Market Use [1074-00-00-0100] When a usage is confined to either the evaluation of an advertisement's concept, idea, copy, view, or audience, or evaluating product appeal to a target audience. ***ex:*** *The client wants to purchase the image for a test market use.* ***plural:*** Test Market Uses

Text Book [2746-01-00-0100] See Textbook ***ex:*** *This text book is for sixth graders.* ***plural:*** Text Books ***preferred term:*** Textbook ***usability:*** Discouraged

Textbook [2746-00-00-0100] A volume in printed or electronic form containing information on one or more subjects used in a real or virtual classroom by students and teachers. ***info:*** Usually includes images. Ancillaries, which require specific licenses, might include other editions, such as instructor handbooks, a student edition, an edition in another language or an electronic edition. Major categories include K-8, high school, college, and professional. ***ex:*** *This textbook is for sixth graders.* ***plural:*** Textbooks ***variation:*** Text Book

Third Party [1735-00-00-0100] Any one individual, company, or organization other than the individuals, companies or organizations involved in the original agreement. ***ex:*** *A third party is interested in an image currently under a time exclusive.* ***plural:*** Third Parties

Three Quarter Page [1503-00-00-0100] A promotional, editorial, or advertising piece that takes up three quarters of a page. ***info:*** A three quarter page image usage license permits use of the image at any size up to three quarters of a page. ***ex:*** *The image was licensed for use at a three quarter page size.* ***plural:*** Three Quarter Pages ***variation:*** Three-Quarter Page

Three-Dimensional [4410-00-00-0100] A flat image having the illusion of depth. ***ex:*** *The image was enhanced to appear as three-dimensional.* ***variation:*** 3-D

Three-Quarter Page [1503-01-00-0100] See Three Quarter Page ***ex:*** *The image was licensed for a three-quarter page.* ***plural:*** Three-Quarter Pages

Thumbnail [1483-00-00-0100] A miniature version of an image larger than a fingernail and smaller than a preview. ***info:*** Frequently used on a web page to represent or be a link to other content (including a larger version of the image). ***ex:*** *My search on the portal resulted in only one thumbnail.* ***plural:*** Thumbnails

Ticket [1226-00-00-0100] A small piece of paper that promises entry into a particular event, such as a concert or a sports game. ***ex:*** *The event ticket includes an image of the team.* ***plural:*** Tickets

TIF [1484-01-00-0100] See TIFF ***ex:*** *Please download the TIF file from our website.* ***plural:*** TIFs

TIFF [1484-00-00-0100] Tagged image file format. A standard digital image file format used for exchanging high quality black and white and color images among computer software. ***info:*** There are several versions, all of which are controlled by Adobe Systems, Inc. Useful for master archive files and derivatives. ***ex:*** *Please download the TIFF file from our website.* ***plural:*** TIFFs ***variation:*** TIF

Time Exclusive [1710-01-00-0100] See Time Exclusivity *ex: The client wants to purchase a time exclusive.*

Time Exclusivity [1710-00-00-0100] A right that, when granted by a licensor to a licensee, limits the right of the licensor (and other parties offering licenses of the work) to license or otherwise permit any third party the right to use the work during a specified time period. *ex: The client wants to purchase time exclusivity. plural: Time Exclusivities variation: Time Exclusive*

Time Period Exclusive [2729-00-00-0100] A right that, when granted by a licensor to a licensee, limits the right of the licensor (and other parties offering licenses of the work) to license or otherwise permit any third party the right to use the work during a specified time period. *ex: The client wants to purchase a time period exclusive. plural: Time Period Exclusives*

Tip On [1042-00-00-0100] A request for subscriber renewals (or other magazine promotion) that is glued onto a magazine cover. *info: Similar to a cover wrap but less expensive. ex: The tip on is postage paid. plural: Tip Ons variation: Tip-On*

Tip-On [1042-01-00-0100] See Tip On *ex: The tip-on is postage paid. plural: Tip-Ons*

Title [3560-00-00-0100] A work published under a specific name. *info: A written work as distinguished from a particular copy. ex: Does your company publish more than one biology title? plural: Titles*

Title Page [1526-00-00-0100] A leaf usually in the front of a work that lists pertinent identifying information about its publication such as the name of the work and the author. *ex: Turn to the title page, just before the table of contents. plural: Title Pages*

TOC [1525-01-00-0100] Abbreviation for Table of Contents *ex: The image will appear in the article and on the TOC.*

Tone [1487-00-00-0100] A color that has been mixed with gray. *ex: The tone of the image was softened to complement the background color. plural: Tones*

Total Exclusive [1323-01-00-0100] See Total Exclusivity *ex: The client purchased a total exclusive. plural: Total Exclusives*

Total Exclusivity [1323-00-00-0100] A right that, when granted by a licensor to a licensee, limits the right of the licensor (and other parties offering licenses of the work) to license any rights in the work

to any third party. *info: The most comprehensive form of exclusivity. ex: The client purchased total exclusivity. plural: Total Exclusivities variation: Total Exclusive*

Trade Advertisement [1075-00-00-0100] Advertising that is directed to specific industries, professions, or special interest groups. *info: Not directed to the general public. ex: The image will be used for a trade advertisement in a specialty magazine that goes to mechanical engineers. plural: Trade Advertisements*

Trade Book [1178-00-00-0100] A book intended for the general public that is sold through retail booksellers. *ex: The trade book using our images is scheduled for publication in the fall. plural: Trade Books*

Trade Dress [1179-00-00-0100] The overall image of a product that can include shape, design, and features such as its size, color, color combinations, and graphics. *info: Includes the particular advertising and marketing techniques used to identify the source of the product. ex: The client is using our image in the product's updated trade dress. plural: Trade Dresses*

Trade Magazine [2807-00-00-0100] A magazine publication that is targeted to the interests of a specific business, profession, or special interest group. *info: Not usually available to the general public. ex: The story will appear in a trade magazine. plural: Trade Magazines*

Trade Paperback [1180-00-00-0100] A book that often closely resembles the original hardcover version and is typically better production quality, larger size and higher priced than a mass market paperback. *info: Intended for sale in retail bookstores. ex: Our illustration will be used on the cover of their new trade paperback. plural: Trade Paperbacks*

Trade Publication [1676-00-00-0100] A magazine or other publication that is targeted to the interests of a specific business, profession, or special interest group. *info: Not usually available to the general public. ex: The article and photos on the latest medical equipment appeared in a trade publication for hospital administrators. plural: Trade Publications*

Trade Show Display [1131-00-00-0100] A large exhibit at an event venue where many related companies or businesses present promotional material and product or service demonstrations. *info: Displays are semi-permanent and typically shipped from show to show. ex: Many photography conferences include a trade show display where the latest in gear and trends can be explored. plural: Trade Show Displays*

Trademark [1324-00-00-0100] A word, phrase, symbol, or other design identifying the source of one product or service from that of another. *info:* Officially registered and legally restricted to the use of the owner or manufacturer. *ex: The trademark appears on the product's packaging.* *plural:* Trademarks

Train Advertising [1854-00-00-0100] A marketing or promotional piece, usually poster-sized or larger, displayed on the interior or exterior of a public transportation vehicle. *info:* May be printed or displayed on monitors or other digital devices. *ex: The campaign includes train advertising.*

Train Terminal Advertising [1846-00-00-0100] A marketing or promotional piece, usually poster-sized or larger, placed on the structure of a public train stop, station, platform, or terminal. *info:* May be printed or displayed on monitors or other digital devices. *ex: The campaign includes train terminal advertising.*

Transfer of Copyright [2711-00-00-0100] A transfer of copyright occurs when the owner of a work (such as a photograph or illustration) passes its interest to another party. Must be in writing and signed by the owner. *ex: The photographer made a transfer of copyright to her picture agency.* *plural:* Transfers of Copyrights

Transit Advertising [1090-00-00-0100] A marketing or promotional piece, usually poster-sized or larger, displayed on the interior or exterior of a public transportation vehicle. *info:* May be printed or displayed on monitors or other digital devices. *ex: The campaign includes transit advertising on taxis and buses.*

Transit Poster [1076-00-00-0100] Large printed advertising sign displayed on the interior or exterior of trains, buses, subways, associated stations, stops, platforms, or shelters as well as taxicabs, airline and car rental terminals. *info:* The more specific transit advertising or transit terminal advertising are preferred. *ex: The transit poster is being printed for display on Boston buses.* *plural:* Transit Posters

Transit Terminal Advertising [1089-00-00-0100] An advertisement, usually poster-sized or larger, placed on the structure of a public transportation stop, station, platform, or terminal. *info:* May be printed or displayed on monitors or other digital devices. *ex: The campaign includes transit terminal advertising at downtown subway stops.*

Translation Rights [4710-00-00-0100] A permission that specifies the languages in which a creative work may be used. *info:* Each separate language must be named in the license agreement. Often confused with international rights and territory rights. *ex: The client is requesting specific translation rights.*

Transparency [1586-00-00-0100] A photograph or image appearing on transparent film (such as slides or Duratrans) rather than on opaque material (such as paper). *ex: Please deliver the image on a transparency.* *plural:* Transparencies

Trim Size [1533-00-00-0100] The outer dimensions of a finished printed work. *ex: The trim size will be six by four inches.* *plural:* Trim Sizes

TV [1130-01-00-0100] Abbreviation for Television *ex: Rights are being negotiated to use his images of Chicago in a TV documentary.* *plural:* TVs

TV Still [2715-00-00-0100] A motionless image used in a broadcast production as editorial or advertising content. *ex: This image is being licensed as a TV Still.* *plural:* TV Stills *variation:* Television Still

TV Use [4700-00-00-0100] A still image used in a TV production as editorial or advertising content. *ex: The image will have a TV Use.* *plural:* TV Uses

Two Page Spread [2687-00-00-0100] A piece that covers adjacent facing pages in a magazine, newspaper, book, or other printed publication. *ex: The advertisement will be a two page spread.* *plural:* Two Page Spreads

UCC [1325-01-00-0100] Abbreviation for Uniform Commercial Code [1325-00-00-0100] *ex: Our contracts are UCC compliant.*

Unauthorized Use [1605-00-00-0100] Use of a work for which a specific license has not been granted. *info:* Considered copyright infringement. The new IPTC core metadata schema has a specific field where usage rights can be stored. These are found in the file info section of a digital file when opened in Adobe Photoshop. *ex: Unless you have a license, that is an unauthorized use.* *plural:* Unauthorized Uses

Underexposure [1488-00-00-0100] When a camera is set so the film or digital imaging sensor receives too little light to adequately record an image. *info:* Dark and badly defined low-contrast images usually result. *ex: The best frame suffered from underexposure and was rejected by the picture editor who wanted to see an image with more contrast.* *plural:* Underexposures

Underrun [1534-00-00-0100] When the number of copies falls below the expected quantity in print production. *ex: The printer will compensate us for the underrun.* *plural:* Underruns

Uniform Commercial Code [1325-00-00-0100] One of the laws drafted by the National Conference of Commissioners on Uniform State Laws and the American Law Institute governing commercial transactions (including sales and licensing, licensing of goods, transfer of funds, commercial paper, bank deposits and collections, letters of credit, bank transfers, warehouse receipts, bills of lading, investment securities and secured transactions). *info:* The Uniform Commercial Code has been adopted wholly or substantially by all states. *ex: Our products are compliant with the Uniform Commercial Code.* *variation:* UCC

Unit Opener [2769-00-00-0100] Special prominent use of an image to designate a new portion of a work. *info:* Often treated as a special design element. *ex: The image will be used as a unit opener.* *plural:* Unit Openers

Universal Product Code [1619-00-00-0100] The barcode (and corresponding number) on products that allows retailers to automatically record the sale of those products. *ex: Look for the universal product code on the side of the package.* *plural:* Universal Product Codes *variation:* UPC

Unlimited Use [1326-00-00-0100] A broad grant of rights that permits utilization across all media types and parameters. *info:* Can be restricted in any usage type or parameter, singly or in groups; can include all uses, all media, all time. *ex: The client wants unlimited use in all media for all time.* *plural:* Unlimited Uses

Unpaid Circulation [1057-00-00-0100] The portion of a magazine or periodical subscription base that received the magazine free of charge. *ex: Many publishers have a small unpaid circulation.* *plural:* Unpaid Circulations

Unpaid Copy [1056-00-00-0100] A magazine given to a recipient at reduced or zero cost and not included in the total, audited, paid circulation numbers of Audit Bureau of Circulations or BPA. *ex: A magazine freelancer generally receives an unpaid copy of each issue of the magazine he/she writes for.* *plural:* Unpaid Copies

Unrestricted Use [2794-00-00-0100] A broad grant of rights that permits usage across all usage types and parameters. *info:* Can be restricted in any usage type or parameter, singly or in groups. *ex: The client asked for an unrestricted use license.* *plural:* Unrestricted Uses

UPC [1619-01-00-0100] Abbreviation for Universal Product Code [1619-00-00-0100] *ex: Look for the UPC on the side of the package.* *plural:* UPCs

Upload [1705-00-00-0100] To transfer digital data or computer software from a computer or other digital device to a server or another device. *ex: We will upload those images in two minutes.* *plural:* Uploads

URL [1688-00-00-0100] Uniform resource locator: an Internet address usually consisting of the access protocol (HTTP), the domain name (e.g., usePLUS. org), and optionally, a path to a file or resource residing on that server. *ex: I will email the URL to you.* *plural:* URLs

Usage [1328-00-00-0100] When a copyrighted work is licensed, the terms of the license that specify the type of media, size of reproduction, duration, and locations in which the work will appear, along with other parameters. *info:* Other parameters include but are not limited to: licensee, licensor, media, quantity, size, placement, industries, regions, languages, restrictions, exclusivity, and duration. *ex: We license images for various types of usage.* *plural:* Usages *variation:* Use

Usage Fee [1639-00-00-0100] A charge made for a work to be shown in a specific media, based on terms in a license or contract agreement. *ex: The usage fee is due in 30 days.* *plural:* Usage Fees

Usage License [1687-00-00-0100] A legal contract or permission outlining the parameters under which a copyrighted work may be used. *ex: The client purchased a usage license for ten images.* *plural:* Usage Licenses

Use [1328-01-00-0100] See Usage *ex: We license images for various types of use.* *plural:* Uses

Variable Data Publishing [1835-00-00-0100] Using digital information to customize content and create a more personalized advertising, marketing, or editorial publication or product. *ex: These sales packages were produced using new variable data publishing technology.* *variation:* VDP

Variance [1665-00-00-0100] A term in a contract, estimate or project bid that cites the amount by which costs may rise or fall. *info:* Often expressed as a percentage of a base amount. *ex: The expense estimate includes a variance of plus or minus twenty percent.* *plural:* Variances

VDP [1835-01-00-0100] Abbreviation for Variable Data Publishing *ex: These sales packages were produced using new VDP technology.*

Vector [1489-00-00-0100] A resolution-independent graphical element or illustration that, without losing detail, can be scaled to any size and printed on any output device at any resolution. *info:* When scaled down in size, vector graphics can sometimes lose fine detail. Clipping paths are vector-based. *ex: The layout includes several pieces of vector art. plural:* Vectors

Vertical [1490-00-00-0100] Perpendicular to the horizon, running up and down, and taller than it is wide. *ex: The image will run as a vertical on the page. plural:* Verticals

Video

(1) Video (Production) [2694-00-01-0100] Technologies associated with the creation, processing and storage of electronic signals representing moving pictures. *ex: He viewed the production on video. plural:* Videos

(2) Video (Media) [2694-00-02-0100] An electronic recording or broadcast of stationary or moving visual images of objects, often in conjunction with audio. Used to distribute and view motion pictures and television programs. *info:* In licensing, refers to media such as VHS videotape, DVD discs, and television broadcasts. *ex: I brought home a video to watch tonight. plural:* Videos

Video Packaging [1228-00-00-0100] The container or wrapping for a consumer DVD or videotape. *ex: Our image is used on the front cover of the video packaging.*

Videotape [1182-00-00-0100] A plastic cassette containing a video. *info:* Usually, video packaging includes images and graphics. *ex: See the videotape to review her images of Maine. plural:* Videotapes

Vignette

(1) Vignette (Book) [1491-00-01-0100] A decorative design placed at the beginning or end of a book or chapter, or along the borders of a page. *ex: This illustration will be used for the vignette at the end of chapter three. plural:* Vignettes

(2) Vignette (Imaging) [1491-00-02-0100] An unbordered image that fades off into the surrounding color at the edges. *ex: The art director asked for a vignette. plural:* Vignettes

(3) Vignette [1491-00-03-0100] (Photo Technical) The tendency of camera lenses to render the corners of an image darker when shot at wide aperture settings. *ex: Please fix the vignette in the lower right and left corners. plural:* Vignettes

Virtual Reality [1798-00-00-0100] Any of a variety of interactive media that allows users to experience a location or subject virtually in three dimensions— without having to actually go to that location or have the subject physically near them. *info:* Most often, a combination of electronic images (either motion or still) and / or audio. *ex: The image is being used as a background in a virtual reality sequence. plural:* Virtual Realities *variation:* VR

Voucher Package [1043-00-00-0100] Inexpensive direct mail advertising offering low-cost introductory magazine subscriptions. *ex: Our image will be used in their voucher package. plural:* Voucher Packages

VR [1798-01-00-0100] Abbreviation for Virtual Reality *ex: The image is being used as a background in a VR sequence. plural:* VRs

Waiver [1330-00-00-0100] The renunciation, repudiation, abandonment, or surrender of some claim, right, privilege, or the opportunity to take advantage of some defect, irregularity, or wrong. *info:* An express or implied relinquishment of a legal right. *ex: If your request for a waiver is denied, you can appeal the denial. plural:* Waivers

Wall Decor [1183-00-00-0100] An image used as decoration on any vertical partition of a home or office. *info:* Wall decor can range from a framed limited-edition print to a wall covering mural. Typically usage is for a set duration of time unless purchased outright. *ex: The photograph is being reproduced for use as wall decor. plural:* Wall Decors

Wallpaper

(1) Wallpaper (Print) [1799-00-01-0100] A decorative paper or vinyl applied to the vertical partitions of rooms. *ex: Rights to the images of patterns in water were sold for use on wallpaper. plural:* Wallpapers

(2) Wallpaper (Electronic) [1799-00-02-0100] In computer parlance, a picture or design covering the background of a display screen on a computer. *ex: Rights to the photographer's images of patterns in water were sold to an ISP for use as wallpaper. plural:* Wallpapers

Warranty [1331-00-00-0100] A promise that a fact is true. *info:* A warranty can authorize, sanction, support, or justify. *ex: The contract includes a warranty that the files will work on our computers. plural:* Warranties

Warranty of Fitness for a Particular Purpose
[5210-00-00-0100] A promise that goods delivered shall be suitable for a specific purpose of the buyer. *info:* Applies to the sale of goods under the Uniform Commercial Code. *ex: The client wanted to ensure that the products would be usable in her business, and so requested that the vendor provide a warranty of fitness for a particular purpose.*

Warranty of Merchantability [5220-00-00-0100]
A promise that goods delivered shall be fit for the ordinary purposes for which they are used. *info:* Applies to the sale of goods under the Uniform Commercial Code. *ex: The client wanted to ensure that the products would be usable in her business, and so requested that the vendor provide a warranty of merchantability.*

Watermark [1492-00-00-0100] Logo, brand mark, or
other visible identification mark superimposed on or impressed into an image, film, or video clip, or on paper. *info:* Watermarks can be made on physical items such as photographic prints or illustrations using different methods or embossing techniques. Digital versions of watermarks can be created that will identify the source of an image or provide additional information about the image. They can be undetectable to the human eye. *ex: Our watermark is in the lower right corner of all our online images.* *plural:* Watermarks

Weather Delay [1077-00-00-0100] Postponement of
a production schedule due to inclement meteorological conditions. *info:* Compensation for weather delays is negotiated in the production contract and is not usually a part of a usage license. *ex: The hurricane forced a two day weather delay.* *plural:* Weather Delays

Web [1696-01-00-0100] Abbreviation for World Wide
Web *ex: A great deal of information is accessible on the web.* *plural:* World Wide Webs *preferred term:* Internet *usability:* Discouraged

Web Address [1698-00-00-0100] Usually, an access
protocol (HTTP), a domain name (e.g., usePLUS.org), and optionally a path to a file or resource residing on that server. *ex: Please send us your web address.* *plural:* Web Addresses *preferred term:* URL *usability:* Discouraged

Web Banner Ad [1132-00-00-0100] A marketing or
promotion announcement embedded in a particular Internet page, usually placed at the top or bottom of the screen. *ex: This web banner ad will be used for two weeks.* *plural:* Web Banner Ads

Web Page [1199-00-00-0100] A single entry of
content from a website on the Internet (World Wide Web) or an intranet composed in HTML, or related markup languages. *info:* A corporate web page on an intranet is visible to the employees within a company and sometimes to contractors. *ex: Here is what the new web page will look like.* *plural:* Web Pages

Web Site [1670-01-00-0100] See Website
ex: You will find contact information on our web site. *plural:* Web Sites

Website [1670-00-00-0100] A collection of Internet
accessible pages interconnected by HTML links, usually including a home page. *info:* All web pages within a website typically exhibit a unified graphical appearance and are physically located on the same server on the Internet. *ex: You will find contact information on our website.* *plural:* Websites *variation:* Web Site

Webzine [1154-02-00-0100] See Ezine *ex: My image is
being used in her webzine, which receives thousands of online visits each month.* *plural:* Webzines

Wedding [1800-00-00-0100] A ceremony at which
a civil or religious marriage occurs. *info:* Often includes a reception event after the ceremony. Images produced at either event by a professional photographer and subsequently delivered to participants are usually licensed for personal use only. *ex: The wedding photographs were shipped to the bride and groom today.* *plural:* Weddings

Week [1664-00-00-0100] A seven day time period. *ex:
His image will be used for newspaper advertisements all week.* *plural:* Weeks

Weekly [3580-00-00-0100] A publication with a unique
title that is issued once every seven days. *ex: Because it is a weekly, the magazine must schedule tight deadlines in order to stay on schedule.* *plural:* Weeklies

Whole Page [2801-00-00-0100] A promotion,
editorial, or advertising piece that takes up one complete leaf in a volume. *info:* A one page image usage license permits use of the image at any size up to the complete page. *ex: The ad will be a whole page.* *plural:* Whole Pages *preferred term:* Full Page [2800-00-00-0100] *usability:* Discouraged

Wholesaler [1590-00-00-0100] A company that
receives products from manufacturers, distributes them to retail outlets, processes returns, and engages in marketing and in-store service. *ex: Our newest product was shipped to the wholesaler yesterday.* *plural:* Wholesalers

Wild Posting [1801-00-00-0100] Advertising sign displayed at construction sites. *ex: The band's concert attendance got a huge boost from the wild posting campaign.* *plural:* Wild Postings

Work

(1) Work (Legal) [4180-00-01-0100] As used in copyright and licensing, an original expression, such as a photograph or illustration, fixed in any tangible medium from which it can be perceived, reproduced, or otherwise communicated, either directly or with the aid of a machine or device. *info:* A work may be protected by copyright if it is: literary, musical, dramatic, pantomime, choreographic, pictorial, graphic, sculptural, a motion picture, audiovisual, a sound recording and/or architectural. *ex: The work is unique, so the license to use it may be more expensive.* *plural:* Works

(2) Work (Production) [4180-00-02-0100] A duty or obligation to produce something of value or provide a service, or the act of fulfilling such a duty or obligation. *info:* Work is typically offered in exchange for consideration, often monetary. *ex: It's going to take a great deal of work to get that shot.* *plural:* Works

Work for Hire [1659-01-00-0100] See Work Made For Hire *ex: The image was made by an employee of the company and is a work for hire.* *plural:* Works For Hire

Work Made for Hire [1659-00-00-0100] A defined term under the U.S. Copyright Act (17 USC 101) meaning (1) a work prepared by an employee within the scope of his or her employment; or (2) a work specially ordered or commissioned for use as a contribution to a collective work, as a part of a motion picture or other audiovisual work, as a translation, as a supplementary work, as a compilation, as an instructional text, as a test, as answer material for a test, or as an atlas, if the parties expressly agree in a written instrument signed by them that the work shall be considered a work for hire. *ex: The image was made by an employee of the company who understood that it would be a work made for hire.* *plural:* Works Made For Hire *variation:* Work For Hire

Work Print [4020-00-00-0100] An image or photograph provided to a client for reference and comment, before final versions are made or delivered. Typically not of reproduction quality. *ex: A work print was sent to the client for approval.* *plural:* Work Prints

World Rights [1332-00-00-0100] In an image license agreement, the right to reproduce a work throughout the planet. *info:* May be limited by language (e.g. World rights, English language.) *ex: A license for world rights to 40 images was purchased.* *usability:* discouraged

World Wide Web [1696-00-00-0100] The complete set of documents residing on all Internet servers that are accessible to computer users. *ex: A great deal of information is accessible on the World Wide Web.* *plural:* World Wide Webs *variation:* Web, WWW

Worldwide Use [4730-00-00-0100] Use that allows for reproduction in any country in the world. *ex: The book company purchased rights for worldwide use.* *plural:* Worldwide Uses

Wrap [2707-00-00-0100] A special promotional cover attached to the outside of a magazine, often used on special sample copies or for subscription renewal. *ex: To attract attention, the wrap is bright orange.* *plural:* Wraps

Wrap Around [1493-00-00-0100] Usually refers to an image or illustration used on the cover of a magazine or book or other printed matter that occupies full front and full back or a major portion, such as the front, spine and part of the back cover. *ex: The image will be used as a wrap around on the cover of our next book.* *plural:* Wrap Arounds

Wrapper [2708-00-00-0100] A special promotional cover attached to the outside of a magazine, often used on special sample copies or for subscription renewal. *ex: To attract attention, the wrapper is bright orange.* *plural:* Wrappers

Writing [1723-00-00-0100] A document with meaningful letters or characters that constitutes readable printed matter. *ex: Put the changes in writing, and have all the parties sign off on them.* *plural:* Writings

Written Instrument [1712-00-00-0100] A composed or published legal document that defines rights, duties, entitlements, or liabilities. *info:* While a contract can be a written instrument, a written instrument is not necessarily a contract. *ex: I have a written instrument which promises payment once the images are used.* *plural:* Written Instruments

WWW [16960200-0100] Abbreviation for World Wide Web *ex: A great deal of information is accessible on the WWW.* *plural:* WWWs *preferred term:* Internet *usability:* Discouraged

YA Book [1553-01-00-0100] Abbreviation for Young Adult Book *ex: The YA Book was borrowed from the school library.* *plural:* YA Books

Year [1509-00-00-0100] 52 continuous weeks, 12 continuous months, or 365 continuous days. *info:* A year must start from a given date, usually the date of a contract. *ex: The image will be used for one year.* *plural:* Years

Young Adult Book [1553-00-00-0100] A volume designed and written for preteens and teens. *ex: The 13-year-old girl borrowed a young adult book from the school library.* *plural:* Young Adult Books *variation:* YA Book

PROPOSED TERMS

After approval and first publication of the PLUS Glossary version 1.0 in 2005, industry stakeholders continued to submit additional terms for consideration by PLUS. In addition, certain uses of terms within the new PLUS Media Matrix standard will require additional contextual definitions in the next version of the Glossary. In the next round of industry review, PLUS will circulate these new terms. Definitions will be derived by industry consensus during the review process, and thus are not listed here. To participate in the review process, visit the Contact section of the PLUS website at www. useplus.org, where you may also sign up for the PLUS mailing list, so that PLUS may notify you of any future Glossary revisions.

Adhesive Tag
Adshel Poster
Airborne Display
Aliasing
Ancillary
Animal Handler
Annual Review
Apparel
Art Display
ATM Card
Baby Wrangler
Back Side
Backdrop
Bank Card
Bestseller
Bill Insert
Birthday Book
Blank Note Book
Body Content
Body of Advertisement
Body of Content
Body of Program
Body of Works
Both Sides
Bound in Insert
Broad International Region
Broadcast
Bulletin
Bus Panel
Bus Poster
Bus Rear Display
Bus Wrap

Business Envelope
Business Greeting Card
Business Invitation
Business Stationery
Camera-Ready
Car Preparation
Cardbound
Case Card
Clause
Cloning
Closing Sequence
Commercial Defamation
Commercial Vehicles
Commercial Website
Compensation
Compliment Slip
Computer Wallpaper
Confidentiality Agreement
Content Body
Continuity Publishing
Corporate Brochure
Corporate Calendar
Corporate Greeting Card
Corporate Magazine
Corporate Poster
Coupon Packs
Custom Published Magazine
Datebook
Design Element
Diary
Disclaimer of Warranty
Discount

Document, Documentation
Door Side Poster
E&O
Editorial Website
Educational
Educational Ancillary Product Materials
Educational Film Set
Educational Program
Educational Publishing
Electronic
Email Format
Emailshot
Entertainment Program
Entertainment Programming
Errors and Ommissions
Event
Exclusive Contract
Feature Film
Finished Art
Flat Rate Fees
Folder
Forward
Front Page
Front Side
Full Area
Full Screen
Full Surface Area
Full Term of Copyright
Gallery Exhibition
Game
Giclee Print

Gift Box
Gift Card
Glossy
HSB
Illustrated Guide
In Theater Screen Ad
Industrial Photography
Infomercial
Inside
In-Store Poster
Insurance, Insure
Internal Presentation
ISDN
Item
Kiosk
Lab Manual
Landing Page
Life of Event
Life of Item
Life of Product
Life of Publication
Limited Buyout
Liquidation for Unlicensed
    Use
Live Presentation
Lossy Compression
Made For TV Movie
Magazine Reprints
Major City
Map
Marketing Materials
Material Exclusive Contract
Merchandise
Metro Area
Metropolitan Area
Minor City
Mobile Billboard
Mugs
Multi-Page
Multiple
Music Video
New Edition
News Program
Non Broadcast Pilot
Non-Exclusive
Non-Exclusive Contract
Nonexclusivity
Non-Profit Program
Novelty Products
On-Air Promotion
One Side
Outtakes
Overprint
Package Exterior
Package Interior
Panel Presentation
Password Protected Electronic
    Book

PDF
Perpetuity
Personal Website
Photo Album
Photocomposed
Photojournalism
Plates
Politically Incorrect
Postcard Book
Price Fixing
Product
Product Packaging
Promo Cards
Promotional Calendar
Promotional Ecard
Quarterly Report
Recordable Media
Reference Book
Restraint of Trade
Retail Book
Retail Calendar
Retail Packaging
Retail Postcard
Retail Poster
Right to Use an Image
Rotating Billboard
Sales Presentation
Scholarly Journal
Service Charge
Shelflife
Shelter Advertising
Short Film
Spectacular
Stadium Advertising
Stage Performance
Stamp
Station Poster
Sticker
Still Use
Study Print
Tattoo
Telephone Book
Telephone Kiosk
Television Programming
Terminal Advertising
Textiles
Thumbnail Sketches
Title Sequence
Toy
Trade Secrets
Trade Show Presentation
Trade Website
Trading Cards
Training Materials
Transport
Transport Advertising
Transport Poster
Underground

Version
Viewers
Wallscape
Web Interstitial Ad
Webcast
Wholesale Packaging
Widget
Wrap Around Cover
Wrap Around Dust Jacket

NOTES

NOTES

www.ingramcontent.com/pod-product-compliance
Lightning Source LLC
Chambersburg PA
CBHW022112170526
45157CB00004B/1596